ISEE

ENGLISH
1ST EDITION

IVY GLOBAL, NEW YORK

This publication was written and edited by the team at Ivy Global.

Editor: Laurel Perkins
Layout Editor: Sacha Azor
Producers: Lloyd Min and Junho Suh

About Ivy Global

Ivy Global is a pioneering education company that provides a wide range of educational services.

E-mail: info@ivyglobal.com
Website: http://www.ivyglobal.com

CONTENTS

CHAPTER 6: VOCABULARY BUILDING **269**

CHAPTER 7: ANSWER KEYS **355**

INTRODUCTION

CHAPTER 1

HOW TO USE THIS BOOK

SECTION 1

Welcome, students and parents! This book is intended for students preparing for the Verbal Reading, Reading Comprehension, and Essay sections of the Lower, Middle, or Upper Level Independent School Entrance Exam (ISEE). For students applying to many top private and independent schools in North America, the ISEE is a crucial and sometimes daunting step in the admissions process. By leading you step-by-step through the fundamental content and most effective strategies for the ISEE, Ivy Global will help you build your confidence and maximize your score on this important exam.

This book is right for you if:

- you are applying to a private or independent school that requires the ISEE for admission
- you will be in grades 4-5 (Lower Level), 6-7 (Middle Level), or 8-11 (Upper Level) when you write the ISEE
- you would like to learn and practice the best strategies for the Verbal Reasoning, Reading Comprehension, and Essay sections of the ISEE
- you are a parent, family member, or tutor looking for new ways to help your Lower, Middle, or Upper-Level ISEE student

We know that no two students are exactly alike—each student brings a unique combination of personal strengths and weaknesses to his or her test preparation. For this reason, we've tailored our preparation materials to help students with a specific subject area or goal. Ivy Global's *ISEE English* walks students through the best strategies for the ISEE Verbal Reasoning and Reading Comprehension sections, plus a step-by-step approach to the Essay section and a thorough vocabulary and writing skills review. This book includes:

- an up-to-date introduction to the ISEE's administration, format, and scoring practices
- targeted strategies for students new to standardized tests, including study schedules, pacing, and stress management
- a complete introduction to the ISEE Verbal Reasoning and Reading Comprehension sections, explaining in detail what concepts are tested and what types of questions are asked

- the most effective strategies to approach each type of question on these sections, including advanced strategies for Upper-Level students
- a step-by-step approach for the Essay, preparing students to write responses that will stand out in the admissions process
- a thorough review of all of the fundamental concepts you will need to know for the ISEE English sections, including vocabulary, grammar, and literary terminology
- 500 core vocabulary words to prepare for the level of vocabulary tested by the ISEE, plus innovative and fun strategies to make vocabulary building part of your daily life
- over 800 practice questions and drills, grouped into targeted practice sets for each concept and difficulty level

Work through the material that is appropriate to your level. If you are a Lower Level student, work through all of the material except any content marked "Middle Level" or "Upper Level." If you are a Middle Level student, work through all of the material except any content marked "Upper Level." If you are an Upper Level student, review all of the basic material before you look at the "Upper Level" content. The three levels have the same basic format, so both younger and older students will benefit from learning the same fundamental strategies.

Finally, keep in mind that every student has a different learning style. If you come across a strategy or a concept that you find challenging, circle it and move on. You might find that some of the other strategies work better for you, and that is okay! Pick the strategies that are the best fit for your learning style and add them to your toolkit for writing the ISEE. You can always come back to more difficult material with the help of a trusted adult or tutor.

To get started, continue reading for an overview of the ISEE and some general test-taking advice. Good luck in this exciting new step for your education!

ABOUT THE ISEE

The **ISEE (Independent School Entrance Exam)** is a standardized test administered to students in grades 1-11 to help determine placement into certain private and independent schools. Many secondary schools worldwide use the ISEE as an integral part of their admissions process. The ISEE is owned and published by the Educational Records Bureau.

You will register for one of four ISEE tests, depending on your grade level:

- The **Primary Level** exam is for students currently in grades 1-3.
- The **Lower Level** exam is for students currently in grades 4-5.
- The **Middle Level** exam is for students currently in grades 6-7.
- The **Upper Level** exam is for students currently in grades 8-11.

The Primary Level exam is administered only with the use of a computer, and includes auditory content. All other levels may be taken on a computer or in a paper-and-pencil format. Among levels, the exams differ in difficulty, length, and the types of questions which may appear. The Lower Level exam is shorter than the Middle or Upper level exams.

WHEN IS THE TEST ADMINISTERED?

Administration dates for the ISEE vary between test locations. ISEE test sites and administration dates can be found online, at ERBlearn.org. In addition to taking the test at a school that administers large group tests, students applying to grades 5-12 can register to take the ISEE at a Prometric Testing Center, which administers computer-based exams.

HOW MANY TIMES CAN I TAKE THE TEST?

Students may only take the ISEE once per admission season. The version of the test doesn't matter: a student who has taken a paper-and-pencil test may not take another test on a computer, and a student who has taken a computer-based test may not take another test in a paper-and-pencil format.

HOW DO I REGISTER?

The easiest and fastest way to register is to complete the **online application**. Visit www.ERBlearn.org to register for an exam in your location. It is also possible to register over the phone by calling (800) 446-0320 or (919) 956-8524, or to register by mail. To register by mail, you must complete and submit the application form available only in the printed ISEE student guide. Visit www.ERBlearn.org to order a printed copy of the ISEE student guide.

WHAT IS THE FORMAT OF THE ISEE?

The Lower, Middle, and Upper Level ISEE exams consist of four scored sections (**Verbal Reasoning**, **Quantitative Reasoning**, **Reading Comprehension**, and **Mathematics Achievement**), plus an **Essay** that is used as a writing sample. The format of the test differs based on the level of the exam:

LOWER LEVEL			
Section	**Questions**	**Length**	**Topics Covered**
Verbal Reasoning	34	20 min	Synonyms, Sentence Completion
Quantitative Reasoning	38	35 min	Logical Reasoning, Pattern Recognition (Word Problems)
Reading Comprehension	25	25 min	Short Passages
Math Achievement	30	30 min	Arithmetic, Algebra, Geometry, Data Analysis
Essay	1	30 min	One age-appropriate essay prompt
Total testing time: 2 hours 20 minutes			

MIDDLE AND UPPER LEVEL			
Section	**Questions**	**Length**	**Topics Covered**
Verbal Reasoning	40	20 min	Synonyms, Sentence Completion
Quantitative Reasoning	37	35 min	Logical Reasoning, Pattern Recognition (Word Problems and Quantitative Comparison)
Reading Comprehension	36	35 min	Short Passages
Math Achievement	47	40 min	Arithmetic, Algebra, Geometry, Data Analysis
Essay	1	30 min	One age-appropriate essay prompt
Total testing time: 2 hours 40 minutes			

Except for the Essay, all questions are **multiple-choice** (A) to (D). You are not normally allowed to use calculators, rulers, dictionaries, or other aids during the exam. However, students with documented learning disabilities or physical challenges may apply to take the test with extra time, aids, or other necessary accommodations that they receive in school. For more information about taking the ISEE with a documented disability, visit the ISEE website at ERBlearn.org.

HOW IS THE ISEE SCORED?

All of the multiple-choice questions on the ISEE are equal in value, and your **raw score** for these sections is the total number of questions answered correctly. There is no penalty for incorrect answers.

Within each section, there are also 5-6 **experimental questions** that do not count towards your raw score for the section. The ISEE uses these questions to measure exam accuracy and to test material for upcoming exams. You won't be told which questions are the experimental questions, however, so you have to do your best on the entire section.

Your raw score for each section is then converted into a **scaled score** that represents how well you did in comparison with other students taking the same exam. Scaled scores range from about 760-950 for each section, with total scaled scores ranging from about 2280-2850.

The **Essay** is not scored, but is sent to the schools you are applying to as a sample of your writing skills. Admissions officers may use your essay to evaluate your writing ability when they are making admissions decisions.

Scores are released to families, and to the schools that families have designated as recipients, within 7-10 business days after the test date. Scores will be mailed to the address you provided when registering for the ISEE, and to up to six schools and/or counselors. You may request expedited score reports, or send score reports to additional schools or counselors, for an additional fee.

WHAT ARE THE ISEE PERCENTILES AND STANINES?

The ISEE score report also provides **ISEE percentile** rankings for each category, comparing your performance to that of other students in the same grade who have taken the test in the past three years. If you score in the 60th percentile, this means you are scoring higher than 60% of other students in your grade taking the exam.

These percentile rankings provide a more accurate way of evaluating student performance at each grade level. However, the ISEE percentiles are a comparison against only other students who have taken the ISEE, and these tend to be very high-achieving students. Students should not be discouraged if their percentile rankings appear low.

The following chart shows the median (50th percentile) ISEE scores for students applying to grades 5-12.

MEDIAN SCORES (ISEE 50TH PERCENTILE) FOR 2012					
Level	Grade Applying To	Verbal Reasoning	Quantitative Reasoning	Reading Comprehension	Mathematics Achievement
Lower Level	5	840	843	843	848
	6	856	856	848	863
Middle Level	7	868	865	869	871
	8	878	873	883	876
Upper Level	9	879	878	880	882
	10	883	882	886	886

Level	Grade Applying To	Verbal Reasoning	Quantitative Reasoning	Reading Comprehension	Mathematics Achievement
Upper Level	11	886	885	889	890
	12	881	884	880	889

The ISEE score report also includes **stanine** rankings. A stanine is a number from 1-9 obtained by dividing the entire range of students' scores into 9 segments, as shown in the table below:

PERCENTILE RANK	STANINE
1 – 3	1
4 – 10	2
11 – 22	3
23 – 39	4
40 – 59	5
60 – 76	6
77 – 88	7
89 – 95	8
96 – 99	9

Stanine scores are provided because small differences in percentile rankings may not represent a significant difference in ability. Stanines represent a range of percentile rankings, and are intended to provide a better representation of student ability.

HOW DO SCHOOLS USE THE ISEE?

Schools use the ISEE as one way to assess potential applicants, but it is by no means the only tool that they are using. Schools also pay very close attention to the rest of the students' applications—academic record, teacher recommendations, extracurricular activities, writing samples, and interviews—in order to determine which students might be the best fit for their program. The personal components of a student's application sometimes give schools a lot more information about the student's personality and potential contributions to the school's overall community. Different schools place a different amount of importance on ISEE and other test scores within this process, and admissions offices are good places to find how much your schools of interest will weight the ISEE.

Ivy Global

TEST-TAKING STRATEGIES

CHAPTER 2

APPROACHING THE ISEE

SECTION 1

Before you review the content covered on the ISEE, you need to focus on *how* you take the ISEE. If you approach the ISEE *thoughtfully* and *strategically*, you will avoid common traps and tricks planted in the ISEE by the test makers. Think of the ISEE as a timed maze—you need to make every turn cleverly and quickly so that you avoid getting stuck at a dead end with no time to spare.

In this section, you will learn about the ISEE's format and structure; this awareness will help you avoid any surprises or shocks on test day. A very predictable exam, the ISEE will seem less challenging once you understand what it looks like and how it works. By learning and practicing the best test-taking strategies and techniques, you will discover how to work as quickly and intelligently as possible. Once you know what to expect, you can refine your knowledge of the actual material tested on the ISEE, such as the verbal and math skills that are based on your grade level in school.

This section on ISEE strategies will answer your **major questions**:

1. How does the ISEE differ from a test you take in school?
2. What preparation strategies can you learn before you take the ISEE?
3. What strategies can you learn to use during the ISEE?
4. How can you manage stress before and during the ISEE?

In the process of answering your big questions, this section will also highlight key facts about smart test-taking:

- Your answer choice matters—your process does not. Enter your answer choices correctly and carefully to earn points. You have a set amount of time per section, so spend it wisely.
- The ISEE's format and directions do not change, so learn them now.
- All questions have the same value.
- Each level of the ISEE corresponds to a range of grades, and score expectations differ based on your grade level.
- Identify your areas of strength and weakness, and review any content that feels unfamiliar.

- Apply universal strategies—prediction-making, Process of Elimination, back-solving, and educated guessing—to the multiple-choice sections.
- Stay calm and be confident in your abilities as you prepare for and take the ISEE.

HOW DOES THE ISEE DIFFER FROM A TEST YOU TAKE IN SCHOOL?

The ISEE differs from tests you take in school in four major ways:

1. It is not concerned with the process behind your answers. Your answer is either right or wrong: there is no partial credit.
2. You have a set amount of time per section (and for the exam as a whole).
3. It is divided into four levels that correspond to four grade ranges of students.
4. It is extremely predictable given that its format, structure, and directions never vary.

NO PARTIAL CREDIT

At this point in your school career, you have probably heard your teacher remark, "Be sure to show your work on the test!" You are most likely familiar with almost every teacher's policy of "No work, no credit." However, the ISEE completely ignores this guideline. The machine that grades your exam does not care that you penciled brilliant logic in the margins of the test booklet—the machine only looks at your answer choice. Your answer choice is either right or wrong: **there is no partial credit**.

SET AMOUNT OF TIME

You have a **set amount of time per section**, so spend it wisely. The ISEE test proctors will never award you extra time after a test section has ended because you spent half of one section struggling valiantly on a single problem. Instead, you must learn to work within each section's time constraints.

You also must view the questions as equal because **each question is worth the same number of points** (one). Even though some questions are more challenging than others, they all carry the same weight. Rather than dwell on a problem, you should skip it, work through the rest of the section, and come back to it if you have time.

FOUR LEVELS

There are four levels of the ISEE—Primary, Lower, Middle, and Upper—each of which is administered to a specific range of students. The Primary Level is given to students applying to grades 2, 3, and 4; The Lower Level is given to students applying to grades 5 and 6; the Middle Level is given to students applying to grades 7 and 8; and the Upper Level is given to students applying to grades 9, 10, 11, and 12. While you might be used to taking tests in school that are completely tailored to your grade, the ISEE is different: each test level covers content from a specific range of grade levels.

Score expectations differ based on your grade level. You are not expected to answer every question correctly on an Upper Level exam if you are only in eighth grade. Conversely, if you are in eleventh grade, you are expected to answer the most questions correctly on the Upper Level exam because you are one of the oldest students taking that exam.

STANDARD FORMAT

The ISEE is, by definition, a **standardized test**, which means that its format and directions are standard and predictable. While your teachers might change formats and directions for every assessment they administer, you can expect to see the same format and directions on every ISEE.

Ivy Global

WHAT PREPARATION STRATEGIES CAN YOU LEARN BEFORE YOU TAKE THE ISEE?

Now that you are familiar with how the ISEE differs from the tests you take in school, you are ready to learn some test tips. You can prepare for the ISEE by following these three steps:

1. Learn the format and directions of the test.
2. Identify your areas of strength and weakness.
3. Create a study schedule to review and practice test content.

LEARN THE FORMAT AND DIRECTIONS

The structure of the ISEE is entirely predictable, so learn this now. Rather than wasting precious time reading the directions and understanding the format on test day, take the time now to familiarize yourself with the test's format and directions.

Refer to the tables on pages 6 and 7 for an overview of the ISEE's format. Continue reading for specific directions for the Verbal Reasoning, Reading Comprehension, and Essay sections. Specific directions for the Quantitative Reasoning and Mathematics Achievement sections can be found in Ivy Global's *ISEE Math*.

IDENTIFY YOUR STRENGTHS AND WEAKNESSES

To determine your areas of strength and weakness and to get an idea of which concepts you need to review, take a full-length, accurate practice exam to serve as a diagnostic test. Practice exams for the ISEE can be found in Ivy Global's *ISEE Practice*.

Make sure you simulate test day conditions by timing yourself. Then, check your answers against the correct answers. Write down how many questions you missed in each section, and note the topics or types of questions you found most challenging. What was hard about the test? What did you feel good about? Did you leave a lot of questions blank because of timing issues, or did you leave questions blank because you did not know how to solve them? Reflecting on these questions, in addition to looking at your score breakdown, will help you determine your strengths, weaknesses, and areas for improvement.

CREATE A STUDY SCHEDULE

After determining your areas of strength and weakness, create a study plan and schedule for your ISEE preparation to review content. Work backward from your test date until you arrive at your starting point for studying. The number of weeks you have until your exam will determine how much time you can (and should) devote to your preparation. Remember, practice is the most important!

To begin, try using this sample study plan as a model for your own personalized study schedule.

SAMPLE STUDY PLAN

My test date is: _____.

I have _____ weeks to study. I will make an effort to study _____ minutes/hours each night, and I will set aside extra time on _____ to take timed sections.

I plan to take _____ full-length tests between now and my test date. I will study for _____ weeks and then take a practice test. My goal for this test is to improve my score in the following sections:

_____

_____

_____

_____

_____

_____

_____

If I do not make this goal, then I will spend more time studying.

Ivy Global

STUDY SCHEDULE				
Date	Plan of Study	Time Allotted	Time Spent	Goal Reached?
1/1/2013	Learn 5 words and review perimeter of polygons	1 hour	44 minutes	Yes, I know 5 new words and can calculate perimeter!
1/3/2013	Learn 5 words and review area of triangles	1 hour	1 hour	I know 5 new words, but I'm still confused about the area of triangles. I'll review this again next time and ask a teacher, tutor, or parent for help.

WHAT STRATEGIES CAN YOU LEARN TO USE DURING THE TEST?

Once you have grown accustomed to the ISEE through practice, you are ready to learn strategies to use during the ISEE. The following points will prepare you to take the test as cleverly and efficiently as possible:

1. Enter your answer choices correctly and carefully.
2. Pace yourself to manage your time effectively.
3. Learn a strategic approach for multiple-choice questions.

ENTERING ANSWER CHOICES

Whether you are taking a pencil-and-paper or a computer-based exam, you must follow the directions carefully to enter your answers. In school you probably take tests that, for the most part, do not ask you to enter your answers in a specific format. However, the ISEE streamlines the grading process by only reviewing the answers you have entered on your answer sheet or into the computer program. This means that any notes or work you have written on your scratch paper will not be reviewed, and you will only receive credit for entering your answers correctly.

On a computer-based exam, you will click an answer on the computer screen in order to enter your response. Follow the directions carefully to make sure your answer has been recorded. Within each section, you will be able to go back to questions earlier in the section and change your answers. You will also be able to skip questions and come back to them later. However, you will not be able to review questions from sections that come earlier or later in the exam; you will only be able to review your answers for the questions in the section you are currently working on. Make sure all of your answers have been entered correctly before your time is up for the section.

On a pencil-and-paper exam, you will enter your answers on a separate answer sheet. You must grid in your multiple-choice answers onto this sheet using an HB pencil to fill in the circle that corresponds to your answer. This sheet is scanned and scored by a highly sensitive computer. You will also write your Essay on separate lined pages of this answer sheet.

Since you have to take an additional step to record your answers, it is important that you avoid making gridding mistakes. Sadly, many students get confused and mismark their answer sheets. Remember, even if you arrive at the right answer, it is only correct and counted in your favor if you grid correctly on your answer sheet.

To grid correctly and carefully to maximize your points, consider the following tips:

Keep your answer sheet neat. Since your answer sheet is graded by a machine, your score is calculated based on what your marks look like. The machine cannot know what you really meant if you picked the wrong bubble. Stray marks can harm your score, especially if you darken the correct answer but accidentally make a mark that confuses the machine! Avoid this and other errors by consulting the following image, which shows the difference between answers that are properly shaded and those that are not.

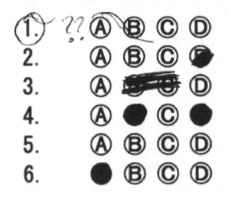

- Answer 1 is *wrong* because no answer is selected and there are stray marks.
- Answer 2 is *wrong* because choice (D) has not been darkened completely.
- Answer 3 is *wrong* because two answers have been selected.
- Answer 4 is *wrong* because two answers have been selected.
- Answer 5 is *neither right nor wrong* because it was left blank.
- Answer 6 is *right* because choice (A) has been darkened properly.

Train yourself to **circle your answer choice in your test booklet**. If you have time to go back and check your answers, you can easily check your circled answers against your gridded ones.

You should also **create a system for marking questions that you skipped** or that you found confusing (see the next section for more information about skipping around). Try circling those question numbers only in your test booklet so that you can find them later if you want to solve them or check your work. Be aware of these questions when gridding answers on your answer sheet.

Finally, **grid your answers in batches of four, five, or six answer choices.** That way, you do not have to go back and forth between your test booklet and your answer sheet every minute. If you choose to use this strategy, keep an eye on the clock—you do not want to get to the end of the section and find you have not gridded any answers. Depending on how much time you have left to check your work (if you happen to finish early), you can either review every problem or spot-check a series of questions on your answer sheet against your test booklet.

TIME MANAGEMENT (PACING)

Manage your time effectively to boost your score. The ISEE has an element of time pressure, so it is important to keep moving on the exam rather than wasting your time on any single question.

You can come back to questions within each section of the ISEE. Each question is only worth one point, regardless of its difficulty. If you are stuck on a problem, you should make your best guess and move on to try to answer another problem. It makes more sense to answer as many questions as possible (and get as many points as possible) rather than spending all your time on one question. If you come across a question you want to come back to, circle it in your question booklet or mark it on your scratch paper. Remember not to make any stray marks on your answer sheet.

By moving quickly through each question of the section, you will ensure that: 1) you see every question in the section; 2) you gain points on questions that are easy for you; 3) you return to more challenging problems and figure out as many as you can with your remaining time. It is also important to note that you might not be able to answer several questions in each section if you are on the younger end of the testing group for your particular test level. In that case, you should make your best guess based on the information you do know, but shouldn't worry if the content is unfamiliar.

Even if you are unsure about a question and want to come back to it later, you should **always make a guess.** The ISEE doesn't take off any points for answering questions incorrectly, so you should never leave a question blank! Even if you guess a completely random answer, you have a small chance of gaining a point. If you can rule out one or two choices that you know are wrong, you have even better odds of guessing the right answer. Therefore, always make a guess on every question, even if you are planning to come back to it later. When your time is up, you want to make sure that you have entered an answer for every question!

Follow this step-by-step process for moving through a section:

1. Look through the section and answer the questions that are easy for you. If a question seems difficult or is taking too long, make a guess and circle it to come back to later.
2. After answering all the easier questions, go back to the questions you have circled and spend some time working on ones that you think you might be able to solve. If you figure out that the answer you originally guessed was incorrect, change that answer on your answer sheet.
3. If you have no idea how to solve a question, leave your best guess as your answer.
4. If you have any time remaining, check your work for the questions you solved.

Ivy Global

STRATEGIES FOR MULTIPLE-CHOICE QUESTIONS

Apply universal strategies—prediction-making, Process of Elimination, back-solving, and educated guessing—to the multiple-choice sections. To illustrate the value of these strategies, read through the following example of a synonym question from the Verbal Reasoning section:

HAPPY:

    (A) delighted

    (B) unhappy

    (C) crazy

    (D) nice

Answer: (A). "Delighted" is the correct answer because it is the word that most nearly means "happy."

Regardless of whether the answer choices are easy, difficult, or somewhere in between, you can use certain tricks and tips to your advantage. To approach ISEE questions effectively, you need to step into the test makers' minds and learn to avoid their traps.

Make predictions. When you see a question, try to come up with an answer on your own before looking at the answer choices. You can literally cover the answer choices with your hand so that you must rely on your own intelligence to predict an answer instead of being swayed by answer choices that you see. If you look at the answer choices first, you might be tempted to pick an answer without thinking about the other options and what the question is asking you. Instead, make a prediction so that you understand the question fully and get a clear sense of what to look for in the answers. In the synonym example above, you could predict that a possible synonym for "happy" would be something like "glad."

Use the Process of Elimination. For each multiple-choice question, you must realize that the answer is right in front of you. To narrow down your answer choices, think about the potential incorrect answers and actively identify those to eliminate them. Even if you can eliminate just one answer, you will set yourself up for better odds if you decide to guess. For the synonym example above, test your prediction of "glad" against the answer choices and immediately eliminate "unhappy" since it is opposite in meaning. You can also probably eliminate "crazy" and "nice" since those words do not match your prediction. This leaves you with "delighted," which is the correct answer.

Try back-solving. This strategy is most useful on the math sections, especially when you are given a complicated, multi-step word problem. Instead of writing an equation, try plugging in the answer choices to the word problem. Take a look at the following question:

Catherine has a basket of candy. On Monday, she eats ½ of all the candy. On Tuesday, she eats 2 pieces. On Wednesday, she eats twice the amount of candy that she consumed on Tuesday. If she only has 4 pieces left on Thursday, how many pieces did she initially have?

    (A) 12

    (B) 14

    (C) 16

    (D) 20

To use back-solving, start with answer choice (C) and plug it into the word problem. If (C) is the correct answer, you are done. If not, you will then know whether you should test (B) or (D). When we start with 16 pieces of candy, we subtract 8 on Monday, then 2 more for Tuesday, and then 4 more for Wednesday. By Thursday, Catherine only has two pieces of candy left, which is less than the amount we wanted. Therefore, we know our answer has to be bigger, so we eliminate choices (A), (B), and (C) and try (D), which works.

(*Fun Fact:* If you think about it, you will have to plug in three answer choices at most to determine the right answer.)

Armed with these strategies, you might feel that the ISEE is starting to look more manageable because you now have shortcuts that will help you navigate the maze of questions quickly and cleverly.

Take a look at this example to practice using the strategies you just read about.

Because Kaitlin was -------- from her soccer game, she went to bed early.

    (A) thrilled

    (B) exhausted

    (C) competitive

    (D) inspired

1. Assess the question and recognize what it is testing. In this case, the question tests whether you can pick a word to complete the sentence.

2. Make a prediction. What about Kaitlin's soccer game would cause her to go to bed early? Maybe it wore her out, so we could look for something like "tired" to go in the blank.

3. Look for inaccurate answer choices and eliminate them. If Kaitlin were "thrilled," "competitive," and "inspired" as a result of her soccer game, this wouldn't explain why she had to go to bed early. Therefore, you can eliminate answers (A), (C), and (D).

4. Make an educated guess, or choose the best answer if you feel confident about the answer. Since you made a fantastic prediction and used Process of Elimination, you only have one choice left: (B). "Exhausted" is the correct answer—you just earned yourself a point!

HOW CAN YOU MANAGE YOUR STRESS?

If you have ever had a big test before, or an important sports match, play, or presentation, then you know what anxiety feels like. Even if you are excited for an approaching event, you might feel nervous. You might begin to doubt yourself, and you might feel as if your mind is racing while butterflies flutter in your stomach!

When it comes to preparing for the ISEE, the good news is that a little anxiety (or adrenaline) goes a long way. Anxiety is a natural, motivating force that will help you study hard in the days leading up to your test. That anxiety will also help you stay alert and work efficiently during the test.

Sometimes, however, anxiety might become larger than life and start to get the best of you. To prevent anxiety and nerves from clouding your ability to work effectively and believe in yourself, you should try some of the suggestions below. Many of these suggestions are good ideas to use in everyday life, but they become especially important in the final week before your test and on test day itself.

- **Relax and slow down.** To center yourself and ease your anxiety, take a big, deep breath. Slowly inhale for a few seconds and then slowly exhale for a few seconds. Shut your eyes and relax. Stretch your arms, roll your neck gently, crack your knuckles—get in the zone of Zen! Continue to breathe deeply and slowly until you can literally feel your body calm down.
- **Picture your goals.** Close your eyes or just pause to reflect on what you want to achieve on test day. Visualize your success, whether that means simply answering all the math questions or getting a top score and gaining acceptance into the school of your dreams. Acknowledge your former successes and abilities, and believe in yourself.
- **Break it down.** Instead of trying to study a whole section at once, break up your studying into small and manageable chunks. Outline your study goals before you start. For example, instead of trying to master the entire Reading Comprehension section at once, you might want to work on one type of passage at a time.
- **Sleep.** Make sure you get plenty of rest and sleep, especially the two nights leading up to your exam!
- **Fuel up.** Eat healthy, filling meals that fuel your brain. Also, drink lots of water to stay hydrated.
- **Take a break.** Put down the books and go play outside, read, listen to music, exercise, or talk to a trusted friend or family member. A good break can be just as restful as a nap. However, watching television will provide minimal relaxation.

On the night before the exam, study only lightly. Make a list of your three biggest fears and work on them, but don't try to learn anything new. Pick out what you are going to wear to the exam—try wearing layers in case the exam room is hotter or colder than you expect. Organize everything you need to bring. Know where the test center is located and how long it will take to get there. Have a nutritious meal and get plenty of sleep!

On the morning of the exam, let your adrenaline kick in naturally. Eat a good breakfast and stay hydrated; your body needs fuel to endure the test. Bring along several pencils and a good eraser. Listen carefully to the test proctor's instructions and let the proctor know if you are left-handed so you can sit in an appropriate desk. Take a deep breath and remember: you are smart and accomplished! Believe in yourself and you will do just fine.

VERBAL REASONING

CHAPTER 3

The ISEE Verbal Reasoning section tests your ability to recognize word meanings and use them logically in a sentence. In this section, you will see two types of questions: synonym questions and sentence completion questions. **Synonyms** are words with similar or same meanings; these questions will give you a word in capital letters and ask you to find another word that means the same thing. **Sentence completion** questions ask you to "fill in the blank" in a sentence; these questions will give you a sentence with a portion missing, and ask you to find a word or short phrase that logically completes the sentence. On the Lower Level exam, you will have 20 minutes to answer 34 questions: 17 synonyms and 17 sentence completions. On the Middle and Upper Level exams, you will have 20 minutes to answer 40 questions: 20 synonyms and 20 sentence completions.

HOW TO APPROACH THE VERBAL REASONING SECTION

Review the following test-taking strategies and study methods to help you prepare for the Verbal Reasoning section as a whole. Then, turn to the following sections on specific strategies for the synonym and sentence completion questions.

TIME MANAGEMENT

You have 20 minutes to complete the section, so you only have half a minute to spend on each question! In this section, as in every section on the ISEE, it is important to pace yourself and be smart about which questions you answer and in what order. First, answer questions with words you know immediately and make your best guess on words you don't know. Then, if you have time, go back and see if you can make a better guess for the words you are less familiar with.

EDUCATED GUESSING

You aren't expected to know the answer to every question in the section. If you don't know the answer to a question, make your best guess, and circle it so you can come back to it later if you have time. You want to make sure that no single question is taking up too much of your time, and that you have enough time to make your best guess on every question. When you come back to the questions you have circled, try your best to figure out a possible answer, and see if you can make a more educated guess.

PROCESS OF ELIMINATION

The Process of Elimination will help you make educated guesses if you are uncertain of the answer. Narrow down your answer choices by crossing out the obviously wrong answers, and make your best guess among the answers that remain.

VOCABULARY BUILDING

Vocabulary building is the best long-term way to improve your Verbal Reasoning score. Work your way through the Vocabulary Building chapter and word list included in this book. Test yourself regularly on your vocabulary, making sure you are reviewing old words as you learn new ones.

SYNONYMS

PART 1

The first half of the ISEE Verbal Reasoning section takes the form of synonyms. In this section, read about the best strategies for approaching this question type.

WHAT ARE SYNONYMS?

Synonyms are words with similar or same meanings. On the ISEE, you will see a word in capital letters and will be asked to find another word that is closest in meaning. Here is an example:

CAUTIOUS:

  (A) different

  (B) careful

  (C) angry

  (D) together

The question is asking you to pick which word among the answer options most nearly means the same thing as CAUTIOUS.

How would you define the word "cautious"? To be cautious means to display caution, or to be careful.

"Different" means "unlike," so (A) is incorrect. "Angry" means characterized by anger, so (C) is incorrect. "Together" can mean "in a group" or "composed and calm," so (D) is incorrect. Therefore, the only correct answer for this question is (B) careful.

Even though this example is a bit easier than some of the questions you will see on the ISEE, you can rest assured that every synonym question will have only **one correct answer**. Before moving onto the next question, be sure to look through all 4 answer choices to make sure you have really selected the correct answer. If multiple answers seem possible, it is your job to test out each answer choice to find which one is the best synonym for the word in capital letters. Be careful—the test will try to trick you by including many words that sound like possible synonyms! Continue reading for some strategies to help you avoid these misleading answer choices and select the best synonym every time.

APPROACHING SYNONYMS

Start by covering up the answer choices and thinking of your own definition for the word in capital letters. If it helps, write your definition down. If you can define the word easily, look for an answer that matches your definition. Try this with the example below:

CHARGE: (*Your definition:* _____)

    (A) release

    (B) accuse

    (C) belittle

    (D) conspire

If no answer choice fits the definition you chose, you might need to look for a different definition of the word.

CHARGE can mean "price" or "fee" (as in the phrase "free of charge"), but here there is no answer choice like "price" or "fee" or "cost."

To find other definitions of a word, come up with many **contexts**—phrases where you might have heard the word before. A word's context is everything in a phrase or sentence that might influence the word's meaning. The word CHARGE can have many different meanings, depending on its context.

It might be helpful to make yourself a bubble chart and think of as many phrases as you can:

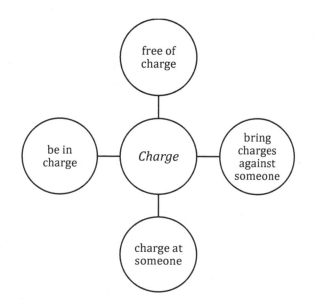

What does CHARGE mean in each of these contexts? To be "in charge" means to have power or be in control; to "charge at someone" means to attack suddenly or assault; and to "bring charges against someone" means to accuse or blame. The correct answer here is (B) accuse.

Exercise #1: For each of the following words, try to come up with three different contexts and write them in the bubble charts. If you run out of room, use a separate sheet of paper. The first word has been filled in for you. If you can think of more than three contexts, draw a new bubble! To check your work for this exercise, look up each word in a good dictionary and see if your contexts related to all of the word's possible meanings.

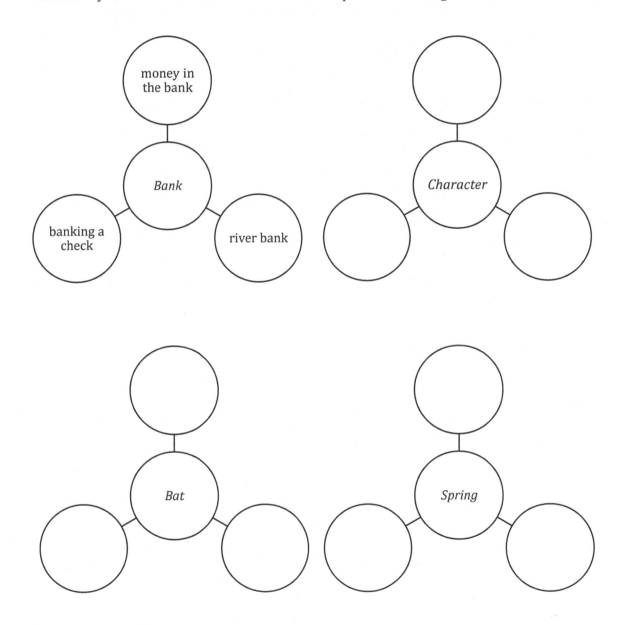

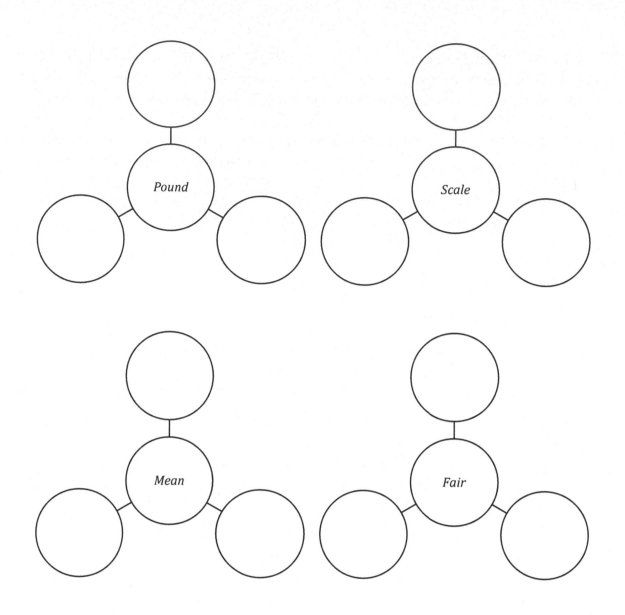

Looking for more words to try out? On a separate piece of paper, try drawing bubble charts for FINE, ROLL, FIGURE, LIE, SOLE, FAST, EXPRESS, and DRIVE. Not all of these words will have three different meanings, and some might have more than three.

USING CONTEXT TO DEFINE UNFAMILIAR WORDS

Coming up with **contexts** can also help you define a word that you only sort of know, or at least match it with an answer choice that makes sense. Look at the following example:

CONSENSUS:

(A) difference

(B) survey

(C) agreement

(D) dispute

Do you know the meaning of CONSENSUS? If not, can you think of a context in which you may have heard it used? Perhaps you have heard it in the context of "come to a consensus" or "arrive at a consensus."

What answer choices make sense in these contexts? Let's test: "come to a difference," "come to a survey," "come to an agreement," and "come to a dispute." The answer that makes the most sense is (C) agreement.

Exercise #2: See if you can come up with a context for each of the following words by writing a phrase you have heard that uses the word.. Then, try to guess a definition of the word based on its context. When you are finished, use a dictionary to check your answers. The first question has been filled out for you.

1. ADVANCE

   Context: advance to the front of the line

   Definition: to move forward. Other definitions: a forward movement ("the advance of civilization"), sent beforehand ("in advance").

2. PROMOTE

   Context:

   Definition:

3. AUTHENTIC

   Context:

   Definition:

4. NARRATE

   Context:

   Definition:

5. ESTABLISH

   Context:

   Definition:

Have you mastered the words above? Try your hand at these more challenging words:

6. LOFTY

   Context:

   Definition:

7. ALLEGIANCE

   Context:

   Definition:

8. SYMPATHETIC

   Context:

   Definition:

9. TESTIMONY

   Context:

   Definition:

10. AILMENT

Context:

Definition:

WORD CONNOTATIONS

A word's **connotation** is its secondary meaning, or the feeling we get from the word. A word can have a positive (+) connotation if it means something good, a negative (-) connotation if it means something bad, or a neutral connotation if it is neither good nor bad. For example, the word "horrible" has a negative connotation, whereas "joyous" has a positive connotation. If you can remember that a word means something positive or negative, you can eliminate answer choices with the opposite connotation. Your context can also help you remember if the word has a positive, negative, or neutral connotation.

Exercise #3: Try to come up with a context for the following words, and use this information to decide whether they have a positive, negative, or neutral connotation. Then, check your connotation with the answer key at the back of the book.. The first question has been filled out for you.

1. TRAGEDY

   Context: coping with the tragedy of Hurricane Sandy

   Connotation: negative

2. IRRITABLE

   Context:

   Connotation:

3. RADIANT

   Context:

   Connotation:

4. HAIL

   Context:

Connotation:

5. BLEAK

Context:

Connotation:

6. INADEQUATE

Context:

Connotation:

7. ADMIRATION

Context:

Connotation:

Have you mastered the words above? Try your hand at these more challenging words:

8. DILAPIDATED

Context:

Connotation:

9. EXEMPLARY

Context:

Connotation:

10. TURMOIL

Context:

Connotation:

11. ECSTASY

   Context:

   Connotation:

12. ABJECT

   Context:

   Connotation:

IF YOU GET STUCK

If you get stuck while solving a synonym question, try some of these strategies to get back on track.

WHAT IF YOU DON'T KNOW A WORD?

Building your vocabulary is the best way to prepare for the words you will see in the ISEE's synonym questions, as well as the rest of the Verbal Reasoning section. Take a look at the Vocabulary Building chapter at the end of the book for the best strategies for learning new words. Then, work your way through as much of the Core ISEE Vocabulary list as you are able, making sure to review old words as you learn new ones.

If you don't know a word in a synonym question, use the strategies we discussed above to try to identify a context for the word and guess at its meaning or connotation. You can also use your knowledge of common word parts—roots, prefixes, and suffixes—to try to relate the word to other words you might know. Take a look at the Word Roots, Prefixes, and Suffixes section in the Vocabulary Building chapter for more information.

You might see words you don't know in the answer choices. Remember that a word is not necessarily wrong just because you don't know it. Look at the words that you do know, and use the **Process of Elimination** to cross off any options that are wrong. Keep in mind that you are looking for the *best* synonym for the word in the question. If you eliminate all of the wrong answers and are left with only one choice, it might be the right answer, even if it is a word you don't know!

If this doesn't work, look at the **types of words** being used in the question. Here is a chart of the most common word types:

TYPES OF WORDS			
Word Type	**Definition**	**Examples**	**Sample Sentence**
Noun	a person, place, or thing: "things" can also include qualities or categories that you might not be able to touch or see	teacher, lawyer, city, Italy, animal, car, water, tool, hunger, comfort, curiosity, trust, emotion, science, art, biology	The young <u>puppy</u> ran quickly.

Verb	an action word: what the subject of the sentence (the main noun) is "doing"	run, hit, dig, carve, learn, hear, enjoy, understand, become, be	The young puppy <u>ran</u> quickly.
Adjective	a word that describes, identifies, or defines a noun	soft, sharp, green, full, loud, wet, happy, thoughtful, diligent, humorous, good	The <u>young</u> puppy ran quickly.
Adverb	a word that describes a verb, adjective, or another adverb: often ends in "-ly"	quickly, desperately, sadly, suddenly, freely, quietly, strangely, well	The young puppy ran <u>quickly</u>.

If you're able to identify the type of words in a synonym question, you can rest assured that the correct answer choice will be the same type of word. For example, if the question stem is a noun, you should cross off any answers that can't be nouns, and guess among the nouns that remain.

WHEN SHOULD YOU GUESS?

Always! You don't lose any points for wrong answers, so you should never leave a question blank. However, it is important to be smart about the way that you guess. Use the Process of Elimination to narrow down your answer choices, and if you are unable to choose between the remaining answers, make your best guess. The more wrong answers you are able to eliminate, the better chance you have of guessing the right answer. If you're not able to use the Process of Elimination to narrow down any of your answer options, then pick any answer and move on. It is more important to spend your time on the questions you do think you'll be able to solve, rather than worrying about the questions where you need to guess.

SYNONYM PRACTICE QUESTIONS

In this section, you will find 245 practice questions to prepare you for the types of synonym questions you might find on the ISEE. There are 6 sets of questions, grouped by difficulty. Pay attention to the difficulty of each set to determine which questions are appropriate for your level.

WARM-UP QUESTIONS

Use these questions to test your familiarity with basic synonym strategies for the Lower, Middle, and Upper Level ISEE.

1. ERROR:

    (A) edit
    (B) fear
    (C) mistake
    (D) pause

2. EXIT:

    (A) open
    (B) leave
    (C) undo
    (D) experience

3. CREATE:

    (A) find
    (B) glimpse
    (C) adore
    (D) make

4. REPLACEMENT:

    (A) substitute
    (B) pretense
    (C) move
    (D) location

5. BOLD:

    (A) old
    (B) daring
    (C) weak
    (D) submissive

6. TRY:

    (A) attempt
    (B) hold
    (C) plow
    (D) put

7. EMBRACE:

    (A) laugh
    (B) scold
    (C) hug
    (D) lug

8. SCARE:

    (A) cry
    (B) frighten
    (C) scold
    (D) shove

9. BOTHER:

    (A) tickle
    (B) snap
    (C) ignore
    (D) annoy

10. STUMBLE:

    (A) hum
    (B) chatter
    (C) trip
    (D) throw

BASIC QUESTIONS

Use these questions to practice the most basic difficulty level you might see on the Lower, Middle, and Upper Level ISEE. The Lower Level exam will include more basic questions than the Middle and Upper Levels.

1. DEMAND:
   (A) punish
   (B) give
   (C) request
   (D) yell

2. SHRIEK:
   (A) ghost
   (B) screech
   (C) whistle
   (D) song

3. CASUALLY:
   (A) unnecessarily
   (B) traditionally
   (C) disrespectfully
   (D) informally

4. HAZY:
   (A) sad
   (B) unclear
   (C) sloppy
   (D) harmful

5. MIRACLE:
   (A) gift
   (B) fortune
   (C) life
   (D) wonder

6. TECHNIQUE:
   (A) point
   (B) engineer
   (C) detail
   (D) method

7. INSPECT:
   (A) answer
   (B) plan
   (C) examine
   (D) require

8. ATTRACT:
   (A) annoy
   (B) refuse
   (C) interest
   (D) surprise

9. REALITY:
   (A) vision
   (B) theory
   (C) truth
   (D) persistence

10. DECEIVE:
   (A) clarify
   (B) predict
   (C) control
   (D) mislead

11. REGRETFUL:

   (A) enraged

   (B) sorry

   (C) stubborn

   (D) gleeful

12. DETACH:

   (A) separate

   (B) attack

   (C) torture

   (D) drop

13. CRATER:

   (A) cavity

   (B) lake

   (C) sphere

   (D) moon

14. FERTILE:

   (A) productive

   (B) deserted

   (C) warm

   (D) sympathetic

15. REFRESH:

   (A) polish

   (B) caress

   (C) practice

   (D) renew

16. COMBINE:

   (A) join

   (B) whisk

   (C) list

   (D) visit

17. CONSTRUCT:

   (A) carry

   (B) explain

   (C) destroy

   (D) build

18. VILE:

   (A) tasty

   (B) disgusting

   (C) strong

   (D) syrupy

19. DEFINITELY:

   (A) certainly

   (B) endlessly

   (C) likely

   (D) formally

20. APPEAR:

   (A) learn

   (B) seem

   (C) paint

   (D) simplify

21. ENCOUNTER:

   (A) betrayal

   (B) meeting

   (C) story

   (D) celebration

22. CATEGORIZE:

   (A) replace

   (B) classify

   (C) recount

   (D) found

23. COMPROMISE:

(A) bargain

(B) possibility

(C) ending

(D) trick

24. SOLITUDE:

(A) weariness

(B) forgetfulness

(C) isolation

(D) concern

25. FRAIL:

(A) shy

(B) imaginary

(C) expensive

(D) weak

26. FASCINATE:

(A) pacify

(B) imitate

(C) amuse

(D) interest

27. APPROACH:

(A) scare

(B) advance

(C) observe

(D) criticize

28. HUMOROUS:

(A) comic

(B) plump

(C) good

(D) ill

29. HUMBLE:

(A) boastful

(B) hungry

(C) quiet

(D) modest

30. PREDICT:

(A) relate

(B) confuse

(C) maneuver

(D) foretell

31. CONFESS:

(A) disappoint

(B) imprison

(C) admit

(D) reject

32. TRIUMPH:

(A) happiness

(B) truth

(C) obstacle

(D) victory

MEDIUM QUESTIONS

Use these questions to practice the medium difficulty level you might see on the Lower, Middle, and Upper Level ISEE. Questions like these will make up a majority of the Lower Level synonym section, and a smaller portion of the Middle and Upper Level sections.

1. FATIGUE:

   (A) service
   (B) exhaustion
   (C) relief
   (D) excitement

2. ADMIRING:

   (A) appreciative
   (B) wonderful
   (C) secretive
   (D) memorable

3. DREAD:

   (A) fear
   (B) animation
   (C) wish
   (D) fog

4. CLARITY:

   (A) desire
   (B) error
   (C) clearness
   (D) shine

5. AGENDA:

   (A) plan
   (B) effect
   (C) invitation
   (D) unit

6. PACT:

   (A) hymn
   (B) agreement
   (C) family
   (D) interest

7. HUE:

   (A) idea
   (B) interval
   (C) shade
   (D) shift

8. ERA:

   (A) extent
   (B) period
   (C) character
   (D) measurement

9. ASSIST:

   (A) need
   (B) prevent
   (C) support
   (D) create

10. REBEL:

    (A) prolong
    (B) invent
    (C) destroy
    (D) disobey

11. DEVOUR:

   (A) consume
   (B) insist
   (C) collect
   (D) expand

12. MANUAL:

   (A) boundary
   (B) guide
   (C) machine
   (D) heavy

13. POSTPONE:

   (A) consider
   (B) delay
   (C) confuse
   (D) mention

14. VOCALLY:

   (A) patiently
   (B) intriguingly
   (C) calmly
   (D) outspokenly

15. UNIFIED:

   (A) important
   (B) inspiring
   (C) together
   (D) national

16. RATIONALLY:

   (A) generously
   (B) peacefully
   (C) strictly
   (D) reasonably

17. BENEFIT:

   (A) energize
   (B) enhance
   (C) compose
   (D) lessen

18. ABUSE:

   (A) buoy
   (B) care
   (C) harm
   (D) partake

19. CONFIDE:

   (A) hide
   (B) rescue
   (C) entrust
   (D) develop

20. UTILIZE:

   (A) correct
   (B) invent
   (C) use
   (D) alter

21. PRODUCE:

   (A) create
   (B) expand
   (C) protect
   (D) impact

22. INQUIRE:

   (A) discover
   (B) question
   (C) reply
   (D) command

23. EXTINCT:

    (A) dull

    (B) short

    (C) completed

    (D) dead

24. OPTIMISTIC:

    (A) hopeful

    (B) cheerless

    (C) flawless

    (D) excellent

25. SACRIFICE:

    (A) complain

    (B) forgo

    (C) refuse

    (D) pray

26. BOUND:

    (A) unrestricted

    (B) restrained

    (C) confident

    (D) deep

27. THRILL:

    (A) surprise

    (B) excite

    (C) satisfy

    (D) annoy

28. NEUTRAL:

    (A) mental

    (B) unbiased

    (C) untrue

    (D) conservative

29. HORRID:

    (A) moist

    (B) massive

    (C) terrible

    (D) wasteful

30. BASHFULLY:

    (A) confidently

    (B) cruelly

    (C) hurtfully

    (D) shyly

31. LIMITATION:

    (A) constraint

    (B) range

    (C) speed

    (D) minimum

32. THOROUGH:

    (A) thoughtful

    (B) physical

    (C) complete

    (D) inefficient

33. HESITATION:

    (A) pause

    (B) moment

    (C) surge

    (D) boredom

34. RENEW:

    (A) sparkle

    (B) finish

    (C) clean

    (D) regenerate

35. REVEAL:

   (A) repair
   (B) expose
   (C) intersect
   (D) seek

36. ABSTRACT:

   (A) conceptual
   (B) healthy
   (C) unintentional
   (D) loose

37. FUNDAMENTAL:

   (A) accidental
   (B) additional
   (C) basic
   (D) hilarious

38. INSTINCTIVE:

   (A) detestable
   (B) favorable
   (C) intuitive
   (D) forgiving

39. CHUCKLE:

   (A) laugh
   (B) deride
   (C) grin
   (D) daydream

40. RARE:

   (A) old
   (B) uncommon
   (C) best
   (D) flawed

41. WRITHE:

   (A) enliven
   (B) wriggle
   (C) digress
   (D) grumble

42. ELDERLY:

   (A) fresh
   (B) employed
   (C) senior
   (D) decent

43. BIZARRE:

   (A) treasured
   (B) unhealthy
   (C) magical
   (D) unusual

44. LINGER:

   (A) tickle
   (B) remain
   (C) depart
   (D) select

45. ALTER:

   (A) sustain
   (B) offer
   (C) preserve
   (D) adjust

46. REVOLVE:

   (A) rotate
   (B) block
   (C) rethink
   (D) guide

47. EXHAUSTED:

(A) odorous
(B) depleted
(C) disappointed
(D) confused

48. SERIOUS:

(A) unfortunate
(B) important
(C) irresponsible
(D) angry

49. PARADE:

(A) procession
(B) holiday
(C) festival
(D) dance

50. CURRENT:

(A) antique
(B) contemporary
(C) useful
(D) electric

51. PURPOSE:

(A) finding
(B) expectation
(C) realization
(D) intent

52. REPOSE:

(A) death
(B) silence
(C) pomp
(D) rest

53. MATURE:

(A) capable
(B) developing
(C) adult
(D) decayed

54. CLARIFY:

(A) describe
(B) confuse
(C) orate
(D) explain

55. SYNOPSIS:

(A) letter
(B) diagnosis
(C) summary
(D) argument

56. SURLY:

(A) unfriendly
(B) mournful
(C) hopeful
(D) nostalgic

57. REMOTE:

(A) sophisticated
(B) respectful
(C) distant
(D) unimportant

58. EJECT:

(A) expel
(B) forgive
(C) ignore
(D) measure

59. NURTURE:

(A) commence

(B) soil

(C) nourish

(D) please

60. IMPACT:

(A) problem

(B) argument

(C) consequence

(D) conclusion

DIFFICULT QUESTIONS

Use these questions to practice the more advanced questions you might see on the Lower, Middle, and Upper Level ISEE. The Upper Level exam will include more difficult questions than the Middle and Lower Level exams.

1. VIVID:
   (A) beneficial
   (B) intense
   (C) living
   (D) upbeat

2. ELATED:
   (A) curious
   (B) delayed
   (C) delighted
   (D) grieving

3. CONVENTIONAL:
   (A) assembled
   (B) constructive
   (C) representative
   (D) customary

4. CONVERGE:
   (A) visit
   (B) overlook
   (C) align
   (D) unite

5. COUNSEL:
   (A) restraint
   (B) assembly
   (C) advice
   (D) committee

6. SKEPTICALLY:
   (A) doubtfully
   (B) intriguingly
   (C) sneakily
   (D) certainly

7. RECREATION:
   (A) regulation
   (B) gathering
   (C) production
   (D) amusement

8. ALLEVIATE:
   (A) injure
   (B) relieve
   (C) remove
   (D) believe

9. AGGRAVATE:
   (A) improve
   (B) dismiss
   (C) agitate
   (D) cultivate

10. IMPLY:
    (A) suggest
    (B) concern
    (C) define
    (D) suppress

11. ECCENTRIC:

   (A) perceptible
   (B) uniform
   (C) exciting
   (D) unusual

12. AMPLIFY:

   (A) indulge
   (B) intensify
   (C) hinder
   (D) compress

13. ILLUMINATE:

   (A) brighten
   (B) distort
   (C) flicker
   (D) glance

14. VEND:

   (A) acquire
   (B) sell
   (C) influence
   (D) catch

15. COMPOSURE:

   (A) lapse
   (B) arrangement
   (C) collectedness
   (D) harmony

16. INVERT:

   (A) reunite
   (B) reverse
   (C) transmute
   (D) calculate

17. GULLIBLE:

   (A) naive
   (B) deceptive
   (C) discerning
   (D) edible

18. QUIVER:

   (A) convulsion
   (B) inquiry
   (C) target
   (D) tremble

19. PONDER:

   (A) consider
   (B) dabble
   (C) ascertain
   (D) propose

20. MOURN:

   (A) torment
   (B) devastate
   (C) awaken
   (D) grieve

21. JUVENILE:

   (A) childish
   (B) criminal
   (C) jovial
   (D) compassionate

22. FUSION:

   (A) electricity
   (B) mixture
   (C) disorientation
   (D) duration

23. PROPORTION:

    (A) expanse

    (B) category

    (C) ratio

    (D) quality

24. SILKEN:

    (A) snide

    (B) bright

    (C) valuable

    (D) smooth

25. ROUT:

    (A) trip

    (B) perish

    (C) defeat

    (D) exhibit

26. ASSESS:

    (A) interrogate

    (B) determine

    (C) speculate

    (D) nominate

27. NULL:

    (A) veritable

    (B) mundane

    (C) nonexistent

    (D) corresponding

28. DISCLOSE:

    (A) insult

    (B) estimate

    (C) refrain

    (D) reveal

29. CONCISE:

    (A) contrary

    (B) decisive

    (C) specific

    (D) terse

30. CONTRACT:

    (A) shorten

    (B) dilute

    (C) uphold

    (D) absorb

31. FRINGE:

    (A) interior

    (B) edge

    (C) minimum

    (D) skirt

32. CREVICE:

    (A) closure

    (B) fissure

    (C) insight

    (D) warning

33. AIL:

    (A) afflict

    (B) interfere

    (C) aid

    (D) whine

34. EMBELLISH:

    (A) cleanse

    (B) resonate

    (C) decorate

    (D) individualize

35. ROTATION:
   (A) cycle
   (B) system
   (C) teamwork
   (D) formation

36. SERIAL:
   (A) granular
   (B) vicious
   (C) flying
   (D) recurring

37. MAKESHIFT:
   (A) dingy
   (B) valueless
   (C) improvised
   (D) unreliable

38. ANIMATE:
   (A) enliven
   (B) bewilder
   (C) hypnotize
   (D) organize

39. ADAMANT:
   (A) flexible
   (B) demonstrative
   (C) evident
   (D) obstinate

40. DISPERSE:
   (A) flourish
   (B) scatter
   (C) deduce
   (D) garner

41. IMMORAL:
   (A) dishonest
   (B) absurd
   (C) farcical
   (D) chaste

42. CHRONICLE:
   (A) dream
   (B) prospect
   (C) exhibit
   (D) narrative

43. SUBSIDE:
   (A) diminish
   (B) advance
   (C) descend
   (D) immerse

44. FAVOR:
   (A) dislike
   (B) halt
   (C) prefer
   (D) agree

45. INNOVATE:
   (A) jumble
   (B) pioneer
   (C) standardize
   (D) associate

46. INTRICATE:
   (A) confusing
   (B) systematic
   (C) distinctive
   (D) elaborate

47. INTERVENE:

    (A) arrange

    (B) suspend

    (C) mediate

    (D) permit

48. EMIT:

    (A) escape

    (B) enclose

    (C) inhale

    (D) expel

49. JEER:

    (A) heckle

    (B) whimper

    (C) incite

    (D) celebrate

50. TOIL:

    (A) contrast

    (B) imitate

    (C) pressure

    (D) labor

51. EXCAVATE:

    (A) withstand

    (B) unearth

    (C) occupy

    (D) surrender

52. ECLECTIC:

    (A) confined

    (B) assorted

    (C) rhythmic

    (D) perpetual

53. MAR:

    (A) despise

    (B) taint

    (C) contemplate

    (D) denounce

54. ADVERSE:

    (A) unstable

    (B) fortunate

    (C) unfavorable

    (D) invalid

55. LACKLUSTER:

    (A) ferocious

    (B) authoritarian

    (C) dull

    (D) dissatisfied

MIDDLE LEVEL CHALLENGE QUESTIONS

Use these questions to practice the most challenging questions you might see on both the Middle Level and Upper Level exams. These questions would very rarely appear on the Lower Level.

1. ALOOF:

    (A) advantageous
    (B) lofty
    (C) abiding
    (D) distant

2. BREVITY:

    (A) ardency
    (B) shortness
    (C) triviality
    (D) respiration

3. SUPERFLUOUS:

    (A) cursory
    (B) resplendent
    (C) extra
    (D) mellifluous

4. ANIMOSITY:

    (A) hostility
    (B) disposition
    (C) altruism
    (D) vitality

5. REMINISCE:

    (A) repress
    (B) depreciate
    (C) begrudge
    (D) recollect

6. DIGRESS:

    (A) dawdle
    (B) implicate
    (C) adjourn
    (D) deviate

7. PLAUSIBLE:

    (A) arbitrary
    (B) dubious
    (C) credible
    (D) laudable

8. CRITERION:

    (A) supposition
    (B) fulfillment
    (C) certainty
    (D) standard

9. ABYSMAL:

    (A) faithful
    (B) appalling
    (C) explicable
    (D) infallible

10. POTENT:

    (A) feckless
    (B) powerful
    (C) auspicious
    (D) insidious

11. ADVERSITY:

    (A) inquisition
    (B) misfortune
    (C) grief
    (D) intonation

12. IMPAIR:

    (A) criticize
    (B) acquire
    (C) harm
    (D) conjoin

13. OBSCURE:

    (A) indispensable
    (B) tangible
    (C) uncovered
    (D) cryptic

14. AMBIGUOUS:

    (A) explicit
    (B) unclear
    (C) mystical
    (D) grandiose

15. INCOMPETENT:

    (A) inconsistent
    (B) pacifist
    (C) pertinent
    (D) unskillful

16. PIOUS:

    (A) radical
    (B) articulate
    (C) secular
    (D) devoted

17. SOMBER:

    (A) deficient
    (B) melancholy
    (C) faulty
    (D) drowsy

18. DISSUADE:

    (A) confront
    (B) invalidate
    (C) insult
    (D) deter

19. INNATE:

    (A) inherent
    (B) acquired
    (C) deprived
    (D) miniscule

20. DELUSION:

    (A) opinion
    (B) misconception
    (C) extravagance
    (D) propensity

21. BENIGN:

    (A) harmless
    (B) insufficient
    (C) vacant
    (D) misshapen

22. BEWILDER:

    (A) commence
    (B) deceive
    (C) confuse
    (D) banish

23. ASSIMILATE:

(A) recognize
(B) interpret
(C) negotiate
(D) incorporate

24. EFFUSIVE:

(A) obese
(B) harmonious
(C) overflowing
(D) integrative

25. REMORSE:

(A) compunction
(B) aversion
(C) sentiment
(D) misfortune

26. ANALOGOUS:

(A) uncompromising
(B) corresponding
(C) disparate
(D) synthetic

27. APPEASE:

(A) commemorate
(B) censure
(C) impede
(D) satisfy

28. SLANDER:

(A) admonish
(B) debate
(C) defamation
(D) approval

29. CONTINGENT:

(A) worldly
(B) tentative
(C) dependent
(D) imperceptible

30. PERUSE:

(A) browse
(B) bypass
(C) overlook
(D) reprocess

31. DAUNT:

(A) instigate
(B) broadcast
(C) revoke
(D) intimidate

32. DEXTERITY:

(A) assurance
(B) aptitude
(C) adroitness
(D) slyness

33. CONVICTION:

(A) belief
(B) facility
(C) concept
(D) imprisonment

34. ALIENATE:

(A) abduct
(B) baffle
(C) relinquish
(D) estrange

35. ERADICATE:

   (A) neglect
   (B) repurpose
   (C) dismay
   (D) remove

36. PARODY:

   (A) spoof
   (B) tact
   (C) illustration
   (D) competition

37. EXACERBATE:

   (A) abolish
   (B) ostracize
   (C) worsen
   (D) flaunt

38. PROLIFIC:

   (A) irrational
   (B) uncouth
   (C) zealous
   (D) fruitful

39. DORMANT:

   (A) anxious
   (B) inactive
   (C) domestic
   (D) fatigued

40. SPORADIC:

   (A) crowded
   (B) calculating
   (C) fitful
   (D) bountiful

41. ADHERE:

   (A) elude
   (B) cling
   (C) deteriorate
   (D) disown

42. ELOQUENTLY:

   (A) tranquilly
   (B) expertly
   (C) verbosely
   (D) articulately

43. ABYSS:

   (A) chasm
   (B) ignorance
   (C) accumulation
   (D) vehemence

44. AMIABLE:

   (A) appropriate
   (B) adroit
   (C) opposed to
   (D) agreeable

45. HEINOUS:

   (A) horrifying
   (B) empathetic
   (C) suspended
   (D) unyielding

46. WANE:

   (A) misguide
   (B) embolden
   (C) decrease
   (D) disconcert

47. AFFINITY:

(A) poise
(B) candor
(C) attraction
(D) subversion

48. AVERSE:

(A) accommodating
(B) opposing
(C) disproportionate
(D) variable

49. CURTAIL:

(A) astonish
(B) persevere
(C) ridicule
(D) abbreviate

50. EMULATE:

(A) astound
(B) imitate
(C) reinforce
(D) misrepresent

UPPER LEVEL CHALLENGE QUESTIONS

Use these questions to practice the most challenging questions that you might see on the Upper Level exam. These questions would very rarely appear on the Middle or Lower Levels.

1. CHOLERIC:

   (A) benevolent
   (B) irritable
   (C) sickly
   (D) vociferous

2. GARRULOUS:

   (A) talkative
   (B) combative
   (C) derogatory
   (D) taciturn

3. JOCUND:

   (A) fortuitous
   (B) masculine
   (C) cheerful
   (D) ascetic

4. AMBIVALENT:

   (A) lavish
   (B) cranky
   (C) certain
   (D) irresolute

5. ABHOR:

   (A) request
   (B) irritate
   (C) hate
   (D) corrupt

6. FURTIVE:

   (A) changing
   (B) secretive
   (C) malignant
   (D) defiant

7. AUDACIOUS:

   (A) puzzling
   (B) distressed
   (C) daring
   (D) unnecessary

8. GREGARIOUS:

   (A) sociable
   (B) volatile
   (C) reckless
   (D) agrarian

9. DOGMATIC:

   (A) superficial
   (B) opinionated
   (C) liberal
   (D) canine

10. BELLIGERENT:

    (A) noble
    (B) exuberant
    (C) aggressive
    (D) stubborn

11. PRETENTIOUS:

   (A) priceless
   (B) nonchalant
   (C) careful
   (D) pompous

12. RECALCITRANT:

   (A) incongruous
   (B) reluctant
   (C) noisy
   (D) disobedient

13. AFFABLE:

   (A) disrespectful
   (B) weak
   (C) insignificant
   (D) friendly

14. LAMENT:

   (A) subdue
   (B) scrutinize
   (C) bemoan
   (D) sever

15. FRUGAL:

   (A) economical
   (B) negligible
   (C) atrocious
   (D) blundering

16. FICKLE:

   (A) headstrong
   (B) vacillating
   (C) outrageous
   (D) fabricated

17. INSINUATION:

   (A) division
   (B) suggestion
   (C) junction
   (D) transgression

18. COMPLACENT:

   (A) stagnant
   (B) servile
   (C) redundant
   (D) contented

19. GLUTTONOUS:

   (A) guilty
   (B) greedy
   (C) cynical
   (D) murderous

20. INSOLENTLY:

   (A) fervently
   (B) rudely
   (C) narcissistically
   (D) tastelessly

21. LETHARGIC:

   (A) sluggish
   (B) thorough
   (C) soothing
   (D) authoritative

22. RAMPANT:

   (A) illogical
   (B) kinetic
   (C) obedient
   (D) uncontrolled

23. MITIGATE:

   (A) save
   (B) forfeit
   (C) relieve
   (D) merge

24. INADVERTENT:

   (A) detailed
   (B) nomadic
   (C) accidental
   (D) truthful

25. DESPONDENT:

   (A) obsessive
   (B) abominable
   (C) hopeless
   (D) regretful

26. OSTENTATIOUS:

   (A) affectionate
   (B) generous
   (C) showy
   (D) avian

27. ABATE:

   (A) obliterate
   (B) coalesce
   (C) placate
   (D) dwindle

28. BANAL:

   (A) commonplace
   (B) whimsical
   (C) prosperous
   (D) obligatory

29. CONDONE:

   (A) spread
   (B) nourish
   (C) accept
   (D) confirm

30. LISTLESS:

   (A) quiet
   (B) hidden
   (C) unruly
   (D) languid

31. PRECOCIOUS:

   (A) incoherent
   (B) magnificent
   (C) advanced
   (D) childlike

32. GERMANE:

   (A) poignant
   (B) applicable
   (C) familiar
   (D) contaminated

33. CORPULENT:

   (A) squalid
   (B) stout
   (C) mortal
   (D) wealthy

34. ARCANE:

   (A) secret
   (B) overused
   (C) royal
   (D) obsolete

35. INANE:

   (A) dingy
   (B) silly
   (C) crazed
   (D) barren

36. HAPHAZARD:

   (A) emotional
   (B) fractional
   (C) disorganized
   (D) argumentative

37. DISTENDED:

   (A) offensive
   (B) splendid
   (C) unsettled
   (D) swollen

38. BALEFUL:

   (A) helpful
   (B) menacing
   (C) contemptuous
   (D) compliant

SENTENCE COMPLETION

PART 2

SENTENCE COMPLETION STRATEGIES

The second half of the ISEE Verbal Reasoning section takes the form of sentence completion questions. In this section, read about the best strategies for approaching this question type.

WHAT IS SENTENCE COMPLETION?

Sentence completion questions are "fill-in-the-blank" questions. On the ISEE, you will see a sentence with a portion missing, and you will need to pick a word or phrase that logically completes the sentence. Here is an example:

> A sloth's fur provides --------, which enables the sloth to blend into surrounding leaves and trees.
>
> (A) warmth
> (B) camouflage
> (C) nutrition
> (D) environment

This question is asking you to select the word that would make the most sense with the entire sentence. Let's look at the answer options one by one. A sloth's fur could provide warmth, but warmth wouldn't allow the sloth to blend into surrounding leaves and trees, so (A) is incorrect. A sloth's fur doesn't provide nutrition or an environment, and neither allow the sloth to blend into its environment, so choices (C) and (D) are incorrect.

Therefore, the only correct answer for this question is (B) camouflage. "Camouflage" means something that allows a person or animal to blend in with its surroundings, so this word best fits the meaning of the whole sentence.

Regardless of the difficulty of the question, every sentence completion question on the ISEE will have only **one correct answer**. Before moving onto the next question, be sure to look through all 4 answer choices to make sure you have really selected the correct answer. If multiple answers seem possible, it is your job to test out each answer choice to find which one best completes the sentence as a whole. Be careful—the test will try to trick you by including many words that sound like they could *possibly* fit with the sentence, but aren't actually the *best* fit! Continue reading for some strategies to help you avoid these misleading answer choices and select the best answer every time.

APPROACHING SENTENCE COMPLETION

LOOK FOR CLUES

Start by covering up the answer choices and reading the entire sentence to yourself, skipping over the blanks. Try to get a sense of the sentence's main message, even with the missing words.

Then, think of a way that you might complete the sentence. Circle or underline **clues** nearby in the sentence that could help you identify what type of words should go in the blanks. Does part of the sentence define the words you are looking for, or does it give you contrasting information? Are there any positive or negative words in the sentence that could tell you the type of words you are looking for?

WRITE YOUR OWN WORDS

When you have an idea of what types of words could complete the sentence, write them down. Then, uncover the answer choices and look for an answer that matches the word or words you wrote down.

Let's give this strategy a try with the example from the previous page:

> A sloth's fur provides --------, which enables the sloth to blend into surrounding leaves and trees.

Before looking at the answer choices again, can we identify any clues in this sentence that would give us an idea of what word should go in the blank? The sentence gives us two clues: we're looking for something a sloth's fur can provide, and something that would allow the sloth to blend into its surroundings. Let's underline these clues and come up with our own word to go in the blank. We might try something like "disguise":

> A sloth's <u>fur provides</u> *a disguise*, which enables the sloth to <u>blend into surrounding leaves and trees</u>.

Now we can look at the answer choices and decide which one best matches the word "disguise." Here are the answer choices again:

(A) warmth

(B) camouflage

(C) nutrition

(D) environment

"Warmth," "nutrition," and "environment" aren't close in meaning to the word "disguise," so (A), (C), and (D) are probably incorrect. However, "camouflage" is a type of disguise used by soldiers and other people or animals to blend into their environments. Therefore, (B) is a likely answer.

PLUG IT IN

When you have chosen a likely answer for the question, the last step is to test your answer by **plugging it in** to the rest of the sentence to make sure that it fits. In order to be completely sure that you have chosen the best answer, plug in all of the other choices as well. This will help you make sure that you have really chosen the **best fit** for the entire sentence.

Let's plug all of the answer choices for our example problem back into the sentence in order to make sure that (B) is really the best fit:

✘ (A) A sloth's fur provides *warmth*, which enables the sloth to blend into surrounding leaves and trees.

✓ (B) A sloth's fur provides *camouflage*, which enables the sloth to blend into surrounding leaves and trees.

✘ (C) A sloth's fur provides *nutrition*, which enables the sloth to blend into surrounding leaves and trees.

✘ (D) A sloth's fur provides *environment*, which enables the sloth to blend into surrounding leaves and trees.

The only sentence that makes sense is (B), so we can be confident that (B) camouflage best completes the meaning of the entire sentence.

TYPES OF CLUES

Identifying clues in each sentence completion question will help you pick the one correct answer choice to complete the sentence. When you are looking for these clues, you'll want to pay attention to certain types of words that provide information about the structure and tone of the sentence. Let's look at these different types of clues now.

DEFINITIONS AND SYNONYMS

When you are reading a sentence, pay close attention to any part of the sentence that provides a **definition** or **synonym** of the missing words or phrases. As we saw in the previous section, a synonym is a word that shares the same meaning as another word. For instance, take a look at the sample question below:

A good diplomat must demonstrate -------- by handling difficult situations in a sensitive manner.

    (A) enthusiasm

    (B) decision

    (C) tact

    (D) politics

In this example, the most important clue is the second part of the sentence: *handling difficult situations in a sensitive manner*. This gives us a good idea for the definition of the missing word, which should have something to do with sensitivity and consideration.

Looking at the answer choices, we can see that (A) enthusiasm, (B) decision, and (D) politics don't fit this definition. Diplomats may need to be enthusiastic in some cases, and may need to be involved in making decisions and handling politics, but none of these words means "handling difficult situations in a sensitive manner." The only word that fits this definition is (C) tact, which means sensitivity in dealing with people or issues. Therefore, (C) is the best answer.

Exercise #1: For each sample sentence below, circle or underline the part of the sentence that defines or provides a synonym for the missing word. Then, write your own word or phrase to complete the sentence. Have a trusted reader check your work.

   1.   Many of William Shakespeare's plays were --------, depicting entertaining characters in amusing situations.

My word or phrase:

2. Providing a home for a wide variety of fish, mollusks, crustaceans, and other ocean species, coral reefs are some of the most diverse -------- on the planet.

    My word or phrase:

3. The gray wolf is usually a -------- animal, travelling and hunting in packs instead of on its own.

    My word or phrase:

4. The painter Mark Rothko was known for using -------- colors, which were so intense that they seemed to radiate off of the canvas.

    My word or phrase:

5. Most varieties of algae are -------- organisms, lacking complex cells and organs.

    My word or phrase:

6. During the Industrial Revolution, inventors contributed to many important technological --------, which included new methods for more efficient textile manufacturing, water power, and iron production.

    My word or phrase:

7. A reflex is a(n) -------- reaction, spontaneous and not controlled by conscious thought.

    My word or phrase:

8. During the early 20th century, Pablo Picasso's style of painting grew more diverse as he -------- different theories, techniques, and ideas.

    My word or phrase:

TONE WORDS

When you are looking for clues, pay attention to any positive or negative words in the sentence. These might tell you something about the **tone** of the sentence—that is, whether the sentence is describing something positive or negative. This information can help you decide whether the missing word or phrase should be positive, negative, or neutral.

Here's an example:

> The long hours, tedious tasks, and stressful work environment made Susanne --------.
>
> (A) motivated to do her best work.
> (B) dissatisfied with her job.
> (C) optimistic about her future.
> (D) unaware of her surroundings.

What tone words did you find in this sentence? The sentence describes Susanne's work as "long," "tedious," and "stressful," which are all negative words. Therefore, we can guess that Susanne's work makes her feel somewhat unhappy.

Based on this information, we can eliminate answer choices (A) and (C), because "motivated" and "optimistic" are both positive words: it isn't very likely that a tedious and stressful job would make Susanne feel motivated or optimistic. We can also eliminate choice (D), because "unaware of her surroundings" doesn't fit with the sentence as a whole: why would a stressful environment make Susanne unaware of what is going on around her? Therefore, the best answer choice is (B). "Dissatisfied" is a negative word, and it makes sense that long hours and tedious, stressful work would make Susanne feel dissatisfied with her employment.

Exercise #2: For each of the following sentences, circle any tone words, and identify whether the tone is positive or negative. Then, try to come up with your own word or phrase to complete the sentence. Have a trusted reader check your work.

1. A winner of the 1964 Nobel Peace Prize, Martin Luther King, Jr. is internationally -------- as a leader in the African-American Civil Rights Movement.

    Tone:

    My word or phrase:

2. The young Thomas Jefferson was a -------- student, who applied himself seriously to his studies and completed his university degree in only two years.

Tone:

My word or phrase:

3. The giant panda population has -------- as a result of low birthrates and the destruction of its natural habitat.

   Tone:

   My word or phrase:

4. With many important discoveries in geometry and number theory, the ancient Greeks helped -------- the field of mathematics.

   Tone:

   My word or phrase:

5. The 2010 Haiti Earthquake caused major damage and heavy casualties, making it one of the most -------- earthquakes in the country's history.

   Tone:

   My word or phrase:

6. U.S. President Andrew Johnson made many -------- decisions while in office, which sparked widespread public debate and disagreement.

   Tone:

   My word or phrase:

TRANSITION WORDS

Transition words are important clues that tell you how the sentence is structured: they let you know whether part of the sentence **supports** an earlier statement, **contrasts** with what came before, or shows **cause and effect**. Looking for transition words will help you decide what words or phrases would fit best with the structure of the sentence as a whole.

Here are some common transition words:

TRANSITION WORDS		
Support	**Contrast**	**Cause and Effect**
and	but	because
in addition	yet	so
as well as	however	therefore
furthermore	though	thus
likewise	although	consequently
similarly	even though	as a result
moreover	despite	in order to
	instead	since
	rather	
	nonetheless	

Let's take a look at how these transition words work. Here's an example of a **supporting** transition word:

> Harriet Tubman played an important role in the fight against slavery; moreover, she was -------- for later generations of African Americans struggling for civil rights.
>
> (A) embattled
> (B) influential
> (C) difficult
> (D) unnecessary

The first part of this sentence tells us that Harriet Tubman was "important" during the fight against slavery, and the second part of the sentence connects her to the American Civil Rights movement. The transition word "moreover" tells us that the second part of this sentence *supports* the first part, so Harriet Tubman must also have been important for later generations of African Americans.

We can immediately eliminate (C) difficult and (D) unnecessary, because neither of these mean something like "important." "Embattled," (A), means "involved in war," which could possibly describe Harriet Tubman's fight against slavery, but does not describe how she was important for later generations. "Influential" means having an important effect (an influence) on another person. Therefore, (B) is the best answer to support the first part of the sentence.

Now let's look at an example of a **contrasting** transition word:

> Although Vincent Van Gogh is now considered one of the most notable painters of the 19th century, his work received very little -------- during his lifetime.
>
> (A) recognition
> (B) style
> (C) history
> (D) criticism

The first part of this sentence tells us that Vincent Van Gogh is now thought of as a "notable" painter, or one that is important or remarkable. The transition word "although" tells us that the second part of the sentence *contrasts* with this first part. Therefore, during his lifetime, Vincent Van Gogh must not have been considered notable.

We can eliminate (B) style and (C) history, because neither word conveys the idea that Vincent Van Gogh's work was not considered notable. "Criticism," (D), is a negative word, but when we plug it back into the sentence it doesn't actually contrast with the first part: "his work received very little criticism during his lifetime" means that people did not judge his work or disapprove of it. Therefore, (A) is the best answer: "his work received very little recognition during his lifetime" means that his work was not noticed or appreciated when he was living. This contrasts well with the first part of the sentence, which states that his work is noticed and appreciated today.

Finally, here's an example of a **cause and effect** transition word:

> Because agricultural and industrial practices have -------- many of the world's rainforests, the habitats of many rare rainforest species are disappearing.
>
> (A) driven
> (B) explored
> (C) opposed
> (D) destroyed

The first part of this sentence tells us that agriculture and industry are doing something to rainforests, and the second part of the sentence tells us that many rainforest species are losing their habitats. The transition word "because" sets up a *cause-and-effect* relationship: the rainforest species are losing their habitats *because* of the effect of agriculture and industry. If the species' habitats are disappearing, we can conclude that agriculture and industry are somehow harming the rainforests.

We can eliminate (A) driven and (B) explored, because neither of these convey harmful actions towards the rainforests. "Opposed," (C), is a negative word, but it doesn't fit in the context of the sentence. It doesn't make sense for something to "oppose" a natural entity like a rainforest, and this word also doesn't directly explain why the habitats of rainforest species would be disappearing. Therefore, the best answer is (D) destroyed: if agriculture and industry have destroyed many rainforests, this would have a clearly harmful effect on the habitats of rainforest species.

Exercise #3: In each of the sentences below, there are two possible transition words or phrases. For each sentence, circle the word or phrase that best fits with the structure of the sentence as a whole. Check your answers in the answer key at the back of this book.

1. Mark considers himself a generally optimistic person, *and / even though* he sometimes worries about the future.

2. Robert Frost grew up in the city, *but / so* he became famous for poems about rural life and the natural world.

3. The architect did not want his new building to clash with the other buildings in the neighborhood; *likewise / instead*, he wanted his building to look like it belonged.

4. Amanda spent many hours diligently practicing the piano; *however / as a result*, her skills improved significantly.

5. Gymnast Kerri Strug is known for her strong performance during the 1996 Olympic Games *despite / as well as* a severe ankle injury.

6. Porpoises do not share the same diet as dolphins; *nonetheless / therefore*, the two species are not competitors for food supplies.

7. *Although / Because* most actors don't achieve recognition until they are adults, the actress Shirley Temple was well-known for her many television and film roles as a child.

8. It is complicated to design experiments that accurately test animal intelligence; *furthermore / consequently*, experiments with certain wild animals are very expensive to run.

SPECIAL QUESTION TYPES

Most sentence completion questions on the ISEE only ask you to fill in one blank to complete the sentence. However, if you are taking the Lower Level or Upper Level exam, there are two other special question types that you might see. We'll take a look at strategies for these types of questions now.

PHRASE RESPONSES: LOWER LEVEL ONLY

On the Lower Level test, the last 6 sentence completion questions of the Verbal Reasoning section will be **phrase responses**. These questions ask you to complete a sentence with a full phrase, rather than a word or two. The questions will give you the beginning of a sentence, and you'll need to pick the best phrase to finish the sentence.

Here's an example:

Because the school bus was delayed, the students --------.

    (A) sat in the front seat

    (B) were late to school

    (C) had pizza for lunch

    (D) handed in their homework

A phrase response question is just like any other sentence completion question. All we need to do is look for clues in the sentence, make a guess for how the sentence should be finished, and pick the answer choice that best fits with the entire sentence.

In the example question above, the transition word "because" tells us that this is a cause-and-effect sentence: the first part of the sentence is causing some effect to occur. What type of effect would a delayed school bus have on the students? If the school bus were delayed, we can guess that the students were also delayed.

We can eliminate choices (A), (C), and (D) because a delayed school bus wouldn't likely cause students to sit in the front seat, have pizza, or hand in their homework. The only answer that makes sense is (B), because a delayed school bus could very possibly make students late for school.

As you can see, phrase response questions aren't any harder than any other sentence completion questions. Just remember to look for transition words that tell you something about the sentence structure, and then pick an answer that is the best fit for that structure.

PAIRED WORD RESPONSES: UPPER LEVEL ONLY

On the Upper Level test, the last 9 questions of the Verbal Reasoning section will be **paired word responses**. Instead of filling in one blank in the sentence, these questions ask you to fill in two blanks. The answer choices will be pairs of words, and you will need to select the answer choices where *both* words are the best fit for the whole sentence.

Here's an example:

> Although the African-American cultural revival known as the Harlem Renaissance was -------- in the Harlem neighborhood of New York City, it also -------- many writers and artists in Africa and the Caribbean.
>
> (A) centered ... hindered
>
> (B) overlooked ... affected
>
> (C) rooted ... inspired
>
> (D) unknown ... compelled

Paired word responses are slightly more complicated than other sentence completion questions, but the process for solving them is the same. First, look for clues in the sentence that will help you guess what type of words should go in the blanks. Pay close attention to any words in the sentence that point to a certain relationship between the two words. Then, take a look at your answer choices, and **work on one word at a time**. Eliminate any answers that don't fit in the first blank, and only look at the remaining answers to decide which word would fit in the second blank.

In the sentence above, it looks like the first blank is describing a relationship between the Harlem Renaissance and the Harlem neighborhood. Because they share a name, we can guess that the Harlem Renaissance and the Harlem neighborhood might be closely connected in some way. Therefore, we're looking for a word that would describe this close connection. We can look at the first word in each of our answer options and eliminate any choices that don't make sense. (B) overlooked and (D) unknown don't convey the sense of a close relationship, so we can cross them out. We're left with (A) centered and (C) rooted, which both seem like they might work.

Now that we've narrowed down our answer choices for the first blank, we have to look for clues to determine how this word is related to the second blank. The first part of the sentence starts with "Although," which tells us that there is some sort of contrast or surprise in this sentence. If the Harlem Renaissance was centered or rooted in Harlem, we wouldn't expect it to have a big effect on people in Africa and the Caribbean. However—this is the surprise!—the word "also" tells us that the Harlem Renaissance somehow had a *similar* effect on those areas as it did in Harlem. Because the Harlem Renaissance seemed to be central to Harlem, we can predict that the second blank must also mean something positive or important.

Now that we've identified a possible meaning for the second word, we can choose between answers (A) and (C). The second word in answer (A) is "hindered," which means "held back"—not something positive or important. However, the second word in answer (C) is "inspired," which does match the meaning we're looking for. When we plug answer (C) back into the sentence, we see that it is the best fit for both words: "Although the African-American cultural revival known as the Harlem Renaissance was *rooted* in the Harlem neighborhood of New York City, it also *inspired* many writers and artists in Africa and the Caribbean."

IF YOU GET STUCK

If you get stuck while solving a sentence completion question, try some of these strategies to get back on track.

WHAT IF YOU DON'T KNOW A WORD?

If you don't know a word in the sentence, try using your knowledge of **context** to guess at a relationship. For example, let's pretend the question is "A barometer is an instrument that -------- pressure," and you don't know what "barometer" means. Even if you don't know the exact meaning of "barometer," you may notice that it ends in "meter." Do you know any other words that end in meter? You probably know the word "thermometer," which measures temperature, so you might be able to guess that a barometer is another type of measuring device. From the words given in the sentence, it would make sense to guess that a barometer measures pressure. Now you can test your answer choices to see if your guess makes sense—if there is an answer choice that means something like "measure," you're probably on the right track.

If the answer choices contain words you don't know, don't assume that these answer choices are automatically wrong. First, use the **Process of Elimination** to narrow down your answer options based on the words you do know. Remember that you are looking for the **best fit**—if none of the other answer options seem exactly right, perhaps the answer with the unfamiliar word is the right one after all.

Keep in mind that the best way to prepare for unfamiliar words in the sentence completion section (and the entire Verbal Reasoning section) is to learn as much vocabulary as possible beforehand. Spend time working through the Vocabulary Building chapter at the end of this book. The more words you know, the more questions you will be able to answer!

WHEN SHOULD YOU GUESS?

For the whole ISEE exam, you should always guess. Never leave a question on the ISEE blank! Remember to use the Process of Elimination to narrow down your answer options and increase your odds of guessing the right answer. Then, make your best guess and move on. Don't waste time worrying about whether or how to guess—it is important that you have enough time to get through the section and give every question a shot.

Ivy Global

SENTENCE COMPLETION PRACTICE QUESTIONS

In this section, you will find 174 practice questions to prepare you for the types of sentence completion questions you might find on the ISEE. There are 6 sets of questions, grouped by difficulty. Pay attention to the difficulty of each set to determine which questions are appropriate for your level.

WARM-UP QUESTIONS

Use these questions to test your familiarity with basic sentence completion strategies for the Lower, Middle, and Upper Level ISEE.

1. Ethan was uncomfortable in large crowds and was most -------- when he could be alone.

   (A) happy
   (B) afraid
   (C) guilty
   (D) bored

2. She tried to keep the different ingredients for her dish -------- so their flavors would not get mixed together.

   (A) accused
   (B) separated
   (C) observed
   (D) spoiled

3. Because Natalie had always loved animals, --------.

   (A) she had never had any pets.
   (B) her mother made her go to soccer practice.
   (C) she studied them in her free time.
   (D) she did not think her friend's puppy was cute.

4. The Mountain Bluebird gets its name because it often lives on the tallest -------- of a mountain.

    (A) talon
    (B) pit
    (C) peak
    (D) lake

5. John thought the movie would be boring and --------, so he was very surprised by the plot twist at the end.

    (A) predictable
    (B) realistic
    (C) active
    (D) harmful

6. Although Ed bought all the materials to make a model airplane, --------.

    (A) he loved building things.
    (B) he never found the time to build it.
    (C) his father enjoyed building models with him.
    (D) he bought screws, nails, wood, and other useful things.

7. After moving in, Sarah -------- all the furniture in the house so that it looked the way she wanted it to.

    (A) preferred
    (B) hauled
    (C) arranged
    (D) measured

8. People still remember President Abraham Lincoln as -------- because he always insisted on telling the truth.

    (A) fake
    (B) honest
    (C) harsh
    (D) clear

9. If Lorna had studied the water cycle, --------.

    (A) she would have been excited to go home after school.
    (B) her mother would have reminded her to study.
    (C) she would have been able to describe it on the test.
    (D) she would not have known the difference between condensation and evaporation.

10. Even though Emily Dickinson is a famous poet today, --------.

    (A) she wrote almost 1,800 poems.
    (B) she was not well known while she was alive.
    (C) her poems were very short
    (D) she sent many poems and letters to her friends and family.

BASIC QUESTIONS

Use these questions to practice the most basic difficulty level you might see on the Lower, Middle, and Upper Level ISEE. The Lower Level exam will include more basic questions than the Middle and Upper Levels. Phrase responses will only occur on the Lower Level.

1. After negotiating the price with the car salesman, David and Pete -------- a yellow convertible.

    (A) purchased
    (B) salvaged
    (C) debated
    (D) approximated

2. While millions of people around the world have heard of the Taj Mahal, --------.

    (A) Shah Jahan used new techniques to build it.
    (B) it was built as a tribute to Shah Jahan's wife.
    (C) only a small percentage of people have actually seen it.
    (D) many scholars have tried to explain why the monument is so popular.

3. Jane and Monica made a pact to stay friends forever, and they fulfilled this -------- by remaining friends until the ends of their lives.

    (A) vow
    (B) parody
    (C) devotion
    (D) incision

4. It is important to discuss the -------- of an experiment so that other researchers can know what steps to follow when repeating it.

    (A) methods
    (B) defenses
    (C) specks
    (D) communications

5. After she saw her dog chew through her pillows, Hannah realized that only training would stop the animal's -------- behavior.

    (A) weary
    (B) unruly
    (C) stationary
    (D) comical

6. Because the reservoir contained the town's drinking water, --------.

    (A) no one was allowed to swim in it.
    (B) people thought it seemed spooky at night.
    (C) different reservoirs serve different purposes.
    (D) Lucy spent long hours reading in the park near it.

7. For her submission to an architecture design contest, the architect -------- a plan for a new kind of skyscraper.

   (A) developed
   (B) inspired
   (C) competed
   (D) pressured

8. Katie -------- her older sister by pulling her hair and calling her names.

   (A) pacified
   (B) tormented
   (C) detested
   (D) entrusted

9. Although Helen Keller was both deaf and blind, --------.

   (A) Anne Sullivan was her teacher.
   (B) she learned to communicate with others.
   (C) it was challenging for her to learn sign language.
   (D) she had scarlet fever at the age of two.

10. Ted was so cheerful and good-spirited that he laughed -------- at everyone's jokes, even the bad ones.

    (A) blandly
    (B) identically
    (C) aggressively
    (D) heartily

11. Because the king had -------- that his neighbors were weak, he was surprised to discover that they actually had strong armies.

    (A) inquired
    (B) assumed
    (C) overthrew
    (D) revealed

12. Although the rest of her family was not particularly musical, Annette had a -------- for playing the piano.

    (A) talent
    (B) dialect
    (C) tact
    (D) distress

13. The trade of -------- pets such as tigers, lions, and wolf-hybrids is illegal, yet people still import these animals from foreign countries.

    (A) domestic
    (B) exotic
    (C) aquatic
    (D) alarmed

14. Clara's passion for exploring in the wild led her to --------.

    (A) venture deep into the forest.
    (B) attempt to read difficult books.
    (C) boast of never having traveled outside her town.
    (D) contest those who said they knew less about animals than she did.

15. Because Anna Pavlova was such an -------- dancer, she became one of the most famous ballerinas in the world.

    (A) endangered

    (B) obvious

    (C) accomplished

    (D) exasperated

16. As a responsible pet owner, Anna never -------- to feed her hamster.

    (A) suffocated

    (B) neglected

    (C) prevented

    (D) desired

17. Although many of Jules Verne's books discuss his characters' --------, Verne himself traveled very little in his life.

    (A) myths

    (B) voyages

    (C) illustrations

    (D) strategies

18. Using clever deception, the -------- fox was able to outwit the hunter.

    (A) highbrow

    (B) somber

    (C) cunning

    (D) superb

19. While many think that Watson and Crick were the first to identify DNA's double helix, --------.

    (A) they worked together on this discovery.

    (B) Maurice Wilkins was their research assistant at the time.

    (C) some argue that Rosalind Franklin made this discovery before them.

    (D) they were honored for their findings with a Nobel Prize in 1962.

20. For Madeline, completing the entire marathon was an -------- on its own; she was proud to have finished, and it did not matter how long she had taken.

    (A) achievement

    (B) ideal

    (C) obstacle

    (D) enhancement

21. While some celebrities are --------, others frequently boast about their talents.

    (A) eager

    (B) peculiar

    (C) bitter

    (D) humble

22. Henry David Thoreau wanted a life away from civilization, so he --------.

    (A) wrote the book *Walden*.
    (B) went to live in the woods on his own.
    (C) worked as an elementary school teacher before moving to Concord.
    (D) influenced many prominent thinkers, including Martin Luther King.

23. When the employers realized that their employee had swindled them, they were so -------- that they could not think clearly.

    (A) cautious
    (B) serious
    (C) furious
    (D) nervous

24. After the captain lost her compass, she found it very difficult to -------- her ship.

    (A) terminate
    (B) innovate
    (C) inundate
    (D) navigate

25. All of the author's works revolve around a main character and her trusted --------, who accompanies her on her adventures.

    (A) antagonist
    (B) pedestrian
    (C) companion
    (D) duplicate

26. Alice's life was so busy as an adult that she often thought back to her carefree childhood, when --------.

    (A) she had no worries.
    (B) she never had time to relax.
    (C) her mother gave her many chores.
    (D) her school life had been very problematic.

27. After an apple fell onto Sir Isaac Newton's head, he had the -------- that gravity is what causes objects to fall.

    (A) jubilation
    (B) frustration
    (C) hesitation
    (D) realization

28. After being cooped up in a classroom for hours, it can be quite -------- for students to go play outside.

    (A) liberating
    (B) abolishing
    (C) challenging
    (D) reassuring

29. It is only after a hypothesis is tested many times that --------.

    (A) it can be considered proven.
    (B) it should not be tested on animals.
    (C) it will be doubted by the scientific community.
    (D) researchers will test it in an experiment.

30. Sharon was shocked to discover that someone had left the stove on; it was -------- that nothing had caught on fire.

    (A) fortunate
    (B) absurd
    (C) graceful
    (D) exquisite

31. The mistake that Brian had made on the exam only became -------- to him after he left the classroom.

    (A) gigantic
    (B) apparent
    (C) edible
    (D) visual

32. When Hernando Cortez destroyed the Aztec capital, he cruelly -------- the trust of his peaceful Aztec guides.

    (A) elongated
    (B) believed
    (C) betrayed
    (D) rejected

33. After running the race, Caroline felt -------- until she restored her energy with a large meal.

    (A) reliable
    (B) sluggish
    (C) aimless
    (D) immense

34. Because mosquitoes can transmit malaria, --------.

    (A) they are often found in the woods.
    (B) it is wise to protect oneself from them.
    (C) Sir Ronald Ross was the one who discovered their role in this disease.
    (D) they can be impossible to avoid.

35. Cece was greatly -------- when she had to do her colleague's work for him.

    (A) perplexed
    (B) reassured
    (C) relieved
    (D) aggravated

36. Gorillas live in troops, in which the -------- adult males dictate what the troop should do.

    (A) insecure
    (B) confined
    (C) collaborative
    (D) dominant

37. The thin pieces of caramel were so -------- that they kept breaking as Natalia lifted them off the tray.

    (A) brittle
    (B) deficient
    (C) adhesive
    (D) diverse

38. Craig suspected that Angelina was -------- the truth from him and trying to mislead him.

(A) requiring
(B) integrating
(C) concealing
(D) restoring

39. The actor's rendition of the role was so -------- and passionate that the audience could not take their eyes off him.

(A) hazy
(B) inauthentic
(C) intense
(D) bland

40. Jack had a reputation for pulling pranks; it was as though his -------- had made him famous.

(A) bias
(B) mischief
(C) courtesy
(D) toil

41. While many scientists had previously -------- whether or not the earth revolved around the sun, Copernicus settled the controversy by proving this theory true.

(A) dissolved
(B) absorbed
(C) admired
(D) debated

42. Once she realized there was no way for her to -------- the situation, Jessica decided to accept it.

(A) alter
(B) bewilder
(C) approximate
(D) mutter

43. Whenever Jan spent a long time away from home, her cats became -------- and mewed with distress.

(A) fretful
(B) timid
(C) beneficial
(D) gleeful

44. The terrible fate of the main characters in Shakespeare's *Hamlet* make this play one of his saddest --------.

(A) pacts
(B) tragedies
(C) legends
(D) novels

45. Before airplanes replaced railroads as the nation's primary cargo carriers, railroads were --------.

(A) an unpopular form of transportation.
(B) a form of travel inaccessible to many people.
(C) built by immigrant populations across the United States.
(D) the main method for transporting goods across the United States.

MEDIUM QUESTIONS

Use these questions to practice the medium difficulty level you might see on the Lower, Middle, and Upper Level ISEE. Questions like these will make up much of the Lower Level and Middle Level sentence completion sections, and a smaller portion of the Upper Level section.

1. The carpenters were -------- to find that the materials for their new project were not present at the construction site, as this setback would prevent them from meeting their deadline.

   (A) discontinued
   (B) dismayed
   (C) distorted
   (D) dispersed

2. Rivers can cause a gradual erosion of the land, resulting in a deep ------- carved into the landscape over time.

   (A) altitude
   (B) barrier
   (C) gorge
   (D) wilderness

3. Because the elephant's appetite was so large, the zookeepers -------- its bin of food every day.

   (A) replenished
   (B) justified
   (C) loathed
   (D) diminished

4. Joan knew that her roommates would be very upset that she was moving, so she -------- breaking the news to them.

   (A) subsided
   (B) condoned
   (C) dreaded
   (D) counseled

5. Because Pierre Curie was interested in Marie Curie's work on radiation, he began -------- with her experiments, and the two became scientific collaborators.

   (A) presenting
   (B) hindering
   (C) assisting
   (D) experiencing

6. The lawyer successfully -------- her client against accusations by the prosecution.

   (A) confined
   (B) defended
   (C) savored
   (D) faltered

7. The Declaration of Independence was -------- approved by all thirteen colonies in 1776, with not a single vote opposing it.

(A) recklessly

(B) controversially

(C) unanimously

(D) desperately

8. Charles Dickens showed a -------- for different viewpoints by including both aristocrats and paupers as the main characters of *A Tale of Two Cities*.

(A) hardship

(B) neglect

(C) concern

(D) distrust

9. Although he investigated them thoroughly, Jason could think of no -------- explanation for the ghostly noises he heard in the house every night.

(A) audible

(B) complex

(C) ghastly

(D) plausible

10. The Nobel Laureate did not swagger or act in any unseemly way, but received his prize with humility and --------.

(A) wrath

(B) envy

(C) dignity

(D) anguish

11. Langston Hughes had an exceptional ability to -------- poetry that accurately depicted the struggles of working-class African Americans.

(A) signify

(B) compose

(C) flatter

(D) resemble

12. At Meg's dinner party, she fed her guests so -------- that they left feeling completely full.

(A) scantily

(B) benignly

(C) conventionally

(D) liberally

13. Although he did not invent the first electric light bulb, Thomas Edison's design was inexpensive and durable, making it more -------- to produce on a large scale.

(A) predictable

(B) practical

(C) impressive

(D) industrious

14. The people -------- for many months when their beloved leader passed away.

(A) supposed

(B) prophesied

(C) repressed

(D) lamented

15. Shakespeare's plays often include comical fools whose ------- lighten the mood after more serious scenes.

    (A) jests
    (B) deaths
    (C) contracts
    (D) presents

16. Paul spoke -------- about the guitarist's abilities, pointing out all of his wrong notes and sloppy technique.

    (A) quietly
    (B) condescendingly
    (C) soothingly
    (D) frequently

17. Through his invention of the metric system, Antoine Lavoisier -------- chemistry by making it quantitative instead of qualitative.

    (A) infiltrated
    (B) evaded
    (C) depleted
    (D) transformed

18. Although Homer's *Odyssey* begins by discussing Telemachus, the story soon begins to focus on Odysseus, its true --------.

    (A) narrator
    (B) guardian
    (C) protagonist
    (D) monarch

19. Whenever Arnold felt --------, he looked through old photographs and reminisced about times long gone.

    (A) nostalgic
    (B) indifferent
    (C) gratified
    (D) steadfast

20. In their search for sources of renewable energy, engineers have designed less expensive turbines that -------- electricity from wind power.

    (A) generate
    (B) display
    (C) exemplify
    (D) persevere

21. When Julia disobeyed her curfew, her mother gave her a sharp --------.

    (A) banter
    (B) fallacy
    (C) rebuke
    (D) jurisdiction

22. Because poachers and animal rights activists have opposing goals regarding the protection of endangered animals, there are frequent -------- between the two groups.

    (A) hindrances
    (B) disputes
    (C) perspectives
    (D) receptions

23. Ernest Hemingway's descriptions of life as a soldier are so -------- that readers feel like they are experiencing these events along with him.

(A) spontaneous

(B) insolent

(C) vivid

(D) broad

24. Considering the amount of work left to be done, Nuria's estimate that the project would be finished in an hour was probably too --------.

(A) immaculate

(B) lucrative

(C) sincere

(D) optimistic

25. The revolutionary Toussaint L'Ouverture fought to free the ------- of Haiti, which had been under French rule for decades.

(A) colony

(B) utopia

(C) industry

(D) victory

26. During the Industrial Revolution, factory workers were often -------- of necessities such as clean air and water.

(A) deceived

(B) converted

(C) evacuated

(D) deprived

27. Gregor Mendel -------- genetic research by studying plant reproduction in novel and innovative ways.

(A) augmented

(B) pioneered

(C) ferreted

(D) grappled

28. After his defeat at the Battle of Waterloo, Napoleon was banished from France and sent to live as a lonely -------- on the island of St. Helena.

(A) exile

(B) tyrant

(C) legislator

(D) inventor

29. Although the twins spoke very little to anyone else, they talked -------- with each other.

(A) hesitantly

(B) wordlessly

(C) incessantly

(D) viciously

30. Even though the lawyer -------- her argument, the jury still did not understand what she was attempting to explain.

(A) languished

(B) clarified

(C) obscured

(D) inherited

31. Michelangelo's ------- paintings on the ceiling of the Sistine Chapel demonstrate his skill at depicting minute details.

(A) rustic
(B) haphazard
(C) intricate
(D) decisive

32. In the 1800s, many Americans were deeply ------- against minorities, and this bias is reflected in the caricatures of foreigners often found in editorial cartoons.

(A) enamored
(B) censored
(C) uprooted
(D) prejudiced

33. Though initially unenthusiastic and -------, the two countries' representatives eventually met to discuss their complaints

(A) feisty
(B) elegant
(C) solemn
(D) reluctant

34. Many of Sinclair Lewis's stories were ------- that parodied the lives of middle-class Americans in the 19th century.

(A) quests
(B) satires
(C) elegies
(D) incidents

35. In its efforts to combat ------- currency, the government has added features to its paper money that are almost impossible to copy.

(A) barren
(B) massive
(C) gaudy
(D) counterfeit

36. The devastating disease known as the Black Plague was an ------- that swept across Europe in the Middle Ages, affecting large populations of people.

(A) apathy
(B) immunity
(C) epidemic
(D) altercation

37. Although elks are very large animals, they can move around large obstacles with surprising speed and -------.

(A) puzzlement
(B) agility
(C) patience
(D) congeniality

38. The mysterious smile on the face of Leonardo Da Vinci's *Mona Lisa* inspires many viewers to ------- about her thoughts and feelings.

(A) muse
(B) vilify
(C) surpass
(D) admire

39. Because Leo Tolstoy was opposed to war, his writings often addressed the -------- of pacifism.

    (A) pseudonym
    (B) theme
    (C) cipher
    (D) excerpt

40. Readers criticized the author for -------- about issues in his book instead of discussing them objectively.

    (A) ranting
    (B) invading
    (C) adapting
    (D) impeding

41. As an influential -------- for the United States government, Henry Kissinger was able to open negotiations with both China and the Soviet Union.

    (A) traitor
    (B) graduate
    (C) novice
    (D) diplomat

42. After moving away from his home country, Sam realized that it would take a while for him to feel comfortable and to fully -------- to a foreign culture.

    (A) assimilate
    (B) foster
    (C) chastise
    (D) hover

43. Although the author received widespread acclaim for her new novel, she felt uncomfortable with so much public attention and maintained a -------- attitude when discussing her work.

    (A) furious
    (B) pessimistic
    (C) modest
    (D) pompous

44. If the smallpox vaccine is --------, a small amount of the vaccine can be sufficient for a large population.

    (A) erupted
    (B) diluted
    (C) studied
    (D) esteemed

45. Because neither the Tudors nor the Stuarts would relinquish their claim to the throne of England, the -------- between the two houses lasted for many generations.

    (A) decree
    (B) feud
    (C) sequel
    (D) flaw

Ivy Global

DIFFICULT QUESTIONS

Use these questions to practice the more advanced questions you might see on the Lower, Middle, and Upper Level ISEE. The Upper Level exam will include more difficult questions than the Middle and Lower Level exams. Paired word responses will only occur on the Upper Level.

1. Roald Dahl's stories often feature unique characters, such as the ------- Uncle Oswald who refuses to follow society's rules.

   (A) eccentric
   (B) stodgy
   (C) elite
   (D) ornate

2. Because Sacha was fastidious about cleaning her house, it was always in -------- condition.

   (A) luscious
   (B) pristine
   (C) robust
   (D) noxious

3. When exploring archeological sites, visitors must step -------- so they do not destroy any fragile structures or artifacts.

   (A) gingerly
   (B) feasibly
   (C) excruciatingly
   (D) overtly

4. Due to the efforts of Winston Churchill, Britain's Prime Minister during the Second World War, the country's war preparations -------- after Germany invaded Norway.

   (A) escalated
   (B) dedicated
   (C) evaded
   (D) preserved

5. Jim had a talent for one-person theatre, but he struggled with -------- because he found it difficult to interact convincingly with other actors.

   (A) abbreviations
   (B) dialogues
   (C) commodities
   (D) idioms

6. Through his diligent and -------- observations of particles' trajectories, Ernest Rutherford discovered that atoms have nuclei.

   (A) pithy
   (B) ardent
   (C) conscientious
   (D) durable

7. After a devastatingly -------- harvest, the farmer had very little produce to sell at the market.

    (A) tiresome
    (B) extreme
    (C) meager
    (D) subtle

8. With the United States involved in both national and international conflicts, the 1950s were a -------- time for the country.

    (A) fastidious
    (B) tumultuous
    (C) ravenous
    (D) judicious

9. Ms. Puccia spoke so -------- that her voice grated against her students' ears.

    (A) mournfully
    (B) inventively
    (C) serenely
    (D) stridently

10. Impressionist painters were so committed to their work that neither critical nor audience opposition could -------- them to change their painting style.

    (A) cavort
    (B) dissect
    (C) compel
    (D) thwart

11. Through her influential writings on the status of women, Simone de Beauvoir became a -------- figure in the 20th century feminist movement.

    (A) prominent
    (B) rational
    (C) despicable
    (D) impetuous

12. While DNA reveals its orderly structure during replication, most of the time it appears as an -------- mass.

    (A) ambitious
    (B) ambidextrous
    (C) ambivalent
    (D) amorphous

13. Once Elise became -------- at programming, it was possible for her to create new computer programs with very little effort.

    (A) adept
    (B) brash
    (C) desolate
    (D) urbane

14. Anthony Burgess's controversial novel *A Clockwork Orange* was banned by several countries because its language was seen as -------- and offensive.

    (A) fruitless
    (B) distasteful
    (C) exquisite
    (D) scarce

15. During the Revolutionary War, Major John Andre and Benedict Arnold arranged a -------- so they could meet and exchange information.

(A) blockade

(B) revenue

(C) siege

(D) rendezvous

16. At first, Daniel found Todd's claim --------, but after some thought he decided that it was actually quite plausible.

(A) preposterous

(B) eventful

(C) sinister

(D) residual

17. Jane Austen's novels frequently feature women who speak --------, defying social expectations that they hide their true opinions.

(A) bluntly

(D) vigorously

(C) delicately

(D) resentfully

18. During the Second World War, many scientists fled oppressive conditions in Germany in order to seek -------- in more peaceful countries such as the United States.

(A) siege

(B) pinnacle

(C) sanctuary

(D) education

19. Lauren spent so long -------- between the two options that her friends grew impatient with her inability to make a decision.

(A) vacillating

(B) meddling

(C) jeering

(D) aggregating

20. Although for many years scientists feared that the Asiatic lion might go extinct, its population is now -------- in a protected national reserve.

(A) ailing

(B) vending

(C) flourishing

(D) luring

21. After her scrupulous study of the judicial codes, Kiara began to -------- legal arguments as proof for every claim she made.

(A) mystify

(B) invoke

(C) defend

(D) court

22. Known for her exceptional bravery, Joan of Arc -------- led the French Army during the Hundred Years' War.

(A) contritely

(B) rationally

(C) audaciously

(D) effusively

23. The writer examined the issue so
-------- that readers were
disappointed by his lack of detail.

(A) superficially

(B) shrewdly

(C) menacingly

(D) exaltedly

24. Because Galileo's scientific findings
-------- official doctrine, religious
leaders demanded that he be
imprisoned.

(A) revered

(B) restored

(C) refuted

(D) reinforced

25. The -------- of new information each
day made it hard for the journalists
to keep up with the case.

(A) plight

(B) authority

(C) onslaught

(D) endeavor

26. Thomas Jefferson supported
universal freedom yet owned slaves,
a fact that many consider an
unsolvable --------.

(A) opinion

(B) insight

(C) contradiction

(D) hazard

27. After she finally managed to leave
the conference, Naina -------- to the
airport and was just barely on time
for her flight.

(A) entrusted

(B) hastened

(C) formulated

(D) assented

28. By -------- her presentation with new
research from her laboratory, Chloe
hoped to convince any critics who
had been skeptical of her findings.

(A) afflicting

(B) augmenting

(C) embarking

(D) recovering

29. Farmers often rotate the use of their
fields, growing crops in some fields
but leaving others -------- so they can
be used in the next season.

(A) sown

(B) cultivated

(C) specific

(D) fallow

30. An enthusiastic -------- of the arts,
Giovanni di Medici of Florence
funded the construction of the
Basilica of San Lorenzo.

(A) egotist

(B) antagonist

(C) utilitarian

(D) patron

31. During the Civil Rights Movement, many activists refused to back down from their cause, and they showed -------- towards those who tried to stop them.

(A) fatigue
(B) aspiration
(C) defiance
(D) creed

32. Edward soon realized that the ------- odor emanating from his fridge was coming from the moldy cheese.

(A) haggard
(B) bountiful
(C) pungent
(D) contagious

33. When Archimedes was suddenly -------- by the idea of buoyancy, it is said that he shouted "Eureka!"

(A) struck
(B) tapered
(C) presumed
(D) meandered

34. A well-known personality in the most fashionable circles of London, the author Oscar Wilde was famous for his wit, style, and --------.

(A) reticence
(B) height
(C) flair
(D) banality

35. Saul could not -------- why anyone would want to climb the -------- mountain, whose icy cliffs and frequent avalanches kept most explorers away.

(A) comprehend ... transcendental
(B) inquire ... influential
(C) germinate ... deadly
(D) fathom ... treacherous

36. Although he lived in a time when racism was rampant, Mark Twain took a strong -------- against all forms of discrimination.

(A) buttress
(B) atrocity
(C) hindrance
(D) stance

37. Although some in the scientific community had been skeptical about the existence of black holes, Stephen Hawking's new definitive evidence removed any -------- doubts.

(A) thriving
(B) lingering
(C) economizing
(D) stagnating

38. The work of -------- such as Henry Ford, who manufactured the first automobile, was -------- to the economic growth of the Industrial era.

(A) innovators ... crucial
(B) administrators ... inaugural
(C) ingénues ... commemorative
(D) imposters ... pivotal

39. By imagining the future of a British government whose -------- surveillance keeps all of its citizens under total control, George Orwell's book *1984* warned its readers about the dangers of totalitarianism.

(A) pervasive

(B) hypothetical

(C) porous

(D) abstract

40. During the eighteenth century, royal marriages were often made for --------, so that both kingdoms could benefit from the relationship.

(A) hardship

(B) convenience

(C) concept

(D) doctrine

41. In part because Pablo Picasso's Cubist paintings -------- from the artistic styles of his time, they were considered unique masterpieces and continue to be -------- today.

(A) assessed ... lauded

(B) deviated ... celebrated

(C) distinguished ... annihilated

(D) differentiated ... abhorred

42. Research facilities that do not treat their animal subjects -------- are often the object of -------- by animal welfare activists.

(A) compassionately ... .adoration

(B) humanely ... scrutiny

(C) confidingly ... ramification

(D) voraciously ... observation

43. In their struggle for Indian independence, followers of Mahatma Gandhi -------- violence and promoted pacific resistance.

(A) advocated

(B) rankled

(C) modified

(D) renounced

44. Oliver Cromwell's Puritan regime turned away from the -------- ways of the previous English monarchs; instead, the Puritans embraced a policy of austerity.

(A) extravagant

(B) tenacious

(C) resistant

(D) abundant

45. Gertrude Stein held frequent and -------- gatherings in her home in order to encourage the diligence and -------- of authors seeking critiques of their work.

(A) imperative ... renown

(B) sporadic ... disgrace

(C) recurrent ... dedication

(D) impromptu... indifference

MIDDLE LEVEL CHALLENGE QUESTIONS

Use these questions to practice the most challenging questions you might see on both the Middle Level and Upper Level exams. These questions would very rarely appear on the Lower Level.

1. During the Revolutionary War, soldiers often -------- civilian homes to use as military headquarters.

   (A) incited
   (B) expedited
   (C) appropriated
   (D) feinted

2. The author was surprised that her book had changed to such a large degree when it was edited; she had not expected the editors' alterations to be so --------.

   (A) cursory
   (B) substantive
   (C) impulsive
   (D) perplexing

3. When he heard the positive news, Harrison's -------- changed from distressed to overjoyed.

   (A) countenance
   (B) felicity
   (C) charisma
   (D) fervor

4. Although earlier scientists had suggested that some diseases were caused by invisible micro-organisms, it was Louis Pasteur's well-controlled experiments that -------- proved this theory true.

   (A) prudently
   (B) incongruously
   (C) periodically
   (D) indubitably

5. Although he is now famous worldwide, in his own time the artist El Greco was -------- to a lowly position in the Spanish art community.

   (A) relegated
   (B) extolled
   (C) lampooned
   (D) predicated

6. Even when told that she would be arrested for sitting at the front of the bus, the activist Rosa Parks ignored this -------- and did not give up her seat.

   (A) hiatus
   (B) superlative
   (C) paradox
   (D) ultimatum

7. Zaara tried to remain -------- under stress; she never complained or made any sign that she felt pressured.

    (A) insightful

    (B) detrimental

    (C) stoic

    (D) whimsical

8. Because resources were scarce and heavily rationed during the Second World War, British families were -------- in their consumption of food and other materials.

    (A) frugal

    (B) implausible

    (C) mediocre

    (D) opulent

9. Jane Goodall's early -------- for animals led her to research chimpanzees later in life.

    (A) inflection

    (B) affinity

    (C) conflagration

    (D) impudence

10. The doctor's book used such -------- language that it was accessible only to other doctors, and the general public found it entirely confusing.

    (A) superfluous

    (B) aesthetic

    (C) esoteric

    (D) intact

11. The oral polio vaccine created by Albert Sabin virtually -------- the presence of polio in the Americas.

    (A) obliterated

    (B) satiated

    (C) reified

    (D) succumbed

12. While it can be hard for people to -------- themselves off of bad habits, it is possible to succeed if they are industrious and persistent in their efforts.

    (A) verify

    (B) wean

    (C) twinge

    (D) reprimand

13. J.J. Thomson's model of the atom did not include a nucleus, and it therefore became -------- when the atomic nucleus was discovered.

    (A) tangible

    (B) vociferous

    (C) instantaneous

    (D) obsolete

14. By examining her characters' struggles, anxieties, and biases, the author Jhumpa Lahiri presents a -------- portrayal of immigrant psychology and behavior.

    (A) nuanced

    (B) trivial

    (C) brief

    (D) coarse

UPPER LEVEL CHALLENGE QUESTIONS

Use these questions to practice the most challenging questions that you might see on the Upper Level exam only. These types of questions will not occur on the Middle or Lower Levels.

1. Unfazed by the -------- thrown in its path by powerful supporters of slavery, the abolitionist movement grew steadily and -------- during the mid-nineteenth century.

    (A) hypotheses ... incorrigibly
    (B) buttresses ... imprudently
    (C) impediments ... inexorably
    (D) misconceptions ... impertinently

2. Even at a very young age, Louisa May Alcott showed a natural -------- for writing, and this passion did not diminish or -------- as she grew older.

    (A) anecdote ... deter
    (B) proclivity ... cease
    (C) aptitude ... elucidate
    (D) dowry ... trivialize

3. The politician was known for a generally pleasant and -------- demeanor, so those who watched his latest debate were shocked by his -------- attack on his opponent.

    (A) cordial ... itinerant
    (B) disparaging ... exultant
    (C) caustic ... aggravating
    (D) affable ... vitriolic

4. While many had believed the extinction of the Black Rhinoceros was --------, efforts by conservationists successfully -------- this event and prolonged the survival of the species.

    (A) imminent ... forestalled
    (B) forthcoming ... complemented
    (C) repulsive ... deteriorated
    (D) debatable ... confounded

5. Playwright Aphra Behn -------- her already angry critics when she included themes in her works that they considered -------- and inappropriate to discuss.

    (A) exacerbated ... acute
    (B) daunted ... dormant
    (C) incensed ... taboo
    (D) reiterated ... inapt

6. The museum president acknowledged a large donation in a speech teeming with sentimental commonplaces, and many felt that these -------- statements did not do justice to the benefactor's --------.

    (A) lurid ... sympathy
    (B) mundane ... lassitude
    (C) gruesome ... magnanimity
    (D) trite ... largesse

7. One of the -------- of the Modernist movement in literature was a shift away from traditional literary themes and a focus on -------- subject matter.

   (A) trends ... orthodox
   (B) tendencies ... novel
   (C) denominations ... innovative
   (D) shams ... legendary

8. After Alfred Wegener -------- the theory that the continents once formed a single landmass before breaking apart and drifting to their present locations, many scientists thought his idea was absurd and refused to -------- it.

   (A) proposed ... endorse
   (B) parried ... accept
   (C) scrutinized ... reprove
   (D) negotiated ... criticize

9. At the -------- of her fame and influence, the movie star sometimes smiled -------- when she remembered how much simpler her life had been away from the public's attention.

   (A) affront ... reticently
   (B) bane ... ebulliently
   (C) abyss ... taciturnly
   (D) apex ... wistfully

10. Alice Paul's enthusiasm for women's suffrage was so -------- that even after imprisonment she fought for women's rights with --------.

    (A) ardent ... zeal
    (B) habitual ... apathy
    (C) brusque ... fanaticism
    (D) vehement ... tryst

11. While many today remember Edgar Allen Poe for his -------- and mysterious stories, during his time his literary criticism was his most -------- work.

    (A) byzantine ... juxtaposed
    (B) livid ... nudged
    (C) cryptic ... commended
    (D) demure ... rued

12. After an arduous day at work, Jodi's -------- eyes were soothed by the sight of her daughter happily picking flowers outside, and she smiled to see such a pleasant --------.

    (A) stolid ... bauble
    (B) weary ... tableau
    (C) synthetic ... malady
    (D) tawdry ... precinct

13. Although there was no -------- of evidence that the earth was round, some people did not -------- this fact until the globe was circumnavigated in the 1500s.

    (A) dearth ... concede
    (B) surfeit ... eradicate
    (C) scarcity ... rebuff
    (D) corrosion ... forsake

14. Because Queen Marie Antionette lived in luxury during a time when many French citizens were suffering, she was widely -------- for her frivolous and -------- lifestyle.

(Λ) censured ... decadent

(B) emancipated ... jovial

(C) patronized ... vulgar

(D) denounced ... vital

15. A strong -------- of environmental conservation, President Franklin D. Roosevelt introduced many new -------- to government regulations that ensured better protection for the nation's wildlife.

(A) adversary ... improvements

(B) eminence ... declines

(C) potency ... certifications

(D) advocate ... reforms

READING
COMPREHENSION

CHAPTER 4

INTRODUCTION

The ISEE Reading Comprehension section tests your ability to understand short passages from a variety of different sources. If you are taking the ISEE Lower Level, you will answer 25 total questions based on 5 passages (5 questions per passage). If you are taking the ISEE Middle or Upper Levels, you will answer 36 total questions based on 6 passages (6 questions per passage). Genres may include informative passages, persuasive passages, and narrative passages. You will be asked to answer questions about the author's main idea, supporting information, argument organization, and writing style. You may also be asked to infer conclusions not explicitly stated in the passage by expanding logically on the author's argument. However, you will never need to rely on any of your own prior knowledge about the material; all of the information needed to answer these questions will be given directly in the passage.

APPROACHING THE READING SECTION

TIME MANAGEMENT

Pace yourself carefully. You are only given points for answering the questions, not reading the passages, so don't spend too long reading any one passage. Focus on the shorter passages first and save the longer passages for last. If you are unsure about a question, make your best guess and move on—you can always come back to the question if you have time at the end. If you are close to running out of time, see if there are any questions you can answer quickly by reading just a few lines in the passage, and make your best guess on any other questions you have left.

Read quickly, trying to understand the main points of the passage rather than the small details. Don't waste time trying to understand every piece of information in the passage. If something doesn't make sense to you, try to get an overall sense of what the author is saying and move on.

ANSWER QUESTIONS OUT OF ORDER

Answer questions about the main idea or the main purpose first, and then turn to questions that ask about specific details in the passage. If a question looks like it will take a long time to answer, make your best guess, circle it, and come back to it if you have time at the end of the section.

PROCESS OF ELIMINATION

Use the **Process of Elimination** to narrow down your answer choices, eliminating answers that are obviously wrong or have nothing to do with what is being asked. Then decide among the remaining answer choices which one best answers the question. Remember that you are being asked to find the best answer, not the one that immediately seems correct. Check all of the possible answer choices before making your selection.

VOCABULARY BUILDING

Use your practice reading passages to help develop your vocabulary. Circle words you don't understand, look them up, and add them to your vocabulary flashcards or journal.

CRITICAL READING STRATEGIES

The Reading Comprehension section on the ISEE doesn't only test whether you are able to understand a passage. The section also tests whether you are able to read **critically**, which means examining and interpreting what the passage means as a whole. This means that you should look not only for the facts of the passage, but also what the author is saying about those facts and how the author is saying it.

For every passage you read, ask yourself:

1. What are the author's **topics**, or the key details being discussed in this passage?
2. What is the author saying about these topics, or what is the **main point** of the passage?
3. What is the author's **purpose** in this passage?

In this section, we'll discuss how to go about answering these questions. We'll take a look at several strategies that will build your critical reading skills and help you become a more active reader for the ISEE. Because you have a unique learning style, some of these strategies might work better for you than others. Identify the strategies that help you the most, and practice using these for each new passage you read.

UNDERSTANDING THE PASSAGE

Your first step to understand the passage is to identify the basic facts that the author is discussing. As you read, stop yourself after each paragraph and take the time to mentally **summarize** the basic facts that you have read. Summarizing these basic facts **in your own words** is important because it allows you to prove to yourself that you have really understood what the passage is saying. The questions on the ISEE might also ask you to recognize concepts from the passage in slightly different words, so you can't rely on the exact words that the author uses.

THE 5 W'S

What is the best way to quickly summarize the passage? You may have heard about the **5 w's**: "who," "what," "where," "when," and "why." As you read, ask yourself these five questions:

1. **Who** is involved in this passage? Look for any people being discussed and think about who might be writing this passage.

2. **What** is being discussed in this passage? Look for the major concepts in each section of the passage.

3. **Where** are the events in this passage taking place? Look for any important places that are being discussed.

4. **When** are the events in the passage taking place? Look for any clues that might tell you the dates of the events taking place. Also see if you can guess when the author might have written the passage.

5. **Why** is the information in this passage important? In other words, how are the ideas in the passage connected, and what purpose or main point is the author illustrating with all of these details? We'll discuss this in greater detail in the next section.

KEY WORDS

As you read, underline the **key words** that answer these questions in the passage. Be an **active reader** and read with your pencil! Underlining as you read will improve your concentration and keep you focused on the most important information in the passage. Identify whether the words you underline answer the questions "who," "what," "where," "when," or "why."

As you read, also pay close attention to how the author connects information within the passage. Underline any **transitional words** or phrases that the author uses to move from one idea to another. The author might use words like "additionally," "furthermore," or "consequently" to show how one idea follows from or supports another. She might use words like "but," "yet," or "however" to show how one idea contrasts with another.

Take a look at the example passage below. What key words would you underline to answer the questions "who," "what," "where," "when," and "why"? What other transitional words would you underline? You might try something like this:

1   The duck-billed platypus is a
2 small animal, native to Australia,
3 with many unusual characteristics. It
4 is a very odd-looking animal; in fact,
5 when Europeans first heard about
6 the platypus, many thought such an
7 odd-looking animal must be a fraud.
8 Its head and feet are like a duck's, its
9 body is like a weasel's, and its tail is
10 like a beaver's. Its webbed feet help it
11 swim, its odd-shaped tail helps it to
12 store fat, and its duck-like beak helps
13 it find food in rivers.
14   A platypus is a mammal, but is
15 remarkably unlike almost every
16 other mammal. The platypus lays
17 eggs; it doesn't give birth like other
18 mammals. Also, although all
19 mammals give their young milk, the
20 platypus has an unusual way of doing
21 this: it actually sweats milk all over
22 its body. But despite these
23 differences, the platypus has fur, like
24 other mammals.
25   Finally, the platypus has some
26 amazing abilities. The platypus can
27 see electricity: it senses electricity
28 coming from other animals in the
29 water and uses this ability to catch
30 food and avoid predators. The
31 platypus also has venomous spurs on
32 its feet that allow it to defend itself.
33 An animal that gets too close to the
34 platypus's feet will be injected with a
35 venom.

Let's see how these key words helped us answer the 5 w's for this passage:

1. **Who** is being discussed in this passage? This passage is about the duck-billed platypus, which is the first word we underlined.

2. **What** is being discussed in this passage? This passage focuses on several unusual characteristics of the duck-billed platypus: its odd looks, difference from other mammals, and amazing abilities. We underlined these characteristics in the passage.

3. **Where** are the events in this passage taking place? The passage says that the duck-billed platypus lives in Australia, so we underlined that place in the passage.

4. **When** are the events in this passage taking place? This passage doesn't specifically tell us this information. But because the passage is written in the present tense, we can assume that it is talking about a type of animal that is alive today.

5. **Why** is the information in this passage important? We underlined the transitional words "but," "despite," and "finally" in order to keep track of how the ideas in this passage support or contrast with each other. We'll talk about the author's main idea and purpose in the next section, but all of the information included in this passage seems to be describing *why* the platypus is unusual.

You might have decided that other concepts are also important, and might have underlined some additional words. However, don't underline too many words in any paragraph! Only focus on the *key* words, those that are the most important and those that answer the 5 w's for the passage.

Exercise #1: Read the following passages and underline the key words that answer the questions "who," "what," "where," "when", and "why," as well as any transitional words or phrases. Then, use these key words to answer the 5 w's in your own words. Have a trusted reader check your work.

1   A banana split is an ice cream-
2   based dessert. In its classic form, it is
3   served in a long dish called a boat. A
4   banana is cut in half lengthwise and
5   laid in the dish. There are many
6   variations, but the classic banana
7   split is made with scoops of vanilla,
8   chocolate and strawberry ice cream
9   served in a row between the split
10 banana. Pineapple topping is
11 spooned over the strawberry ice
12 cream, chocolate syrup over the
13 vanilla, and strawberry topping over
14 the chocolate. It is garnished with
15 crushed nuts, whipped cream, and
16 maraschino cherries.
17   David Evans Strickler, a 23-
18 year-old apprentice pharmacist at
19 Tassel Pharmacy in Latrobe,
20 Pennsylvania, invented the banana-
21 based triple ice cream sundae in
22 1904. The sundae originally cost 10
23 cents, twice the price of other
24 sundaes. It quickly caught on with
25 students of nearby Saint Vincent
26 College, who spread news of the
27 sundae by word-of-mouth.
28   Walgreens is credited with
29 spreading the popularity of the
30 banana split. The early drug stores
31 operated by Charles Rudolph
32 Walgreen in the Chicago area
33 adopted the banana split as a
34 signature dessert. If Walgreens had
35 offered only the standard goods,
36 customers might have been just as
37 satisfied having their prescriptions
38 filled somewhere else. But Walgreens
39 offered them something special: the
40 banana split.

1. **Who** is being discussed in this passage?

2. **What** is being discussed in this passage?

3. **Where** are the events in this passage taking place?

4. **When** are the events in this passage taking place?

5. **Why** is the information in this passage important?

1   Sunscreen is a lotion, spray, or
2 gel applied to the skin to help protect
3 against sunburn. The chemicals in
4 sunscreen absorb or reflect some of
5 the sun's ultraviolet radiation. The
6 effectiveness of sunscreen is called
7 its Sun Protection Factor, or SPF.
8 Sunscreens with a higher SPF
9 provide more protection against UV-
10 B rays, the ultraviolet radiation that
11 causes sunburn.
12   Medical organizations such as
13 the American Cancer Society
14 recommend the use of sunscreen
15 because it can help prevent certain
16 skin cancers associated with sun
17 exposure. However, many
18 sunscreens do not offer the full
19 protection needed to reduce the risk
20 of skin cancer. This is because many
21 sunscreens do not block UV-A rays,
22 another form of ultraviolet radiation
23 that does not cause sunburn but can
24 still increase the risk of skin cancer.
25 Broad-spectrum sunscreens have
26 been designed to address this
27 concern by protecting against both
28 UV-A and UV-B radiation.

6. **Who** is being discussed in this passage?

7. **What** is being discussed in this passage?

8. **Where** are the events in this passage taking place?

9. **When** are the events in this passage taking place?

10. **Why** is the information in this passage important?

ANALYZING THE PASSAGE

Understanding the 5 w's of the passage will help you with your basic comprehension. The next step to becoming a critical reader is to understand how these basic facts are organized.

PARAGRAPH TOPICS

Within each paragraph of a passage, some facts will be more important than others. The **topic** of a paragraph is its main focus. As you read, think about how the key words you underlined might support the main topic of each paragraph.

Let's walk through the duck-billed platypus passage again. Here, we'll use the key words we underlined to identify the topic of each paragraph:

- The topic of the first paragraph is the unusual way the duck-billed platypus looks. We can tell this by the first couple of sentences, where we underlined the key words "unusual characteristics" and "odd-looking." The rest of the paragraph gives us more details about this idea. The platypus's odd looks include its beak, its tail, its feet, and its body. As the paragraph goes on, we are told that some of its odd-looking features have purposes, which we also underlined.

- The second paragraph is about why the platypus is different from other mammals, which was one of our key words. The paragraph goes on to tell some key ways that the platypus is different: it lays eggs and sweats milk. It also tells us one way that the platypus is like other mammals: it has fur.

- The third paragraph is about some special abilities of the platypus: its ability to see electricity and to inject a poisonous substance from its feet. Our key words included the phrases "see electricity" and "venomous spurs."

MAIN POINT

After you have discovered the author's topics in a passage, your next step is to identify the author's **main point,** or what the author is saying *about* these topics. The main point helps answer one of the "why" questions of your 5 w's: why is the information in this passage important? All of the information in the passage serves to prove or illustrate one central idea, and this idea is the author's main point. The main point connects all of the paragraphs in the passage and shows how they are working together.

For example, in the duck-billed platypus passage above, we identified the topics of each of the three paragraphs. How would you write a sentence that describes what the author is saying *about* these topics, connecting all three paragraphs? Each paragraph discusses some way that the platypus is an unusual animal. Therefore, you might write:

> *The duck-billed platypus is an unusual animal because it looks strange, is different from other mammals, and has some special abilities.*

Notice how this main point includes the topics of all three paragraphs: they all work together to show how the platypus is unusual!

PURPOSE

Connected to the main point is the passage's **purpose**. This answers another one of the "why" questions of your 5 w's: why might the author have written this passage? What is he or she trying to do? In order to answer this question, think about what type of passage you are reading. Would this passage most likely occur in an encyclopedia? If so, the author's purpose might be to explain or describe something. Would the passage occur in a newspaper? If so, the author might be trying to report an event, or to convince you of something. Would the passage occur in a memoir or an autobiography? If so, the author is probably telling you a story.

Here are the main purposes of most passages you will encounter:

- to explain or describe
- to convince or persuade
- to narrate or tell a story

The duck-billed platypus passage would most likely fall under the first category: you could say that the author's purpose is to *describe* some features of the platypus.

Exercise #2: Re-read the following passages and answer the questions that follow, referring back to your 5 w's in Exercise #1. Have a trusted reader check your work.

1   A banana split is an ice cream-
2   based dessert. In its classic form, it is
3   served in a long dish called a boat. A
4   banana is cut in half lengthwise and
5   laid in the dish. There are many
6   variations, but the classic banana
7   split is made with scoops of vanilla,
8   chocolate and strawberry ice cream
9   served in a row between the split
10 banana. Pineapple topping is
11 spooned over the strawberry ice
12 cream, chocolate syrup over the
13 vanilla, and strawberry topping over
14 the chocolate. It is garnished with
15 crushed nuts, whipped cream, and
16 maraschino cherries.
17   David Evans Strickler, a 23-
18 year-old apprentice pharmacist at
19 Tassel Pharmacy in Latrobe,
20 Pennsylvania, invented the banana-
21 based triple ice cream sundae in
22 1904. The sundae originally cost 10
23 cents, twice the price of other
24 sundaes. It quickly caught on with
25 students of nearby Saint Vincent
26 College, who spread news of the
27 sundae by word-of-mouth.
28   Walgreens is credited with
29 spreading the popularity of the
30 banana split. The early drug stores
31 operated by Charles Rudolph
32 Walgreen in the Chicago area
33 adopted the banana split as a
34 signature dessert. If Walgreens had
35 offered only the standard goods,
36 customers might have been just as
37 satisfied having their prescriptions
38 filled somewhere else. But Walgreens
39 offered them something special: the
40 banana split.

1. What are the topics of each paragraph?

    Paragraph 1:

    Paragraph 2:

2. How would you state the main point of this entire passage? Write your answer as a full sentence.

3. How would you describe the purpose of this passage?

1   Sunscreen is a lotion, spray, or
2 gel applied to the skin to help protect
3 against sunburn. The chemicals in
4 sunscreen absorb or reflect some of
5 the sun's ultraviolet radiation. The
6 effectiveness of sunscreen is called
7 its Sun Protection Factor, or SPF.
8 Sunscreens with a higher SPF
9 provide more protection against UV-
10 B rays, the ultraviolet radiation that
11 causes sunburn.
12   Medical organizations such as
13 the American Cancer Society
14 recommend the use of sunscreen
15 because it can help prevent certain
16 skin cancers associated with sun
17 exposure. However, many
18 sunscreens do not offer the full
19 protection needed to reduce the risk
20 of skin cancer. This is because many
21 sunscreens do not block UV-A rays,
22 another form of ultraviolet radiation
23 that does not cause sunburn but can
24 still increase the risk of skin cancer.
25 Broad-spectrum sunscreens have
26 been designed to address this
27 concern by protecting against both
28 UV-A and UV-B radiation.

4.   What are the topics of each paragraph?

Paragraph 1:

Paragraph 2:

5.   How would you state the main point of this entire passage? Write your answer as a full sentence.

6.   How would you describe the purpose of this passage?

TRICKY VOCABULARY

As you read, you might find words that you don't recognize. Don't panic! Keep reading, and try to guess the meaning of these words **in context**, by looking for clues nearby in the sentence.

Take a look at the sample sentence below:

> A <u>cacophony</u> of squealing brakes, clanking metal, and a blaring horn announced the train's entrance into the station.

If you don't know the meaning of the word "cacophony," try to guess based on the context of the sentence itself. The words "squealing," "clanking," and "blaring" are all types of unpleasant noise. Based on these clues, you might conclude that "cacophony" is a word to describe a loud, unpleasant noise—and you would be correct!

Here's another example:

> The unexpected result was an <u>anomaly</u>, and additional experiments produced more typical results.

If you don't know what the word "anomaly" means, look at the clues nearby in the sentence. The word is being used to describe an "unexpected result," which is in contrast with "more typical results" later on. Based on this information, you might conclude that an "anomaly" is something unexpected and not typical. Indeed, an "anomaly" is defined as an unusual or unexpected event.

Exercise #3: Read the new passages below, using the critical reading strategies you have practiced. Then, guess a definition for each underlined word based on context. When you are done, look up each word in a dictionary to check whether you guessed correctly. If you don't know any of the other words in the passage, look those up as well!

1   The Mississippi is well worth
2 reading about. It is not a
3 commonplace river, but on the
4 contrary is in all ways remarkable.
5 Considering the Missouri its main
6 branch, it is one of the longest rivers
7 in the world—four thousand three
8 hundred miles. It seems safe to say
9 that it is also the crookedest river in
10 the world, since in one part of its
11 journey it uses up one thousand
12 three hundred miles to cover the
13 same ground that the crow would fly
14 over in six hundred and seventy-five.
15   The difference in rise and fall is
16 also remarkable—not in the upper,
17 but in the lower river. The rise is
18 tolerably uniform down to Natchez
19 (three hundred and sixty miles above
20 the mouth)—about fifty feet. But at
21 Bayou La Fourche the river rises only
22 twenty-four feet; at New Orleans
23 only fifteen, and just above the
24 mouth only two and one half.
25   The Mississippi is remarkable
26 in still another way—its disposition
27 to make prodigious jumps by cutting
28 through narrow necks of land, and
29 thus straightening and shortening
30 itself. More than once it has
31 shortened itself thirty miles at a
32 single jump! These cut-offs have had
33 curious effects: they have thrown
34 several river towns out into the rural
35 districts, and built up sand bars and
36 forests in front of them. The town of
37 Delta used to be three miles below
38 Vicksburg: a recent cutoff has
39 radically changed the position, and
40 Delta is now two miles above
41 Vicksburg.

What meaning might you guess for the underlined words, based on how they are used in the passage?

1. commonplace:

2. uniform:

3. prodigious:

4. rural:

1   I will begin by speaking of my
2 childhood, which is the symbol, so to
3 say, of my whole life, since my love
4 for painting declared itself in my
5 earliest youth. I was sent to a
6 boarding-school at the age of six, and
7 remained there until I was eleven.
8 During that time I <u>scrawled</u> on
9 everything at all seasons; my copy-
10 books, and even my schoolmates', I
11 decorated with marginal drawings of
12 heads, some full-face, others in
13 <u>profile</u>; on the walls of the dormitory
14 I drew faces and landscapes with
15 colored chalks. So it may easily be
16 imagined how often I was
17 <u>condemned</u> to bread and water. I
18 made use of my <u>leisure</u> moments
19 outdoors in tracing any figures on the
20 ground that happened to come into
21 my head. At seven or eight, I

22 remember, I made a picture by
23 lamplight of a man with a beard,
24 which I have kept until this very day.
25 When my father saw it he went into
26 transports of joy, exclaiming, "You
27 will be a painter, child, if ever there
28 was one!"
29   I mention these facts to show
30 what an <u>inborn</u> passion for the art I
31 possessed. Nor has that passion ever
32 diminished; it seems to me that it has
33 even gone on growing with time, for
34 today I feel under the spell of it as
35 much as ever, and shall, I hope, until
36 the hour of death. It is, indeed, to this
37 divine passion that I owe, not only
38 my fortune, but my <u>felicity</u>, because it
39 has always been the means of
40 bringing me together with the most
41 delightful and most distinguished
42 men and women in Europe.

What meaning might you guess for the underlined words, based on how they are used in the passage?

5. scrawled:

6. profile:

7. condemned:

8. leisure:

9. inborn:

10. felicity:

TYPES OF PASSAGES

The ISEE Reading Comprehension section includes five or six short passages that you will need to read and analyze under a time limit. In this section, we'll discuss the three main types of passages you will see on the exam: informative passages, persuasive passages, and narrative passages. Continue reading for specific strategies to help you analyze each type of passage.

INFORMATIVE PASSAGES

Informative passages explain or describe a main topic. You might find an informative passage in an encyclopedia, textbook, or even a newspaper story that informs readers about a recent event. On the ISEE, you might see a wide range of topics covered in informative passages, from science to art to history.

MAJOR COMPONENTS

A common structure for informative passages includes the following components:

- **Introduction:** The opening sentences of a passage normally introduce the reader to the main topic of the passage. However, sometimes the introduction for an ISEE passage will be very brief, and sometimes it might be missing altogether! In that case, it will be up to you to figure out how the ideas in the passage are connected.

- **Body:** In an informative passage, each paragraph will give information about a particular idea related to the main topic. For example, in a passage about ice cream, one paragraph might be about how ice cream is made, and another might detail the history of ice cream. In the previous section, we looked at strategies for identifying the key ideas in each body paragraph.

- **Conclusion:** The final sentences of a passage might summarize the main idea of the passage. However, in an ISEE passage, the conclusion might be very brief or missing altogether.

To illustrate these components, let's take another look at the platypus passage from the last section, which is an informative passage:

1   The duck-billed platypus is a
2 small animal, native to Australia,
3 with many unusual characteristics. It
4 is a very odd-looking animal; in fact,
5 when Europeans first heard about
6 the platypus, many thought such an
7 odd-looking animal must be a fraud.
8 Its head and feet are like a duck's, its
9 body is like a weasel's, and its tail is
10 like a beaver's. Its webbed feet help it
11 swim, its odd-shaped tail helps it to
12 store fat, and its duck-like beak helps
13 it find food in rivers.
14   A platypus is a mammal, but is
15 remarkably unlike almost every
16 other mammal. The platypus lays
17 eggs; it doesn't give birth like other
18 mammals. Also, although all
19 mammals give their young milk, the
20 platypus has an unusual way of doing
21 this: it actually sweats milk all over
22 its body. But despite these
23 differences, the platypus has fur, like
24 other mammals.
25   Finally, the platypus has some
26 amazing abilities. The platypus can
27 see electricity: it senses electricity
28 coming from other animals in the
29 water and uses this ability to catch
30 food and avoid predators. The
31 platypus also has venomous spurs on
32 its feet that allow it to defend itself.
33 An animal that gets too close to the
34 platypus's feet will be injected with a
35 venom.

Does this passage have an introduction? We might call the first sentence of the passage its (very brief) introduction, because it states the main topic of the entire passage: "The duck-billed platypus is a small animal, native to Australia, with many unusual characteristics."

The body of this passage includes the rest of the first paragraph and the next two paragraphs. As we have already seen, each of these paragraphs describes a specific topic related to the main idea: the way the platypus looks, the way it is unlike other mammals, and some of its special abilities.

Does this passage have a conclusion? No—there is no sentence or paragraph at the end that summarizes the main idea of the passage again. This is an example of a passage that ends before its conclusion. It might be incomplete—the author might go on to talk about some more unusual traits of the platypus!

PARAGRAPH STRUCTURE

Many informative passages also have special internal structures within their paragraphs. Just like the passage as a whole, each paragraph has a topic sentence that serves as its introduction. The topic sentence introduces readers to the main idea of the paragraph. The next few sentences can be thought of as the body of the paragraph; they present

       Ivy Global

supporting details related to the topic sentence. Finally, a paragraph might end with a concluding sentence that summarizes the main topic of the paragraph. The **concluding sentence** can also provide a transition to the next paragraph.

For example, let's take a look at the second paragraph of the platypus passage again:

> A platypus is a mammal, but is remarkably unlike almost every other mammal. The platypus lays eggs; it doesn't give birth like other mammals. Also, although all mammals give their young milk, the platypus has an unusual way of doing this: it actually sweats milk all over its body. But despite these differences, the platypus has fur, like other mammals.

The topic sentence of this paragraph is its first sentence: "The platypus is a mammal, but is remarkably unlike almost every other mammal." This sentence tells us that the topic of the paragraph is how the platypus is different from other mammals.

The body of this paragraph includes the second and third sentences, which provide supporting detail about how the platypus is different from other mammals. These details include its egg-laying and milk-sweating habits.

The final sentence of this paragraph might be called its conclusion because it explains why the platypus is still a mammal, despite these differences.

STRATEGIES

When you read an informative passage, ask yourself the same three questions we discussed in the Critical Reading section:

1. What are the author's **topics**, or the key details being discussed in this passage?
2. What is the author saying about these topics, or what is the **main point** of the passage?
3. What is the author's **purpose** in this passage?

The third question should be easy to answer: the purpose of an informative passage is to inform, explain, or describe. To answer the first two questions, review the strategies from the Critical Reading section. Looking for the main structure of the passage and the internal structure of each paragraph will help you locate this information.

Be careful: even if the topic of the passage is familiar to you, don't allow your reading to be swayed by your own opinion or prior knowledge! The ISEE will only test you about what the author is saying. Ignore any information you might already know about the topic and look only at the information on the page in front of you.

Exercise #1: Read the sample informative passage below, and then answer the questions that follow. Ask a trusted reader to check your work.

1	One of the Seven Wonders of	16	per day to remain lush and green. To
2	the Ancient World, the Hanging	17	prevent flooding and erosion from
3	Gardens of Babylon is the only one of	18	the daily watering, Nebuchadnezzar
4	the Wonders that may have been a	19	is reported to have used massive
5	legend.	20	slabs of stone beneath and around
6	The gardens were attributed to	21	the gardens.
7	King Nebuchadnezzar II, who ruled	22	Unfortunately, several
8	the ancient city-state of Babylon	23	earthquakes after the Second
9	between 605 and 562 BCE. He is said	24	Century BCE are said to have
10	to have constructed the gardens to	25	destroyed the gardens. While ancient
11	please his homesick wife, Amytis of	26	Greek and Roman writers
12	Media, who longed for the plants of	27	documented the Hanging Gardens of
13	her homeland. The gardens were so	28	Babylon, there is no definitive
14	massive that they required a	29	archaeological evidence confirming
15	minimum of 8,200 gallons of water	30	their existence.

1. Identify each of the following structural components of the passage as a whole:

   Introduction:

   Body:

   Conclusion:

2. For the second paragraph (lines 6-21), identify the following components:

   Topic sentence:

   Supporting details:

3. What are the author's topics, or the key details being discussed in this passage?

4. What is the author saying about them, or what is the main point of the passage?

5. What is the author's purpose in this passage?

PERSUASIVE PASSAGES

In a **persuasive passage**, the author tries to convince the reader of a specific position or argument. A persuasive passage might come from a political speech, an opinion essay, or a newspaper op-ed or letter to the editor.

MAJOR COMPONENTS

A persuasive passage differs from an informative passage because the author is presenting an opinion about a situation, rather than simply explaining or describing a topic. This opinion is called the author's **thesis**, and an author normally uses specific supporting points or **evidence** to prove his or her thesis. Authors can use **objective evidence**, or facts and statistics from outside sources. Authors can also use **subjective evidence**, or examples from their own experiences. While a persuasive passage written with objective evidence will sound more detached and analytical, a persuasive essay written with subjective evidence will sound more personal.

Persuasive passages follow the same basic structure as informative passages, with a few differences:

- **Introduction**: The opening sentences of a passage normally introduce the reader to the author's main argument and thesis. Just like informative passages, however, the introduction for a persuasive passage on the ISEE might be very brief or missing altogether. In that case, it will be up to you to find the author's main argument and thesis by reading the rest of the passage.

- **Body**: In a persuasive passage, each paragraph will provide a specific reason or example that proves why the author's thesis is true. These paragraphs contain the author's evidence, either from outside sources (objective) or personal experience (subjective).

- **Conclusion**: The final sentences of a passage might summarize the main argument of the passage. However, in an ISEE passage, the conclusion might be very brief or missing altogether.

To illustrate these components, let's take a look at this example persuasive passage:

1 Cell phones have become a
2 staple of modern life. While they
3 have many benefits, such as
4 improved communication, they can
5 also be dangerous and
6 counterproductive.
7 For one, cell phone use while
8 driving is becoming increasingly
9 controversial. Distracted driving has
10 resulted in an alarming increase in
11 the number of car accidents. Because
12 of this, many jurisdictions prohibit
13 the use of mobile phones while
14 driving. Egypt, Israel, Japan, Portugal,
15 and Singapore banned both handheld
16 and hands-free use of a mobile
17 phone; others—including the UK,
18 France, and many U.S. states—
19 banned handheld phone use only,
20 allowing hands-free use.

21 In addition, cell phone use is
22 being closely watched in schools.
23 Because so many students have been
24 using them to cheat on tests and
25 bully others, cell phone use is usually
26 restricted in schools. There are few, if
27 any, benefits to using phones in
28 school; instead, cell phone use in
29 school has threatened the school's
30 security, distracted other students,
31 and encouraged gossip and other
32 social activities that harm learning.
33 Besides being monitored or
34 restricted in cars and schools, many
35 cell phones are banned in school
36 locker room facilities, public
37 restrooms, and swimming pools due
38 to the built-in cameras that most
39 phones now feature.

Does this passage have an introduction? Yes, the first paragraph of the passage states both the main topic of the passage (cell phone usage) as well as the author's position about this topic. The author's thesis is stated in the second sentence: "While they have many benefits, such as improved communication, they can also be dangerous and counterproductive." Based on this thesis statement, we expect that the rest of the passage will prove why and how cell phones can be dangerous and counterproductive.

The body of this passage includes the second, third, and fourth paragraphs. Each of these paragraphs explains a specific situation where cell phones may be dangerous:

- Paragraph 2: Cell phones can be dangerous to use while driving.
- Paragraph 3: Cell phones can be dangerous to use in schools.
- Paragraph 4: Cell phones can be dangerous to use in locker rooms, restrooms, and swimming pools.

In each paragraph, the author provides specific details about why cell phones can be dangerous in each of these situations. All of these details work together as the author's evidence to support her thesis.

Does this passage have a conclusion? No—there is no sentence or paragraph at the end that summarizes the author's thesis and argument again. This is another example of a passage that ends before its conclusion. If the author were to continue the passage, what do you think she would discuss next?

STRATEGIES

When you read a persuasive passage, start by asking yourself the same three questions we discussed in the Critical Reading section:

1. What are the author's **topics**, or the key details being discussed in this passage?
2. What is the author saying about these topics, or what is the **main point** of the passage?
3. What is the author's **purpose** in this passage?

The third question should be easy to answer: the purpose of a persuasive passage is to persuade or convince you of the author's opinion. To answer the first two questions, review the strategies from the Critical Reading section. In addition, help yourself by looking for the main components of the passage: the author's thesis and supporting evidence.

If you're having difficulty understanding the passage, try to imagine who is speaking and whom he or she might be speaking to. Is this the type of passage that would be delivered as a speech or a letter to a group of people, or as a speech or a letter to one specific person? If so, who do you think those people are? What type of situation might have led the author to propose this argument?

If you're having difficulty locating the author's main point or thesis, pay close attention to the author's **tone**. Because a persuasive passage presents an opinion, the author will frequently have a **positive** or **negative** feeling about the topic he or she is discussing. In the cell phone passage above, the author uses words like "dangerous," "counterproductive," "controversial," "alarming," and "threatened" to describe cell phone usage. These words indicate that the author feels negatively about using cell phones in the situations she is describing.

Be careful: even if you disagree with the author's position, don't allow your reading to be swayed by your own opinion! The ISEE will only test you about what the author is saying, so only look at the argument on the page in front of you.

Exercise #2: Read the following sample persuasive passage, and then answer the questions that follow. Ask a trusted reader to check your work.

The purpose of Black History Month is to draw attention and pay tribute to people, organizations, and events that have shaped the history of African Americans and their contributions to American society. In this spirit, we should honor Delta Sigma Theta, a black women's organization that has been fighting for civil rights and making a difference in the lives of many for over a century.

Delta Sigma Theta was founded in 1913 by 22 women at Howard University in Washington. The sorority of college-educated women pledged to perform public service in the black community. Nearly six weeks after its founding, Delta Sigma Theta members took part in the historic Women's Suffrage March in Washington, and were the only African-Americans present. The Deltas have participated in every major civil rights march since.

In addition to its political involvement, Delta Sigma Theta has a strong tradition of community involvement. For years, the sorority's local chapters have funded programs providing assistance to persons in need and promoting academic excellence. The groups work as mentors to young people and provide scholarships to help them pursue their education.

Today, Delta Sigma Theta has 260,000 members. For the next century, these sorority sisters say they will continue to leave their mark on black history while helping transform the lives of young people.

1. Identify each of the following structural components in the passage as a whole:

   Introduction:

   Body:

   Conclusion:

2. What are the author's topics, or the key details being discussed in this passage?

3. What is the author saying about them, or what is the main point of the passage?

4. Who might the author be addressing in this passage?

5. What specific evidence does the author use to support his or her thesis?

6. What is the author's tone in this passage?

NARRATIVE PASSAGES

In a **narrative passage**, the author tells a story about an event or an experience. The types of narrative passages that you will see on the ISEE might be found in memoirs or autobiographies, where the author relates an experience from her childhood or adult life. Often, these stories are meant to illustrate an important aspect of the author's individual background, perspective, or values.

MAJOR COMPONENTS

Narrative passages are different from informative and descriptive passages because they have a very flexible structure. However, like all stories, narrative passages have five main components. We can think of these components in terms of the "5 w's": the who, what, where, when, and why of the story.

- **Characters** are the *who* of the story: the people (and sometimes animals) that exist in the world of the story.
- The **narrator** is another *who* of the story: the person telling the story. The narrator can be a character in the story, or somebody outside of the story.
- The **setting** is *when* and *where* the story takes place.
- The **plot** is *what* happens in the story, or the major events that take place.
- The **conflict** is *why* and *how* the plot moves forward. Often the characters need to achieve something, but there is some sort of obstacle in their way. The plot of the story centers on why and how they choose to overcome this obstacle.

To illustrate these components, let's take a look at this example narrative passage:

1	When I was eleven or twelve	18	climbed into it like a frightened
2	years old, a family of robins nested	19	child. It had made its first journey
3	under our cabin's porch roof. When	20	into the world, but the home tie had
4	the young were about ready to fly, I	21	brought it quickly back. A few hours
5	happened to be watching when one	22	afterward, its heart was braver, its
6	of the birds tried to leave the nest for	23	wings were stronger, and, leaping
7	the first time. Its parents were	24	into the air with a shout, it flew easily
8	encouraging it with calls from some	25	to some rocks several yards away.
9	rocks a few yards away. It climbed	26	Each of the young birds, one at
10	over the edge of the nest, took a few	27	a time, left the nest in this manner.
11	steps forward, then a few more, until	28	There would be the first sudden
12	it could look off into free space. Its	29	panic at being so far from home, the
13	parents apparently shouted, "Come	30	rush back, a second and perhaps a
14	on!" But its courage was not quite	31	third attempt, and then the leap into
15	strong enough; it looked around, and,	32	the air, landing on a nearby bush or
16	seeing how far it was from home,	33	rock. Young birds never go back
17	scampered back to the nest, and	34	home once they have taken flight.

Who is the story's narrator? In other words, who might be telling the story? The narrator seems to be someone who is telling a story about her childhood. Who are the characters in this story? In other words, who is this story about? The narrator as a child is the most important character in the story, but the birds she observes in the passage could also be considered characters.

What is the story's setting? In other words, when and where does the story take place? We can tell that this story took place in the past, when the narrator was eleven or twelve years old, but the exact date isn't specified. The narrator tells us that the story takes place at her family's cabin, specifically on the cabin's porch.

What is the plot of the story, and what is the conflict that moves the plot forward? The narrator is observing a family of young birds who are learning to fly. The first bird is trying to leave the nest for its first time, but needs to build up its courage to take that first leap. The plot centers on how that first bird and its siblings finally gain the courage to leave their home.

STRATEGIES

To find the major components of a narrative passage, simply go back to your "5 w's" and ask yourself the following questions:

- Who are the characters in the story, and who is the narrator telling the story?
- When and where is the story set?

- What happens in the story?
- Why and how does this happen? What conflict do the characters need to overcome?

For some narrative passages, you might not be able to answer all of these questions. For example, the story above didn't tell us the exact date that these events took place. Make sure you only use the information in the story to answer these questions—don't use your own opinion or speculate too much. The ISEE will only ask you about information that can be gathered from the story alone.

Every story has its own **point of view**, which is the perspective of the person telling the story. If you're not sure who might be the narrator of the story, focus on the words the narrator uses to show his or her point of view:

- If the narrator uses the word "I" to tell the story ("I talked to Sarah yesterday"), we call this a **first-person point of view**. The narrator is most likely a character in the story who is interacting with the other characters and taking part in the events.

- If the narrator uses the words "he" or "she" to tell the story ("She talked to Sarah yesterday"), we call this a **third-person point of view**. There are some exceptions, but the narrator is frequently not a character in the story. Instead, the narrator is outside of the story, telling about events that he or she did not take part in.

Finally, in addition to the main components of a story, you might be asked to analyze a major **theme** of a story. A story's theme can be described as its "main idea," or the message it conveys about life and behavior.

For example, let's take a look at the last sentence of the passage above:

Young birds never go back home once they have taken flight.

What does this mean, and why might the narrator make this observation? After watching a family of young birds venture into the world for the first time, the narrator concludes that they will never return home. We don't know exactly why this is important for the narrator. However, because she remembers this experience from when she was a girl, we could guess that looking at these birds made her think about her own process of growing up.

Not every story will have a clear-cut lesson for the reader, so it will be up to you to decide if there is any theme you can take away from the story. Do the characters find success or disappointment, and why might this be? Do the characters end up with a greater understanding of themselves and others? How might the events in the story relate to other events you have experienced in real life? Relating a story to your own life is a great way to better understand the characters, events, and major themes in a story.

Exercise #3: Read the sample narrative passage below, and then answer the questions that follow. Ask a trusted reader to check your work.

1   I remember my first invention
2   very well. There were several of us
3   boys, and we were fond of playing
4   around a mill where they ground
5   wheat into flour. One day the miller
6   called us into the mill and said, "Why
7   don't you do something useful
8   instead of just playing all the time?" I
9   said, "Well, what can we do that is
10   useful?" He took up a handful of
11   wheat, ran it over in his hand and
12   said: "Look at that! If you could
13   manage to get the husks off that
14   wheat, that would be doing
15   something useful!"
16   So I took some wheat home
17   with me and experimented. I found
18   the husks came off without much
19   difficulty. I tried brushing them off
20   and they came off beautifully. Then it
21   occurred to me that brushing was
22   nothing but applying friction to them.
23   If I could brush the husks off, why
24   couldn't the husks be rubbed off?
25   In the mill there was a
26   machine—I don't know what it was
27   for—but it whirled its contents,
28   whatever it was, around in a drum. I
29   thought, "Why wouldn't the husks
30   come off if the raw wheat was
31   whirled around in that drum?" So
32   back I went to the miller and
33   suggested the idea to him.
34   "Why," he said, "that's a good
35   idea." So he called his foreman and
36   they tried it, and the husks came off
37   beautifully, and they've been taking
38   husks off that way ever since. That
39   was my very first invention, and it
40   led me to thinking for myself, and
41   really had quite an influence on my
42   way and methods of thought.

1. Who are the characters in this story?

2. Who is the narrator telling the story?

3. When and where is the story set?

4. What happens in the story?

5. Why and how does this happen? What conflict do the characters need to overcome?

6. Is there any lesson or theme from this story that you can relate to your own life?

Ivy Global

TYPES OF QUESTIONS

Now that you have learned about the types of passages that will appear on the ISEE, let's look at the types of questions that you will be asked about each passage. Questions on the Reading Comprehension section fall into six main categories:

1. Main Idea
2. Supporting Ideas
3. Inference
4. Vocabulary
5. Organization/Logic
6. Tone/Style/Figurative Language

Identifying the type of question will help you pick the best strategy to use. Continue reading to learn specific strategies for each question type.

MAIN IDEA QUESTIONS

Main Idea questions ask about the author's main topic, point, theme, or thesis. The ISEE will include 3-4 Main Idea questions on the Lower Level, and 3-7 Main Idea questions on the Middle and Upper Levels. Some examples of Main Idea questions include:

- What is the main idea, main point, or central idea of this passage?
- What is this passage primarily about?
- What is the purpose of this passage?

STRATEGIES

The best preparation for a Main Idea question is to be a **critical reader**! Review the reading strategies outlined in the Critical Reading section. Remember to summarize in your own words what the author is saying in each paragraph, and take note of any key words or main topics. Then ask yourself, "What are the author's topics, and what is the author saying about these topics?" Look for the answer option that matches your answer to this question.

Remember that the main idea of a passage is the common thread that connects the entire passage, tying all of the paragraphs together. If you have trouble finding the main idea, think about how all of the paragraphs might work together to describe a broader topic. Pay close attention to the first and last sentences of the passage, because they frequently give you information about its main idea.

If you are stuck, use the **Process of Elimination** to narrow down your answer options by crossing out answers that are wrong. First, eliminate any answer choices that are unrelated. If you see an answer option that has little to do with the concepts in the passage, cross it out and move on!

Then, eliminate answer options that are too broad or too specific. If the passage is describing the types of food that turtles eat, the main topic is not simply "turtles" – this is too broad! The passage isn't talking about every aspect of turtles, just about their diet. By contrast, if the passage is describing the history of cars, the main topic is not "Henry Ford" – this is too specific! Henry Ford may be an important person in the passage, but he doesn't summarize the passage as a whole.

EXAMPLE

As an example, let's look at the duck-billed platypus passage again. Now we'll go on to answer a Main Idea question about this passage:

1	The duck-billed platypus is a	19	mammals give their young milk, the
2	small animal, native to Australia,	20	platypus has an unusual way of doing
3	with many unusual characteristics. It	21	this: it actually sweats milk all over
4	is a very odd-looking animal; in fact,	22	its body. But despite these
5	when Europeans first heard about	23	differences, the platypus has fur, like
6	the platypus, many thought such an	24	other mammals.
7	odd-looking animal must be a fraud.	25	Finally, the platypus has some
8	Its head and feet are like a duck's, its	26	amazing abilities. The platypus can
9	body is like a weasel's, and its tail is	27	see electricity: it senses electricity
10	like a beaver's. Its webbed feet help it	28	coming from other animals in the
11	swim, its odd-shaped tail helps it to	29	water and uses this ability to catch
12	store fat, and its duck-like beak helps	30	food and avoid predators. The
13	it find food in rivers.	31	platypus also has venomous spurs on
14	A platypus is a mammal, but is	32	its feet that allow it to defend itself.
15	remarkably unlike almost every	33	An animal that gets too close to the
16	other mammal. The platypus lays	34	platypus's feet will be injected with a
17	eggs; it doesn't give birth like other	35	venom.
18	mammals. Also, although all		

What is the main topic of this passage?

    (A) wildlife of Australia

    (B) odd-looking mammals

    (C) the unusual qualities of the platypus

    (D) why the platypus lays eggs

This question is asking us to find the central concept that is the focus of the entire passage. We can eliminate answer choices (A) and (B), because they are too general. The platypus is both an odd-looking mammal and lives in Australia, but the passage does not mention any other odd-looking mammals or wildlife of Australia. Answer choice (D) can be eliminated because the passage never mentions why the platypus lays eggs, and egg-laying is just one of the behaviors of the platypus discussed in this passage. Answer (C) is the best choice because the entire passage is about how the platypus is unusual.

SUPPORTING IDEA QUESTIONS

Supporting Idea questions ask you to identify specific information that supports the passage's main idea. The ISEE will include 3-6 Supporting Idea questions on the Lower Level, and 5-12 Supporting Idea questions on the Middle and Upper Levels. Some examples of Supporting Detail questions include:

- According to the passage, how did ____ change over time?
- According to the author, ____ happened because …

STRATEGIES

All of the information you need to answer a Supporting Idea question can be found in the passage. Always **go back to the passage** to see where you might find the information you need. If a specific line number is given in the question, re-read that line as well as the lines above and below it.

Sometimes a question won't give you a line number where you can find the answer. In this case, first underline the main points in the question. Then, quickly **skim** the passage to find this information. "Skimming" means only looking over the key words and phrases in the passage, without reading all of the details again. Review pages 118-121 in this book to practice finding key words in a passage. Instead of reading each sentence in full, look only at the most important words: words that answer the 5 w's or provide important transitions and connections between ideas. Pay close attention to special terms and proper nouns, and ignore small connecting words like "the" and "of." Once you have found the information the question is asking about, stop and circle it.

After you have located the information you need, pick the answer choice that best matches what is written in the passage. Be careful: don't rely on your memory, opinion, or background knowledge to answer these questions! Only base your answer off of what the author says in the passage. Circle or star the words or phrases in the passage that support the answer choice you think is correct.

EXAMPLE

As an example, flip back a few pages and take look at the duck-billed platypus passage again. This time we'll go on to answer a Supporting Idea question about this passage:

According to the passage, the platypus's ability to see electricity allows it to

(A) store fat.
(B) poison its predators.
(C) feed its young.
(D) hunt for food.

This question is asking us to locate information in the passage about the platypus's ability to see electricity, and to find what this ability allows the platypus to do. Let's find the exact lines in the passage where this ability is discussed:

The platypus can see electricity: it senses electricity coming from other animals in the water and uses this ability to catch food and avoid predators.

The passage tells us that there are two benefits for the platypus's ability to see electricity: this ability lets it catch food and avoid predators. Looking at the answer choices, we can eliminate (A) and (C), because these lines in the passage say nothing about storing fat or feeding the platypus's young. We can also eliminate choice (B)—although seeing electricity allows the platypus to avoid predators, the passage doesn't say that this particular ability allows it to *poison* predators. Actually, the only time the passage mentions a poisonous substance is in relation to the platypus's feet! Therefore, the best answer choice is (D), because the passage does say that the platypus uses its sense for electricity in order to catch food.

INFERENCE QUESTIONS

Inference questions ask you to make a logical guess or assumption based on the information in the passage. The ISEE will include 4-8 Inference questions on the Lower Level, and 6-14 Inference questions on the Middle and Upper Level. These questions will ask you to interpret the meaning of a phrase, or "read between the lines" to discover what the author implies but does not state directly. You may also need to make a logical prediction about an outcome of an event. Some examples of Inference questions include:

- The author implies that ...

- What can be inferred from lines ___ ?

- By saying ___ , the author is suggesting that ...

STRATEGIES

If the question asks you to interpret a certain phrase, go back to that section of the passage and **re-read it carefully**. Think about why the author would include that image or phrase in the passage. What is the **author's purpose** in including this information? Pick an answer choice that best matches the author's primary purpose in the passage.

Keep in mind that your guess or inference should always logically expand the author's argument. Remember the author's main point in the passage and look for an answer choice that is connected to this main point. Don't be swayed by your own opinion or prior knowledge of the topic, and make sure you can back up any guess with information in the passage.

If you are stuck, use the **Process of Elimination** to narrow down your answer options by crossing out answers that are wrong. First, eliminate any answers that are unrelated to the main idea of the passage. If you see an answer choice that is irrelevant or off-topic, cross it out and move on!

Then, eliminate any answers that aren't supported by the **author's own words** in the passage. If you can't find some words, phrases, or sentences in the passage to support an answer choice, cross it out! Don't rely on interpretations based on your own prior knowledge or personal opinion of the passage. Remember that all answers should be based on what the author says.

EXAMPLE

Let's look back at the duck-billed platypus passage again. This time we'll go on to answer an Inference question about this passage:

The passage implies that the Europeans originally thought the platypus was a fraud because

    (A) the people who brought it back were not trustworthy.

    (B) they could not believe such a strange animal existed.

    (C) they had been tricked before.

    (D) they did not like new ideas.

This question is asking us to guess an explanation for a statement that isn't specifically explained in the passage. To answer this question well, we should re-read the part of the passage that talks about the Europeans' first reaction to the duck-billed platypus:

> It is a very odd-looking animal; in fact, when Europeans first heard about the platypus, many thought such an odd-looking animal must be a fraud.

These lines discuss how odd-looking the platypus is, and the passage connects the platypus's strange appearance with the Europeans' reaction. This should make us suspicious that (B) is the right answer right away: the Europeans probably thought that the platypus was a fraud because it looked so strange. Indeed, there is no evidence at all for any of the other answers—the passage says nothing about the people who brought the platypus back, whether the Europeans had been tricked before, or whether they were receptive to new ideas. Therefore, (B) is the best answer.

VOCABULARY QUESTIONS

Vocabulary questions ask you to define a word as it is used in the context of the passage. The ISEE will include 4-8 Vocabulary questions on the Lower Level, and 5-9 Vocabulary questions on the Middle and Upper Levels. The most typical Vocabulary question is:

- In line _____ , the word "_____" most nearly means ...

STRATEGIES

Vocabulary questions frequently pick a word that has **multiple possible meanings**, and ask you to pick the definition that best matches how the author uses the word in a certain sentence. Because these words often have multiple possible definitions, don't pick an answer until you have re-read the sentence from the passage and can identify how the *author* is using the word! Once you have identified the author's meaning, pick the definition that is the best match. Then, check your answer by plugging it back into the author's sentence, replacing the original word to ensure that it makes sense.

Sometimes, a vocabulary question might ask you to define an old-fashioned word, a technical term, or another type of **tricky vocabulary**. If you don't know the meaning of the word, re-read the surrounding sentences and phrases to see if they contain any clues about what the word could mean. Then, pick the answer choice that best fits with the meaning of the entire sentence or paragraph. Re-read the section on Tricky Vocabulary (pages 126-128) for more exercises on guessing word meanings based on the context of a passage.

If you get stuck, find the original word in the author's sentence and look at each of your answer choices. One at a time, plug them into the author's sentence to replace the author's original word. Then, cross out any options that don't make any sense when you read them in the context of the author's sentence, and make your best guess among the answer choices you have left.

EXAMPLE

Let's take a look at the following Vocabulary question for the duck-billed Platypus passage:

As it is used in line 12, "store" most nearly means

- (A) reserve.
- (B) shop.
- (C) consume.
- (D) buy.

The word "store" has two main meanings. It can refer to a shop or a supply of something that might be needed later, or it can refer to the action of keeping something for later—that is, keeping it in reserve. We can eliminate answers (C) and (D) because "consume" and "buy" aren't possible definitions of "store." However, both (A) and (B) are possible meanings.

To make sure that we pick the meaning used by the author, we need to look at the original sentence in line 12 of the passage:

> Its webbed feet help it swim, its odd-shaped tail helps it to store fat, and its duck-like beak helps it find food in rivers.

What meaning of the word "store" is the author using in this sentence? It looks like the author is using the second meaning: the platypus's tail helps it save fat for later. This would be closer to answer choice (A) reserve. To check our answer, let's plug both (A) and (B) back into the sentence to make sure that (A) is the better fit:

- ✓ its odd-shaped tail helps it to *reserve* fat
- ✗ its odd-shaped tail helps it to *shop* fat

"Shop" doesn't make any sense in this sentence, so we know that (A) reserve is the best choice.

ORGANIZATION/LOGIC QUESTIONS

Organization/Logic questions ask you to identify information about the structure, argument, and function of the passage. The ISEE will include 2-4 Organization/Logic questions on the Lower Level, and 3-5 Organization/Logic questions on the Middle and Upper Levels. You may be asked to identify certain patterns or relationships in the author's argument, and consider what types of evidence are being used. You may also be asked to determine the function of certain paragraphs or sentences in the passage as they relate to the author's main point. Finally, you may be asked to outline the author's structure for the passage as a whole and identify what purpose it serves. Some examples of Organization/Logic questions include:

- Which best describes the organization of the passage?
- The author of the passage does all of the following EXCEPT ...
- The function of the last paragraph (lines ____) is to ...
- The passage provides information to answer which question?

STRATEGIES

Re-read the section on Passage Types to review the different types of structures that occur in these passages. For any passage you read, identify the author's **main point** or **purpose**, and then determine how the different components of the passage work together to convey that main idea.

If the question asks you to analyze a specific line or paragraph of the passage, go back to that section of the passage and **re-read it carefully**. Think about the author's purpose for including that line or paragraph, and determine how this helps the author make his overall point in the passage. Pick an answer choice that best reflects the structure and purpose of the passage as a whole.

Certain questions might ask you to identify how **evidence** is used in the passage. Remember that evidence is specific information that the author uses to support or illustrate her main point. To find the author's evidence, identify the main points in the passage, and then look for the supporting information that serves as "proof" for these points.

Pay close attention to the words *NOT*, *LEAST*, and *EXCEPT* in the questions. When you see one of these words, circle it so you are sure you are answering the question correctly. For example, take a look at the following question:

> Which of the following do NOT appear as evidence in the passage?

This question asks you to sort through the answer options and find the only option that doesn't occur in the passage. These types of questions will often require you to look up multiple pieces of information, so they will take a long time to answer. You may want to save them for the end if you are running short on time.

EXAMPLE

Let's take a look at the following Organization/Logic question for the duck-billed platypus passage:

> Which best describes the organization of the passage?
>
> (A) A topic is defined, and different aspects of this topic are discussed.
> (B) Specific facts are discussed, followed by personal opinions.
> (C) Several different opinions are compared and contrasted.
> (D) An issue is introduced, and events are discussed in chronological order.

This question is asking us to look at the various components of the passage, and to determine how they are working together to form an overall structure. To answer this question, we should first determine the main point or purpose of the passage, and then analyze how each section of the passage supports this main point.

The passage as a whole seems to be focused on different qualities that make the duck-billed platypus unusual. The first paragraph discusses how the platypus looks, the second paragraph discusses why it is not a typical mammal, and the third paragraph discusses some "amazing abilities" of the platypus. The passage's structure contains many specific details that all support a general observation about how the platypus is odd.

Which answer choice best matches the structure that we have identified? Although the passage does contain specific facts, we can eliminate answer choices (B) and (C) because the passage doesn't discuss different opinions about the platypus. The passage also doesn't describe different events in chronological order, so we can eliminate choice (D). The best answer is (A): the passage defines a topic (the platypus), and then discusses different aspects of this topic (its looks, its classification as a mammal, and its special abilities).

TONE/STYLE/FIGURATIVE LANGUAGE QUESTIONS

Tone/Style/Figurative Language questions ask you to analyze *how* the author is writing. The ISEE will include 1-3 Tone/Style/Figurative Language questions on the Lower Level, and 1-4 Tone/Style/Figurative Language questions on the Middle and Upper Levels. You may be asked about the author's **tone**, or his attitude toward the topic— is the author presenting the facts in a neutral manner, or getting emotionally involved? You may also be asked about the **style** or **mood** of the passage—how does the passage evoke certain emotions or images? Finally, you may be asked to identify and interpret **figurative language** in the passage, or the author's use of images, metaphors, and other rhetorical devices. Some examples of Tone/Style/Figurative Language questions include:

- The author's tone could best be described as ...

- The mood of the first paragraph could best be described as ...

- Lines ____ of the passage most likely represent ...

STRATEGIES FOR TONE AND STYLE

Review the section on Passage Types. As you are reading, ask yourself to identify the **style of passage** you are reading and where this passage would most likely be found. Would the passage most likely occur in a history or science textbook? In a diary? In a newspaper? As part of a short story?

Often, the author's **tone** will match the style of the passage. An informative passage, like you might find in a history or science textbook, will most likely be presenting facts. We would describe this tone as neutral, objective, or analytical. A persuasive passage, such as a diary entry or letter to the editor, might be more emotionally involved. The author's attitude toward the subject might be positive or negative. If you are having trouble finding the tone of the passage, look for any **positive or negative words** that might indicate the author's opinion about the topic.

Once you have identified the tone of the passage, you'll need to match it to an answer choice on the ISEE. The ISEE likes to use very challenging vocabulary words to define tone! Prepare yourself by learning all of the words in following chart. If these are unfamiliar, look them up and add them to your vocabulary flashcards or journal.

TONE WORDS			
Positive	**Negative**	**Humorous**	**Neutral**
admiring	bitter	amused	ambivalent
appreciative	critical	comical	analytical
assertive	condescending	flippant	apathetic
authoritative	concerned	ironic	detached
celebratory	contemptuous	mocking	disinterested
enthusiastic	cynical	sarcastic	indifferent
empathetic	disparaging	satiric	informative
exuberant	dubious		matter-of-fact
jubilant	harsh		objective
impassioned	hostile		unbiased
lighthearted	indignant		unconcerned
passionate	outraged		unemotional
reverent	skeptical		
	somber		

STRATEGIES FOR FIGURATIVE LANGUAGE

Within a passage, an author might use **figurative language** to add heightened meaning. Figurative language uses a word's connotation, or the feelings and symbols associated with a word, rather than just its literal meaning. Often these symbols are used to create a particular **mood** in the passage—a certain feeling we get as we are reading. Here are some of the most common types of figurative language.

Imagery uses descriptive words from the five senses to create a vivid image in the reader's mind. For example, the author might describe the sun as "a fiery blaze of gold." This evokes a vivid image of the sun's color, brightness, and heat.

A **symbol** is a word that represents another concept or idea within a poem. For example, an author might talk about the spring in order to symbolize rebirth or renewal. Here are some other very common symbols used in literature:

SYMBOL	MEANING
sleep	death
dreams	fate, the future
light (sun, stars, moon)	good, hope, freedom
dark	evil, magic, the unknown
spring	youth, birth, life
winter	death, dying, old age
owl	wisdom
dove	peace
rose	love, beauty
crown	wealth, royalty
ring	love, commitment

A **simile** is a device that compares two things using the words "like" or "as." For example, an author might say that a man's laugh is "like a thunderclap." From this comparison, we can conclude that the man's laugh is loud, booming, and startling.

A **metaphor** is also a device that compares two things, but does not use the words "like" or "as." Using the example above, the author might say that the man's laugh "is a thunderclap." The author is not saying that the man's laugh is literally caused by a thunderstorm, but that it resembles a thunderclap in its loudness and startling qualities.

Finally, **personification** is a technique that gives human characteristics to animals, objects, or ideas. For example, an author might say that "winter jealously steals the world's warmth." This statement personifies the season of winter by describing it as a thief and giving it the human characteristic of jealousy.

If you are asked about a specific type of figurative language in a passage, think about what type of mood or image it evokes. Then, try to determine why the author chose to use this particular image in order to support his main point or main purpose in the passage.

Ivy Global

EXAMPLE

Now let's take a look at a Tone/Style/Figurative Language question from the duck-billed platypus passage:

> The author's tone in this passage could best be described as
>
> (A) informative
> (B) argumentative
> (C) humorous
> (D) mournful

We could approach this question in several ways. We could re-read the passage with each of the tones in mind, and then eliminate the answers which don't work. However, we could also look at the passage and realize that its main purpose is just to give us information about the platypus. It is not trying to convince us of anything, so we can eliminate answer choice (B). The passage is not humorous, even though there are interesting parts, so we can eliminate (C). The passage is also not mournful, or deeply sad, so we can eliminate (D). We are left with (A), which works well, as the passage is just giving us information.

READING COMPREHENSION PRACTICE QUESTIONS

In this section, you will find 157 questions to prepare you for the types of reading passages you might find on the ISEE. There are 5 sets of questions, grouped by difficulty. Pay attention to the difficulty of each set to determine which questions are appropriate for your level. Read each passage carefully, and answer the questions following each passage on the basis of what is stated or implied in that passage.

BASIC PASSAGES

Use these questions to practice the most basic difficulty level you might see on the Lower, Middle, and Upper Level ISEE. The Lower Level exam will include more basic questions than the Middle and Upper Levels.

1   Every time you turn on a light,
2   you have Thomas Alva Edison to thank.
3   Born in 1847, Thomas Edison was an
4   American inventor and businessman.
5   In 1866, at the age of 19, Edison
6   moved to Kentucky, where he worked
7   at the Associated Press news wire.
8   Edison requested the night shift, which
9   allowed him plenty of time during the
10   day to spend on his two favorite
11   pastimes: reading and experimenting.
12   Edison was a prolific inventor,
13   devising hundreds of new inventions
14   and improvements on existing devices.
15   In Menlo Park, Edison founded the first
16   industrial research lab, where he and
17   an army of experimenters, scientists,
18   and craftsmen invented hundreds of
19   patentable processes and devices—
20   earning him the nickname "The
21   Wizard of Menlo Park." Edison's lab
22   produced numerous inventions that
23   contributed to mass communication,
24   such as a stock ticker, a mechanical
25   vote recorder, a new microphone that
26   improved telephone call quality, and
27   devices for recording and playing
28   music and motion pictures. These
29   devices helped to shape the way that
30   people communicate today.

1. What is the main idea of this passage?

   (A) Thomas Edison had a laboratory in Menlo Park.
   (B) Thomas Edison was a highly influential inventor.
   (C) Thomas Edison loved to read.
   (D) Thomas Edison was a child prodigy.

2. Which phrase most nearly means the same thing as "an army of experimenters, scientists, and craftsmen" (lines 16-18)?

   (A) a well-armed group of experimenters, scientists, and craftsmen
   (B) a small group of experimenters, scientists, and craftsmen
   (C) mostly experimenters, but also scientists and craftsmen
   (D) a large team of experimenters, scientists, and craftsmen

3. Edison requested the night shift at the Associated Press news wire because

   (A) he was too tired to work during the day.
   (B) he wanted to work on his reading and experiments during the day.
   (C) he wanted to work under the cover of darkness.
   (D) he wanted to work alone.

4. According to the third paragraph, Edison was most likely called "The Wizard of Menlo Park" because

   (A) he used magic to invent new devices.
   (B) he and his employees looked like wizards while they were working.
   (C) he convinced the residents of Menlo Park that he had supernatural powers.
   (D) he produced so many inventions in Menlo Park that it seemed like magic.

5. As it is used in line 12, "prolific" most nearly means

   (A) productive.
   (B) scarce.
   (C) friendly.
   (D) nervous.

The 1910 Cuba hurricane – known as the Cyclone of Five Days – was said to be one of the worst tropical cyclones that has ever hit Cuba. The storm formed in the southern Caribbean Sea on October 9, 1910. It grew stronger as it moved northwest. It then made landfall on the western end of Cuba. The storm made a loop over open water, and then began moving towards the United States. After crossing Florida, the storm continued moving close to the southeastern United States and passed out to sea.

The storm caused some damage in Florida, but in the island country of Cuba the storm was one of the worst disasters on record, bringing significant destruction across the island. Strong winds and rain caused flooding in streets, ruined crops, and damaged farms. Thousands of homes were destroyed, many other buildings were damaged, and ships carrying valuable goods were sunk by the storm. It is not known exactly how much damage the storm caused. However, losses in Havana, Cuba's capital city, were over $1 million, and the total amount of damage was probably in the millions. At least 100 people died in Cuba, mostly in lethal mudslides caused by the storm.

6. The primary purpose of the passage is

(A) to describe the climate of the Caribbean Sea.
(B) to compare and contrast the economies of Cuba and Florida.
(C) to give a complete history of hurricanes in the southeastern United States.
(D) to describe one tropical storm's effects on a particular region.

7. All of the following questions can be answered by the passage EXCEPT

(A) Where did the hurricane go after hitting Cuba?
(B) Did anybody die in Florida as a result of the hurricane?
(C) Where did the hurricane first make landfall?
(D) What is Cuba's capital?

8. The author's tone in this passage can best be described as

(A) informative.
(B) pessimistic.
(C) enthusiastic.
(D) humorous.

9. Which of the following statements is true, according to the passage?

(A) The hurricane traveled primarily in a northeastern direction.
(B) The worst damage caused by the hurricane was the sinking of ships.
(C) The majority of hurricane-related deaths in Cuba were caused by mudslides.
(D) The hurricane caused more damage in Florida than in Cuba.

10. With which of the following statements would the author most likely agree?

(A) There are still many questions to be answered about the 1910 Cuban Hurricane.
(B) Cuba will probably never recover from the damage caused by the 1910 Hurricane.
(C) The Cuban Hurricane could likely have been prevented with better planning.
(D) Hurricanes can have a devastating impact on island nations like Cuba.

1   Bacteria are an interesting and
2 numerous form of life. They are the
3 smallest and simplest organisms on
4 Earth. Bacteria are made up of only a
5 single cell, but even just an inch of your
6 skin contains millions of cells. There is
7 room for thousands or even millions of
8 bacteria in even very tiny places.
9   Bacteria can also live in many different
10 sorts of places. They can live in the dirt,
11 in the bodies of larger organisms, or
12 even in such hostile places as storm
13 clouds or boiling water. Bacteria also
14 reproduce very quickly, sometimes as
15 often as once every twenty minutes. For
16 these reasons, there are more
17 individual bacteria than any other sort
18 of organism on the planet.
19   Many people associate bacteria
20 with unsanitary conditions and assume
21 that all bacteria are harmful. There are
22 harmful bacteria that can damage your
23 body and cause illness, but many other
24 kinds of bacteria are harmless or even
25 very helpful. The good bacteria in your
26 body help you to digest food, produce
27 healthy vitamins, and help to fight off
28 harmful bacteria. We have so many
29 harmless bacteria in our bodies that in a
30 healthy person bacteria can outnumber
31 human cells ten to one.
32   Bacteria also play an important
33 role in manufacturing. They are used to
34 make food products like cheese, yogurt,
35 and vinegar. They are also used in
36 many other industrial processes, for
37 purposes as diverse as producing
38 biofuels, separating plant fibers, and
39 controlling pests.

11. The primary purpose of the passage is to

(A) provide information about bacteria.
(B) offer a detailed description of the scientific discovery of bacteria.
(C) explain why bacteria are dangerous and how one can avoid them.
(D) discuss the life cycle of bacteria.

12. Which best describes the way the passage is organized?

(A) A subject is introduced and then described in greater detail.
(B) An opinion is expressed and subsequently refuted in the second paragraph.
(C) A controversial topic is described, and various perspectives are explained.
(D) A series of problems is stated, and solutions to these problems are suggested.

13. With which of the following statements would the author most likely agree?

(A) For most illnesses, bacteria are probably the best medicine.
(B) The human body would function better without bacteria.
(C) Bacteria get too much credit for tasks that are mostly carried out by people.
(D) Bacteria have an underappreciated role in our everyday lives.

14. In line 37, the word "diverse" most nearly means

(A) different.
(B) dangerous.
(C) suspicious.
(D) delicious.

15. Based on information in the passage, which sentence best explains why bacteria are so numerous?

(A) Bacteria are very useful for making products, so we make as many of them as we can.
(B) There are ten times as many bacteria as people, so when people became more numerous so did bacteria.
(C) Bacteria can reproduce very quickly and can live in a wide variety of environments.
(D) Our immune system doesn't kill all bacteria because many bacteria are actually helpful.

16. What is the purpose of the last paragraph?

(A) to outline the role that bacteria play in industry
(B) to summarize the main idea of the passage
(C) to explain how bacteria are important for human health
(D) to show that even dangerous bacteria can be helpful in the proper context

Long ago in Japan lived a brave warrior known to all as Tawara Toda, or "My Lord Bag-of-Rice," but whose real name was Fujiwara Hidesato. This is the story of how Fujiwara came to be known as Tawara Toda.

One day Fujiwara was in search of adventures when he came to the bridge of Seta-no-Karashi. No sooner had he set foot on the bridge than he saw lying right across his path a huge serpent-dragon. Its body was so big that it looked like the trunk of a large pine tree, and it took up the whole width of the bridge. One of its huge claws rested on the railing of one side of the bridge, while its tail lay right against the other. The monster seemed to be asleep, and as it breathed, fire and smoke came out of its nostrils.

At first Fujiwara could not help feeling alarmed at the sight of this horrible reptile lying in his path, for he must either turn back or walk right over its body. He was a brave man, however, and putting aside all fear went forward dauntlessly. Crunch, crunch! he climbed over the dragon's body, and without even one glance backward, he went on his way.

17. Which of the following best describes the main idea of the passage?

(A) While on the journey that inspires him to change his name, Fujiwara confronts a dragon.

(B) Fujiwara nearly loses his life in a deadly fight with a dragon, but he manages to escape.

(C) Fujiwara befriends a seemingly intimidating dragon that turns out to be kind and generous.

(D) A group of villagers offer Fujiwara rice as a gift after he slays a menacing dragon.

18. The dragon in the passage could be described as

(A) angry and violent.

(B) small but dangerous.

(C) powerful but kind.

(D) large and frightening.

19. As it is used in line 27, "dauntlessly" most nearly means

(A) without hope.

(B) without fear.

(C) without looking.

(D) without courage.

20. When Fujiwara encountered the dragon, its tail was

(A) lying against the railing.

(B) scaly and brown.

(C) dangling over the side of the bridge.

(D) 50 feet long.

21. The passage might next discuss

(A) what Fujiwara did before getting to the bridge.

(B) an adventure Fujiwara had on another occasion.

(C) a stranger that Fujiwara meets on the other side of the bridge.

(D) how meeting the dragon led Fujiwara to change his name.

An object one 100th of an inch in diameter is about the smallest thing that can be easily seen by the unassisted eye. Take a piece of card and punch a little hole through it with the point of a small needle, hold it towards a lamp or a window, and you will see the light through it.

This hole will be about one 100th of an inch in diameter, and you will find that you can see it best when you hold it at a certain distance from your eye. This distance will not be far from ten inches, unless you are near-sighted. Now bring it towards your eye and you will find it becomes blurred and indistinct. You will find from this experiment that you cannot see things distinctly when you hold them too close to your eye. In other words, you cannot bring your eye nearer to an object than eight or ten inches and see it well at the same time.

You could see things much smaller than one hundredth of an inch if you could get your eye close enough to them without them appearing blurry. How can that be done? With a microscope.

22. The main purpose of this passage is

 (A) to explain the anatomy and
 function of the human eye.

 (B) to describe the problem that the
 microscope helps to solve.

 (C) to illustrate how the microscope
 was invented.

 (D) to complain about the
 limitations of human sight.

23. According to the passage, things
that are one 100th of an inch are

 (A) easy to see only if you happen to
 be nearsighted.

 (B) the smallest things we can
 easily see without a microscope.

 (C) impossible to see without a
 microscope.

 (D) usually located about eight or
 ten inches away from your eye.

24. According to the passage, what
happens when you bring something
too close to your eye?

 (A) You risk injuring yourself.

 (B) It starts to seem brighter.

 (C) It begins to appear smaller.

 (D) You can't see it clearly.

25. The tone of the passage is

 (A) informative.

 (B) critical.

 (C) fanciful.

 (D) argumentative.

26. In line 19, "distinctly" most nearly
means

 (A) blurry.

 (B) largely.

 (C) clearly.

 (D) distantly.

27. What is the author most likely to
write about next?

 (A) microscopes and how they work

 (B) objects too large to be seen from
 up close

 (C) the effects of near-sightedness

 (D) telescopes and how they work

The olm is a cave-dwelling salamander. Unlike many other amphibians, the olm is almost entirely aquatic. Because it lives predominantly in the water, it breathes with gills, like fish do, and its lungs are poorly developed. Because it lives in the darkness of caves, the olm's eyes are also poorly developed— in fact, they are covered over by skin, and the olm is blind. Instead of using sight, the olm uses very sensitive senses of smell and touch to detect food in its environment.

Prey is scarce in the olm's cave environment, but there are also no other predators, so the olm lives a long, slow life. It does not completely mature until about 16 years of age, which is a very long time for a salamander. Although olms generally avoid conflicts with one another, the males do become territorial when they are ready to breed. However, since there is little food and it takes a lot of energy to fight, territorial males generally settle their disputes with intimidating displays of strength, rather than with violence. At this relaxed pace of life, an olm can live about as long as a human, and much longer than most salamanders. Most olms live an average of 60 to 70 years, and some individuals may live to be over 100.

28. The main purpose of the passage is to

(A) provide information about a particular species of salamander.

(B) explain why the olm lives longer than other salamanders.

(C) describe various types of salamanders, including the olm.

(D) discuss the differences between salamanders.

29. The olm is a type of

(A) fish.

(B) mammal.

(C) amphibian.

(D) herbivore.

30. According to the passage, why don't olms normally fight each other?

(A) Olms that fight each other tend to attract predators

(B) There is no reason to fight when the environment isn't dangerous.

(C) Olms try to live a long time, so they don't like to take risks.

(D) Fighting uses up too much energy in an environment with little food.

31. What does the passage imply about types of salamanders other than olms?

(A) They tend to live in caves.

(B) They tend to have much shorter lives than humans.

(C) They are generally much larger than olms.

(D) They are much more comfortable around humans.

32. In line 4, the word "predominantly" most nearly means

(A) mainly.

(B) sometimes.

(C) unusually.

(D) quietly.

MEDIUM PASSAGES

Use these questions to practice the medium difficulty level you might see on the Lower, Middle, and Upper Level ISEE. Questions like these will make up much of the Lower Level and Middle Level Reading sections, and a smaller portion of the Upper Level section.

1 Bowling is an indoor game
2 played upon an alley with balls and
3 nine or ten pins, but up to the year
4 1840 it was played on a green, like
5 cricket or baseball. One of the chief
6 spots for bowling was the square just
7 north of New York's Battery Park
8 that is still called Bowling Green.
9 After bowling moved indoors, the
10 first covered alleys were made of
11 hardened clay or of slate. Today, they
12 are built up of alternate strips of pine
13 and maple wood, fastened together
14 and to the bed of the alley.
15 Originally, nine pins were used
16 and arranged in a diamond shape,
17 but during the first part of the 19th
18 century the game of "nine-pins" was
19 legally prohibited because of its
20 connection with gambling. This law,
21 however, was soon evaded by the
22 addition of a tenth pin, resulting in
23 the game of "ten-pins," which is what
24 we play today. The ten pins are set
25 up at the end of the alley in the form
26 of a triangle in four rows: four pins at
27 the back, then three, then two, and
28 one as head pin.
29 Several other varieties of
30 bowling are popular in America, the
31 most popular being "Cocked Hat,"
32 which is played with three pins, one
33 in the head-pin position and the
34 others on either corner of the back
35 row. The pins are usually a little
36 larger than those used in the regular
37 game, and smaller balls are used.
38 There is also "Candle Pin," which
39 uses thin pins tapering towards the
40 top and bottom, but is otherwise
41 similar to the regular game. The old-
42 fashioned game with nine pins is still
43 played from time to time under the
44 name "Head Pin."

1. The main subject of this passage is

   (A) the game of bowling and its history.

   (B) the gamed of "Cocked Hat."

   (C) popular American pastimes.

   (D) how bowling survived despite laws prohibiting it.

2. The passage implies that in the 19th century, gambling was

   (A) one of the most popular pastimes in New York.

   (B) only conducted during games of nine-pin.

   (C) regarded as an activity that should be restricted.

   (D) generally legal, but not in the case of nine-pins.

3. According to the passage, some people today still play a version of bowling with nine pins, known as

   (A) Head Pin.

   (B) Nine-pins.

   (C) Candle Pin.

   (D) Cocked Hat.

4. According to the passage, Bowling Green

   (A) was named for its resemblance to a bowling alley.

   (B) was once a very popular spot for outdoor bowling.

   (C) is still the main place to bowl in New York City.

   (D) is the only place where New York City law allowed bowling to be played in the 19th century.

5. Which of the following puts the history of the bowling alley in the right order?

   (A) Bowling started outdoors, then moved into wooden alleys, which were then replaced by clay and stone alleys.

   (B) Bowling started in wooden alleys, then moved outdoors, then returned indoors to clay and stone alleys.

   (C) Bowling started outdoors, then moved indoors to clay and stone alleys, which were then replaced by wooden alleys.

   (D) Bowling started in clay and stone alleys, which were replaced by wooden alleys, then moved outdoors.

6. When the author says that the law "was soon evaded by the addition of a tenth pin" (lines 21-22), she means that

   (A) ten-pin bowling was a good alternative for people who did not want to gamble.

   (B) a tenth pin was added to the game, and as a result the law was rewritten to ban both nine- and ten-pin bowling.

   (C) legislators soon overturned the law against nine-pin bowling because ten-pin bowling, a nearly identical game, was still allowed.

   (D) the law was specifically against the game of nine-pin bowling, so players could continue to bowl legally by adding a tenth pin.

1   The optical microscope, sometimes called the "light microscope," uses visible light and a system of lenses to magnify images of things that are too small to be seen with the naked eye. Optical microscopes are the oldest type of microscope and were designed in close to their present form in the 17th century. Basic optical microscopes can be very simple, although there are many complex designs which aim to improve the clarity and detail of the image produced.

15   Another optical invention of the 17th century was the telescope. Like the microscope, the telescope made it possible to study things that were previously hard or impossible to see— but in this case, because they were too far away, not because of their size. 17th century astronomers relied on telescopes to help them develop new theories about the movements of the distant stars and planets.

26   The first microscopes and telescopes used visible light to make very small or very distant things visible, but in the 20th century, telescopes were developed that use other forms of light, like infrared light and x-rays. Meanwhile, scientists in the 1930s developed an electron microscope that uses electrons instead of visible light to generate magnified images.

7. Which of the following best expresses the main idea of the passage?

(A) The microscope is a powerful tool that significantly advanced the field of medicine.

(B) The 20th century saw many developments in optical technology.

(C) The microscope and the telescope were both invented in the 17th century, and were both developed further in the 20th century.

(D) The original forms of microscopes and telescopes were better than the ones we use today.

8. According to the passage, all of the following is true of optical microscopes EXCEPT

(A) they use visible light to produce magnified images.

(B) they were invented in the 17th century.

(C) they use electrons instead of visible light.

(D) they can be fairly simple or more complex in design.

9. According to the passage, what is another name for the optical microscope?

(A) the light microscope

(B) the megascope

(C) the refractor

(D) the electron microscope

10. The telescope is similar to the microscope in that it

(A) now uses infrared light.

(B) helped people see what they previously could not.

(C) helped scientists develop theories about the stars.

(D) did not use optical light.

11. The passage suggests that "distant stars and planets" (line 25)

(A) are hard to study without the use of a telescope.

(B) were first discovered by astronomers in the 1800s.

(C) orbit the sun.

(D) are easy to see with a microscope.

12. Which of the following would most likely come next in this passage?

(A) a discussion of the invention of television in the 20th century

(B) an argument that the microscope is more valuable to society than the telescope

(C) a biography of the inventor who developed the electron microscope

(D) more detail about the development of 20th century microscopes and telescopes

1   "Who-oo-ee!" The gleeful shout
2   came from the lips of a little girl who
3   stood, with her hands cupped about her
4   lips, on the edge of a streamlet which
5   divided the village of Domremy into
6   two parts. She was a slight little maiden,
7   of some twelve years, and as she gave
8   the call she danced about in the warm
9   sunshine as though unable to keep still
10   from the mere joy of being. Her hair
11   was very dark and very abundant. Her
12   eyes were wonderful for their blueness
13   and the steadfastness of their gaze. Her
14   face, though pretty, was remarkable not
15   so much for its beauty as for the
16   happiness of its expression. She stood
17   still listening for a moment after
18   sending forth her call, and then, as the
19   morning quiet remained unbroken, she
20   sent forth the cry again in a clear, sweet
21   voice that penetrated into the farthest
22   reaches of the village:
23   "Who-oo-ee!"
24   This time the shout was caught up
25   instantly, and answered by many
26   voices. The village wakened suddenly
27   into life, as there poured forth from the
28   cottages a goodly number of boys and
29   girls who came running toward the
30   little maid eagerly. She shook a finger at
31   them reprovingly.
32   "Oh, but you are late," she cried.
33   "Here it is ten of the clock, and we were
34   to start at nine. The day will be half
35   gone before we get to the Tree. I was
36   afraid that you had gone off without
37   me."
38   "Gone without you, Jeanne,"
39   exclaimed one of the girls. "Why, we
40   couldn't have any sport without you! I
41   had to wait for my mother to fix my
42   basket––that is the reason that I was
43   late."
44   "And I! And I!" chimed several
45   other children in a chorus.
46   "Why didn't you pack them
47   yourselves?" demanded Jeanne, who
48   seemed to be a leader among them. "I
49   did mine, and John's and Pierre's too."

13. We can infer from the passage that Jeanne was excited because

(A) she and the other children had planned some fun for the day.

(B) she was the first of the children to get ready for their plans.

(C) the other children liked and respected her.

(D) her basket was the best, since she had prepared it herself.

14. Jeanne is described as having all of the following EXCEPT:

(A) a happy expression.

(B) lots of dark hair.

(C) a strong, pretty voice.

(D) delicate hands.

15. According to the passage, Jeanne most likely "danced about" (line 8) because

(A) she was trying to keep warm in the chilly morning air.

(B) she was glad to be alive.

(C) she was singing a dancing tune.

(D) she was anxious to leave.

16. It can be inferred from the passage that Jeanne shouted in order to

(A) annoy the villagers.

(B) summon the village children.

(C) warn the villagers of an attack.

(D) show off her beautiful singing voice.

17. The phrase "The village wakened suddenly into life" (lines 26-27) describes

(A) the transition of the village from quiet and inactive to busy and full of energy.

(B) the transformation of the village to a living being.

(C) the rise of the sun and beginning of a new day in the village.

(D) the beginning of rush hour in the village.

18. What was the excuse that one of the children gave for being late?

(A) She had to fix her basket by herself.

(B) She had to wait for her mother to fix her a basket to take along.

(C) She had to fix both her own basket and her brothers' baskets as well.

(D) She planned to start at ten o'clock.

Hanami ("flower viewing") is the Japanese custom of enjoying the beauty of flowers, especially cherry blossoms, or sakura. The practice of Hanami is more than a thousand years old, and is still very popular in Japan today. In modern Japan, the practice mainly takes the form of an outdoor party held beneath the blooming trees.

The trees bloom in the spring, and the weather bureau announces the blossom forecast each year as the flowering season approaches. Because the blossoms are very short-lived, those hoping to practice Hanami pay close attention to this forecast. Full bloom usually comes about one week after the opening of the first blossoms. Another week later, the blooming peak is over and the blossoms are falling from the trees.

The practice of Hanami is said to have started during the Nara Period (710-784) when the Chinese Tang Dynasty influenced Japan in many ways, including introducing a custom of gathering to appreciate flowers. At first, Hanami was focused on viewing the ume, or plum blossoms. But the sakura – cherry blossoms – were considered sacred by the Japanese, and began to attract more attention over time, becoming the focus of Hanami.

The Japanese people today continue the tradition of Hanami, gathering in great numbers wherever there are flowering Sakura trees. Thousands of people fill the parks to hold feasts under the trees, and sometimes these parties go on until late at night. Some people also still practice the more ancient form of Hanami, viewing ume, and this practice is called Umemi, or plum-viewing. Umemi parties are usually smaller and quieter than other Hanami parties, and the guests are usually older.

19. Which of the following best expresses the central idea of the passage?

(A) The sakura, or cherry blossom, is a sacred Japanese flower.

(B) Hanami is an ancient Japanese tradition that is still popular today.

(C) Hanami takes place in March and April, when the sakura blossoms appear.

(D) Traditional Japanese religion worships the natural world.

20. Which sentence best explains why the sakura blossom is the focus of the Hanami tradition in Japan today?

(A) Ume trees are no longer planted as frequently as sakura trees.

(B) The Japanese prefer the sakura blossom and have more exciting parties than those who practice Umeme.

(C) When the tradition of Hanami spread to Japan, its popularity caused the sakura to become a sacred flower in Japan.

(D) The sakura blossom was considered sacred in ancient Japan, so it became the focus of the Hanami tradition when the tradition spread to Japan.

21. According to the passage, what is Umeme?

(A) a Japanese custom that celebrates the sakura blossom

(B) an ancient tradition that was common in Japan before Hanami was introduced

(C) a form of Hanami that involves viewing plum blossoms

(D) a new tradition that is becoming more popular than Hanami

22. What difference can we infer between Umeme parties and other Hanami parties?

(A) Umeme parties will probably stop being held over time, while other Hanami parties will continue.

(B) Young people don't like Umeme parties as much as other Hanami parties.

(C) Umeme parties tend to be more sacred religious events.

(D) In ancient Japan, the Tang Dynasty may have outlawed Hanami which took place around sakura trees.

23. Which of the following statements is supported by information in the passage?

(A) The Hanami tradition remains an important part of Japanese culture.

(B) The Hanami tradition is still observed by some but is generally considered obsolete.

(C) Only older Japanese people consider the tradition of Hanami important.

(D) The sakura and ume plants are found only in Japan.

24. How long does the peak blooming season for Hanami parties last?

(A) about a week

(B) through the spring

(C) late into the night

(D) several weeks

1   On September 24, 2013, off the
2 coast of the port city of Gwadar in
3 Pakistan, a new island appeared. The
4 island, named Zalzala Jazeera (or
5 "Earthquake Island") appeared shortly
6 after a powerful earthquake in the
7 region, which killed at least 825 people
8 and left more than 100,000 homeless.
9   The earthquake, a 7.7 on the
10 Richter scale, disturbed large, shallow
11 pockets of natural gas beneath the sea's
12 surface. The pockets of gas heated up,
13 expanded, and pushed towards the
14 surface. Thrusting the mud, sand, and
15 solid rock above them upwards, the
16 expanding gases created what is known
17 as a "mud volcano," and Zalzala Jazeera
18 emerged from the sea. Unlike a lava
19 volcano, mud volcanos are not
20 necessarily hot. The mud oozing up
21 from beneath the surface can be
22 freezing cold. Zalzala Jazeera is cool
23 enough for people to walk on, but that
24 does not mean that it is perfectly safe:
25 the methane gas beneath the island is
26 highly flammable and explosive, and
27 leaks from vents dotted across the
28 island.
29   In the wake of the earthquake's
30 terrible destruction, Zalzala Jazeera has
31 been a blessing to locals. The raising of
32 the sea bed has attracted numerous
33 small fish and the larger fish that prey
34 on them, and fishermen are now drawn
35 to the waters around the island.
36 Tourists also have come from far and
37 wide to see the island, and they pay
38 local boatmen generously to ferry them
39 out to Zalzala Jazeera.
40   But Zalzala Jazeera is an
41 ephemeral island: it appeared
42 suddenly, and will soon disappear.
43 Over time, the gas beneath the island
44 will cool and compress, or escape
45 through the vents on the island's
46 surface, and the mud and stone of the
47 island will recede back into the sea.
48 Erosion will also take a toll, as rains and
49 waves wash off and carry away the
50 loose sand and soft mud that covers the
51 island's surface. In fact, the island has
52 been shrinking back down into the
53 ocean almost since the moment of its
54 appearance. When it first appeared in
55 September, the island stood about 60
56 feet above sea level. Only two months
57 later, the island had dropped down to
58 about 50 feet above sea level. Experts
59 say that the island will most likely
60 vanish within a year.

25. Which sentence best summarizes the main idea of this passage?

(A) Gas pockets beneath the Earth's surface can cause islands to suddenly erupt from the sea, causing risks of fire and explosion.

(B) Although the earthquake which struck Pakistan was a tragic event, it created new economic opportunities for the people of Gwadar.

(C) Not only did the earthquake which struck Pakistan in 2013 kill hundreds of people, it also caused Zalzala Jazeera to begin to sink into the sea.

(D) Zalzala Jazeera is a temporary island off the coast of Pakistan that was formed during a large earthquake by a mud volcano.

26. According to the passage, what is one reason that Zalzala Jazeera is vanishing?

(A) There are no more earthquakes occurring off the coast of Pakistan.

(B) Its muddy surface is being eroded by natural forces.

(C) Tourists are flocking to the island and carrying away bits of stone and sand.

(D) Pockets of gas were disturbed by the earthquake that struck Pakistan.

27. The passage suggests that a 7.7 on the Richter scale represents

(A) the creation of a new island or volcano.

(B) the number of deaths that occurred during an earthquake.

(C) large pockets of natural gas.

(D) an earthquake that is quite powerful.

28. What is the main purpose of the last paragraph?

(A) to explain that Zalzala Jazeera will only be a temporary landmass

(B) to show why it is important for tourists to visit Zalzala Jazeera as soon as they can

(C) to describe the economic benefits created by the appearance of Zalzala Jazeera

(D) to warn readers of the hazards of living on a temporary island

29. As it is used in line 41, the word "ephemeral" most nearly means

(A) fortunate.

(B) surprising.

(C) short-lived.

(D) unpredictable.

30. Which of the following questions CANNOT be answered by the passage?

(A) What does the name "Zalzala Jazeera" mean?

(B) How has Zalzala Jazeera affected tourism and the fishing industry in Gwadar?

(C) How quickly is Zalzala Jazeera sinking back into the sea?

(D) Was Zalzala Jazeera the only temporary island that appeared after the September 2013 earthquake?

A monarch is a supreme leader of a government who usually inherits the position or is appointed by the previous monarch. Queen Elizabeth II is the Queen of the Commonwealth Realms, and she is a constitutional monarch. King Abdullah is the King of Saudi Arabia, and he is an absolute monarch. The difference between an absolute and a constitutional monarchy involves the powers and privileges of the monarch.

In a constitutional monarchy, the monarch is the official head of state and has certain powers and responsibilities as prescribed by law. However, the law itself is created by some other part of the government. In the United Kingdom, which is a part of the Commonwealth Realms, many state powers are granted to Queen Elizabeth by the law, such as the powers to declare war and to make peace. However, most of her powers are delegated to Ministers, who are members of the elected Parliament and govern on her behalf. To the extent that the Queen participates in the operation of the government, she does so only on the advice of the Prime Minister and the Cabinet Ministers, and has a limited role.

In an absolute monarchy, the monarch is the head of state and also has the authority to make laws, including the laws which define his or her rights as monarch. In Saudi Arabia, King Abdullah plays a much stronger role in government than does Queen Elizabeth in the United Kingdom. Although the King delegates many responsibilities to departments and ministers of government, he retains the right to make law by royal decree and appoints many government officials directly. However, there are some political reforms occurring under the reign of King Abdullah, which are shifting some powers and responsibilities from the Monarch to the public. In 2005, Saudi Arabia held its first government elections in more than 40 years. The King did not open his own office up to elections, but he did allow male citizens to vote for some officials.

31. This passage is mainly concerned with

(A) describing two types of monarchs and the differences between them.

(B) explaining why some places are better to live than others.

(C) giving biographical information about modern Kings and Queens.

(D) explaining the role of elections in monarchies.

32. What does the passage imply about elections in a monarchy?

(A) Elections are possible under a monarchy, but not necessarily required.

(B) When a monarch dies, it is usually necessary to elect the next monarch.

(C) Elections are not allowed in monarchies under any circumstances.

(D) In a monarchy, only the Prime Minister may decide whether to hold elections.

33. What is the main difference between a constitutional monarch and an absolute monarch?

(A) Constitutional monarchs are generally elected, but absolute monarchs are appointed by the previous monarch.

(B) Only a constitutional monarch, not an absolute monarch, is allowed to change the constitution.

(C) Absolute monarchs can create or change laws, but constitutional monarchs must follow laws created by other branches of the government.

(D) There can be only one absolute monarch, but there may be several constitutional monarchs.

34. In line 15, "prescribed" most nearly means

(A) diagnosed.

(B) determined.

(C) opposed.

(D) relaxed.

35. Which question could be answered using information in the passage?

    (A) Have there ever been elections in Saudi Arabia?

    (B) Who is the current Prime Minister of the United Kingdom?

    (C) Do Queen Elizabeth II and King Abdullah have friendly diplomatic ties?

    (D) How did King Abdullah become King of Saudi Arabia?

36. What is true of both of the monarchies used as examples in this passage?

    (A) The monarch plays a largely ceremonial role, with most of the real power in other parts of government.

    (B) In elections, only men are allowed to vote on candidates for public office.

    (C) Other than the monarch, all other government officials are elected.

    (D) Many of the official powers of the monarch are delegated to other parts of the government.

DIFFICULT PASSAGES

Use these questions to practice the more advanced questions you might see on the Lower, Middle, and Upper Level ISEE. The Upper Level exam will include more difficult questions than the Middle and Lower Level exams.

1 London's Millennium Bridge
2 was closed for two years after its
3 opening due to an unsettling wobble
4 that earned it the moniker "Wobbly
5 Bridge."
6 The steel suspension bridge,
7 which carries pedestrians across the
8 Thames, was commissioned to
9 celebrate the millennium.
10 Construction began in 1998, with the
11 grand opening on June 10, 2000. The
12 bridge is a total of 1,214 feet long and
13 13 feet wide, and it links Bankside to
14 the City of London. It was nicknamed
15 the "Wobbly Bridge" after flocks of
16 enthusiastic Londoners crossing the
17 bridge on the day of its opening felt
18 an unexpected swaying motion.
19 While some enjoyed the white-
20 knuckle ride, many pedestrians
21 found the sensation to be
22 uncomfortable. The bridge was
23 closed later that day. After two days
24 of maintaining limited access to the
25 bridge, city officials announced that
26 the bridge would be closed for
27 modifications.

28 The tendency of a suspension
29 bridge to sway when troops march
30 over it in step is well known, which is
31 why troops are required to break
32 step when crossing such a bridge.
33 Engineers did not anticipate that
34 pedestrians walking out of step
35 would cause the same wobble, but
36 the bridge's engineers have since
37 identified that this was the source of
38 the problem. If a bridge has a
39 sideways sway, pedestrians crossing
40 the bridge have an unconscious
41 tendency to match their footsteps to
42 the sway. This phenomenon
43 exacerbates the wobble in a manner
44 similar to the synchronized marching
45 of troops.
46 Once the problem was
47 identified, the Millennium Bridge was
48 retrofitted with dampers to minimize
49 the wobble, and reopened in 2002.
50 Although the bridge no longer suffers
51 from the sway that earned it its title,
52 many Londoners still affectionately
53 refer to it as the "Wobbly Bridge."

1. Which sentence best summarizes the central idea of this passage?

   (A) Most people do not enjoy crossing a bridge that sways, even though some do find it to be an exciting experience.

   (B) London's Millennium Bridge initially suffered from an unexpected problem that earned it an unusual nickname.

   (C) It is important for large groups to break step when crossing a bridge.

   (D) London's Millennium Bridge should have been more carefully designed to avoid the problems that damaged its reputation.

2. As it is used in the passage, "exacerbates" (line 43) most nearly means

   (A) weakens.
   (B) confuses.
   (C) intensifies.
   (D) enlightens.

3. According to the passage, what river does the London Millennium Bridge cross?

   (A) Thames
   (B) London
   (C) Bankside
   (D) Rhine

4. Which of the following places the events of the passage into the order in which they occurred?

   (A) Construction of the bridge began; the bridge was commissioned; the bridge was closed to the public.

   (B) Construction of the bridge was finished; the bridge was opened with limited access; the bridge was opened to the entire public; the bridge was closed for two years.

   (C) Construction of the bridge was finished; crowds of London residents crossed the bridge; the bridge was nicknamed the "Wobbly Bridge."

   (D) The bridge was closed to the public; the bridge was re-opened to the public; the bridge was nicknamed the "Wobbly Bridge."

5. According to the passage, what must soldiers do when crossing certain bridges?

   (A) march in a special, dance-like way

   (B) cross one at a time, because the bridge may collapse under too much weight

   (C) stop marching in unison, so that their footfalls do not make the bridge sway too much

   (D) match their footsteps to the sway of the bridge, so that they will not fall off

6. The passage states that the wobble affecting the Millennium Bridge

(A) should have been anticipated by the engineers who built the bridge.

(B) was understood in relation to military movement, but engineers did not know that pedestrians walking out of step could cause the same problem.

(C) was a highly dangerous phenomenon, and the city acted prudently by closing the bridge so quickly.

(D) was identified and corrected within two years, but pedestrians are still nervous about using the bridge.

Alexander Graham Bell is commonly credited as the inventor of the first practical telephone. Bell was the first to obtain a patent, on March 7, 1876, for an "apparatus for transmitting vocal or other sounds telegraphically," after experimenting with many primitive sound transmitters and receivers. Bell managed to get his telephone to work successfully three days after the patent was issued.

Bell did for the telephone what Henry Ford did for the automobile. Although not the first to experiment with telephonic devices, Bell and the companies founded in his name were the first to develop commercially practical telephones around which a successful business could be built and grown. Bell adopted carbon transmitters similar to Edison's transmitters and adapted telephone exchanges and switching plug boards developed for sending telegraphs. Bell succeeded where others failed to assemble a commercially viable telephone system; it can therefore be argued that Bell invented the telephone industry. The Bell Telephone company was established in 1877, and within ten years, over 150,000 people owned telephones in the United States.

The telephone is the most famous and well-remembered of Bell's inventions, and his most commercially successful enterprise, but his scientific interests were broad and he was also responsible for a number of other important inventions and innovations. In a particularly dramatic act of invention, after the shooting of President Garfield in 1881, Bell quickly created a device which he hoped would locate the bullet in the ailing president's body. The device worked perfectly in tests, but was unfortunately unable to locate the bullet, which was lodged too deeply in the body of President Garfield to be found. However, this was the genesis of the metal detector, a device still used widely today.

By Bell's own estimation, his greatest invention was the Photophone, the first wireless telephone, which Bell invented in the late 19th century. Whereas the original telephone used electricity to transmit sound information over wires, the Photophone operated by transmitting a signal with light. The first wireless signal from the Photophone was transmitted in 1880, nearly 20 years before the first radio communications, and around 100 years before light would become a popular medium for the transmission of information through fiber-optic cables.

As his inventions became a ubiquitous part of modern life, Bell accumulated honors and recognition, and is remembered as one of the most influential figures of the late 19th and early 20th century.

7. The primary purpose of this passage is to

(A) compare Alexander Graham Bell to contemporary inventors.

(B) describe the achievements of Alexander Graham Bell.

(C) describe the steps leading up to Bell's greatest invention, the Photophone.

(D) tell the story of the invention of the telephone.

8. As it is used in line 5, "apparatus" most nearly means

(A) gimmick.

(B) map.

(C) garb.

(D) device.

9. It can be inferred from the passage that Henry Ford

(A) made the automobile commercially successful.

(B) was the first person to design a car model.

(C) was much less influential than Bell.

(D) was the first inventor to experiment with the telephone.

10. Which of the following questions does the passage answer?

(A) What did Alexander Graham Bell regard as his greatest invention?

(B) Who was the first scientist to experiment with telephonic devices?

(C) Why did Bell become interested in transmitting sound?

(D) What was Bell's first invention?

11. On the day that Bell filed his patent for the telephone,

(A) other inventors began experimenting with similar devices.

(B) Henry Ford also filed the first automobile patent.

(C) Bell's telephone was not yet working properly.

(D) Bell single-handedly invented the telephone industry.

12. What is the most likely purpose of the last sentence of the fourth paragraph (lines 60-66)?

(A) It provides evidence that the Photophone was superior to radio technology.

(B) It explains the important role played by fiber-optic cables in Bell's inventions.

(C) It characterizes the Photophone as an invention that was ahead of its time.

(D) It demonstrates how long it took for the Photophone to become commercially successful.

1   I was born on February 23, 1685.
2 Even before I could speak, I showed a
3 remarkable fondness for music, and the
4 only toys I cared for were those which
5 were capable of producing musical
6 sounds. My father, however, had no
7 sympathy at all for my love of music; he
8 regarded the art with contempt, as
9 something beneath the serious notice of
10 one who aspired to be a gentleman, and
11 my earnest desire to be taught to play
12 only served to make him angry. He had
13 decided that I was to be a lawyer, and
14 so that nothing should interfere with
15 the carrying out of this plan he refused
16 to allow me to attend school, lest my

17 fondness for music should induce
18 someone to teach me to play. I was
19 therefore compelled to stifle my longing
20 whilst in my father's presence, and
21 content myself with making music in
22 the seclusion of my own chamber. It
23 may seem strange that my mother
24 should not have interposed in order
25 that I should be taught music, but the
26 elderly surgeon ruled our household
27 with a firm hand, which not even his
28 wife's intercession would have made
29 him relax. And how could she have
30 known that her son would grow up to
31 be a respected composer?

13. This passage is primarily concerned with

(A) investigating how the author eventually became a great composer.

(B) portraying the author's father, and explaining why he hated music.

(C) describing the author's challenging childhood.

(D) persuading parents to let their children study music.

14. According to the passage, what was the profession of the author's father?

(A) a lawyer

(B) a surgeon

(C) a gentleman

(D) a property-owner

15. As he is portrayed in this passage, which word best describes the author's father?

(A) musical

(B) insidious

(C) stern

(D) considerate

16. The passage suggests that the author's mother

(A) was an indulgent and accommodating parent.

(B) also wanted the author to become a lawyer.

(C) paid little attention to her son.

(D) was not as disapproving of music as the author's father.

17. As it is used in line 28, "intercession" most nearly means

(A) intervention.

(B) inclusion.

(C) incapacity.

(D) incident.

18. We can infer from the passage that as an adult the author would

(A) become a composer, in spite of his father's wishes.

(B) be forced by his father to become a lawyer.

(C) become a surgeon, just as his father had done.

(D) practice music alone in his private chambers.

Historically and in many parts of the world, women's participation in the profession of medicine has been significantly restricted, although women's practice of medicine, informally, in the role of caregivers, or in the allied health professions, has been widespread. Most countries of the world now guarantee equal access for women to medical education. While gender parity has yet to be achieved within the medical field worldwide, in some countries female doctors outnumber male doctors. This is the case in Canada and will be the case in England in the next six years.

While people often think of Americans like Ann Preston and Elizabeth Blackwell as the first important female physicians, the earliest cited woman doctor dates all the way back to Ancient Egypt. Her name was Merit Ptah. She was born sometime around 2700 BCE, and she is possibly the first named woman in all of science as well. Her picture can be seen on a tomb in the necropolis near the step pyramid of Saqqara. Her son, who was a High Priest, described her as "the Chief Physician."

19. The main purpose of this passage is to

    (A) describe the history and current state of women's participation in medicine.
    (B) provide a detailed account of Merit Ptah's life.
    (C) argue that women should not be allowed to study medicine.
    (D) compare the performance of men and women in the medical field.

20. According to the passage, the number of female doctors worldwide

    (A) is declining compared to the number of male doctors.
    (B) is the same as the number of male doctors.
    (C) is much greater than the number of male doctors.
    (D) is not yet equal to the number of male doctors.

21. According to the passage, which of the following statements is true?

    (A) There are almost as many female doctors as male doctors in Canada.
    (B) Elizabeth Blackwell was the first important female physician.
    (C) Women have only become involved in medicine in the past hundred years.
    (D) Most countries allow women to study medicine.

22. The passage answers all of the following questions EXCEPT

    (A) What nationality were Ann Preston and Elizabeth Blackwell?
    (B) How many children did Merit Ptah have?
    (C) What is one country in which female doctors outnumber male doctors?
    (D) What was the profession of Merit Ptah's son?

23. Although women's participation in medical professions has been restricted, in what informal roles have women practiced medicine?

    (A) as caregivers
    (B) as researchers of medicine
    (C) as surgeons
    (D) as professors of medicine

1 The Seville Fair, or Feria de Abril,
2 is held in the Andalusian capital of
3 Seville, Spain. The fair generally begins
4 two weeks after the Semana Santa, or
5 Easter Holy Week. Today, it is a
6 cherished regional event, with people
7 dressing in the vibrant colors of
8 traditional flamenco garb and
9 celebrating until the wee hours of the
10 morning.
11   The practice of holding festivities
12 two weeks after Easter dates back to
13 the Middle Ages, but the modern Seville
14 Fair began in 1847, when it was
15 originally organized as a livestock fair.
16 In the following year an air of festivity
17 began to transform the fair, due mainly
18 to the emergence of the first three
19 casetas (lavishly decorated marquee
20 tents which are temporarily built on the
21 fairground). During the 1920s, the fair
22 reached its peak and became the
23 spectacle that it is today.
24   The fair officially begins at
25 midnight on Monday and runs six days,
26 ending on the following Sunday. Each
27 day the fiesta begins with the parade of
28 carriages and riders carrying Seville's
29 most eminent citizens. They make their
30 way to the bullring, La Real Maestranza,
31 where the bullfighters and breeders
32 meet. From around nine at night until
33 six or seven the following morning, at
34 first in the streets and later only within
35 each caseta, you will find crowds
36 partying and dancing flamenco,
37 drinking sherry, and eating tapas.

24. This main purpose of the passage is to

   (A) describe the modern Seville Fair and its origins.
   (B) tell a story about the author's experience of the Seville Fair.
   (C) relate the history of celebrations in Seville.
   (D) explain how a simple livestock fair evolved into a great festival.

25. According to the passage, the Seville Fair

   (A) was once very popular but is no longer celebrated.
   (B) reached its current level of popularity in the 1920s.
   (C) is a very somber time in Spain.
   (D) lasts three days and three nights.

26. As it is used in line 29, "eminent" most nearly means

   (A) important.
   (B) distracted.
   (C) inconsequential.
   (D) frustrated.

27. According to the passage, what was responsible for transforming the Seville Fair from a livestock event to a celebratory festival?

   (A) The people of Seville celebrated until the wee hours of the morning.
   (B) The Casino of Seville remained open for the entire duration of the fair.
   (C) Three decorated marquee tents were set up on the fairground.
   (D) The fair officially began at midnight instead of in the morning.

28. It can be inferred from the passage that "flamenco garb" (line 8) is

   (A) a modern style of dress with sleek lines and bright colors.
   (B) an old-fashioned, bright style of dress, suitable for dancing.
   (C) a pious style of dress popular in the 1920s.
   (D) an old-fashioned style of dress worn by the upper-classes .

29. Which of these would the author most likely discuss next?

   (A) recipes for making tapas
   (B) the controversies surrounding bullfighting in Spain
   (C) Seville's eminent citizens from history
   (D) special events that happen during the week of the Seville Fair

1   Bees around the world are under
2 pressure from a mysterious threat
3 called Colony Collapse Disorder. The
4 disorder causes worker bees to
5 abruptly disappear, wiping out about
6 one-third of honey bee hives each year.
7 There are probably several factors
8 contributing to Colony Collapse
9 Disorder, including pesticides,
10 parasites, and viral agents. Now, air
11 pollution might be added to that list.
12   A new study in the journal
13 Scientific Reports finds that exposure to
14 toxic emissions can affect bees' ability
15 to recognize the odor of flowers.
16 Researchers at Britain's University of
17 Southampton focused on honeybees, a
18 species that pollinates farmers' fields.
19 The pollinator relies on its vision and
20 acute sense of smell to do its job, says
21 neurobiologist Tracey Newman, lead
22 author of the study.
23   "Now, it's faced with a sea of
24 chemistry every time it goes out on a
25 foraging expedition," said Newman. "So,
26 what it has to do is it has to decipher
27 and discern between those different
28 chemicals to hone in on the plants that
29 it knows are going to give it the best
30 reward in terms of nectar and pollen."
31   Newman's team wanted to know
32 how pollutants would change that
33 process. Their study asks this question:
34 if flowers are releasing perfumes in an
35 environment that is polluted, is the bee
36 compromised in its ability to find the
37 flowers that it's looking for?
38   "And in particular," Newman
39 added, "what we wanted to know is not
40 the direct impact on the bee itself, but
41 on the flower chemistry that the bee is
42 having to find."
43   She found that nitric oxides in
44 diesel exhaust emissions reacted with
45 chemicals from the flower and changed
46 or destroyed them. As this process
47 interferes with bees' ability to locate
48 one of their primary food sources, it
49 makes troubled hives even more
50 vulnerable, a factor she says has been
51 disregarded in the context of honeybee
52 health, until now.

30. Which sentence best summarizes the main idea of this passage?

(A) Air pollution may be a factor contributing to Colony Collapse Disorder.

(B) Colony Collapse Disorder is a serious threat to agriculture.

(C) The primary cause of Colony Collapse Disorder is air pollution.

(D) Honeybees are an essential part of our food system.

31. Which of the following statements is supported by information found in the passage?

(A) Decreasing air pollution could increase the size of fruits pollinated by honeybees.

(B) Farmers could increase crop yields if they pollinated plants themselves rather than relying on honeybees

(C) Reducing a colony's exposure to air pollution could make it less vulnerable Colony Collapse Disorder.

(D) Due to Colony Collapse Disorder, honeybee colonies are becoming a surprising source of air pollution.

32. Which of the following stressors are also mentioned as a factor in Colony Collapse Disorder?

(A) predatory birds

(B) loss of habitat

(C) water pollution

(D) parasitic organisms

33. As it is used in line 36, "compromised" most nearly means

(A) negotiated.

(B) cooperated.

(C) weakened.

(D) infected.

34. The article provides evidence that air pollution may affect bees' ability to detect flowers by

(A) damaging the sensitive sense organs of the bees.

(B) killing the flowers that bees are trying to locate.

(C) destroying the perfumes of the flowers that bees are trying to find.

(D) making bees more vulnerable to parasites and viruses.

35. What can we infer from the passage about the effects of diesel exhaust?

(A) The bee-killing effects of diesel exhaust are harmful to agriculture but may have advantages in urban areas.

(B) Because it destroys the perfumes of flowers, diesel exhaust interferes with a pollination process important for farming.

(C) The effects of diesel exhaust can be detected in a laboratory but are probably too small to have a major impact on bees in the wild.

(D) Diesel exhaust's harmful effects are probably restricted to small insects, and unlikely to impact human beings.

Ivy Global

MIDDLE LEVEL CHALLENGE PASSAGES

Use these questions to practice the most challenging questions you might see on both the Middle Level and Upper Level exams. These questions would very rarely appear on the Lower Level.

1   Mme. Marie S. Curie—the
2 renowned French-Polish physicist
3 and chemist—arrived in New York
4 on Wednesday on the Olympic.
5 During her speaking tour in the
6 United States, she will receive a gift
7 of 1 gram of radium from a
8 committee of American women who
9 wish to honor the great French
10 chemist for her discovery of that
11 substance with her husband. The
12 Curies announced the existence of
13 the new element—named "radium"
14 from the Latin word "ray"—on
15 December 26 1898. The couple also
16 coined the word "radioactivity."
17   Mme. Curie was born Maria
18 Salomea Sklodowska in Warsaw,
19 Poland. She studied at Floating
20 University in Warsaw and later
21 studied in Paris. Mme. Curie is the
22 first female professor to teach at
23 the University of Paris. She has not
24 forgotten her Polish roots; in fact, she
25 named the first chemical element she
26 discovered—polonium—after her
27 native country of Poland.
28   Mme. Curie proposes to use
29 this gift, which is valued at $100,000,
30 in her attempts to discover new
31 methods for making radium more
32 useful in the treatment of cancer.
33 Mme. Curie is convinced that radium
34 is a cure for cancer, but she corrected
35 erroneous statements published
36 yesterday which made it appear that
37 she believed the substance to be a
38 cure for all types of cancer. "What
39 Mme. Curie said," explained her
40 secretary, "was that radium was a
41 specific treatment for many forms of
42 the disease. She did not wish to be
43 understood as asserting that it could
44 effect a cure in every case."

1. The main purpose of the passage is to

(A) inform the reader that Mme. Curie is being honored for her discovery of radium, which she believes may be a cure for certain types of cancer.

(B) discuss the news that Mme. Curie is correcting local newspapers for misrepresenting her statements about radium.

(C) describe the discovery of a new substance called radium.

(D) analyze the chemical components of radium.

2. Why was Mme. Curie in the United States?

(A) She had come to the United States to purchase radium.

(B) She was visiting the United States to give lectures.

(C) She was born in the United States and was returning home after studying radium in France.

(D) She was moving to the United States permanently to continue her work.

3. Polonium is named after

(A) the country where Mme. Curie was born.

(B) the country where Mme. Curie currently lives and teaches.

(C) the name of the town in which the element was discovered.

(D) the name of the university at which the element was discovered.

4. According to the passage, the "substance" mentioned in line 10 is

(A) a chemical mixture used to make explosives.

(B) a type of cancer with many different symptoms.

(C) an Olympic medal.

(D) a new chemical element with important medical applications.

5. Which of the following statements is true, according to the passage?

(A) Mme. Curie was employed at the University of Paris at a time when the school had only male professors.

(B) Mme. Curie discovered radium single-handedly, with no other collaborators or assistance.

(C) When Mme. Curie arrived in New York, she gave a committee of American women 1 gram of radium.

(D) Radium was the first element that Mme. Curie discovered.

6. What is Mme. Curie's position on the use of radium to treat cancer?

(A) It is dangerous and should not be attempted.

(B) In the future, radium will be used to cure every kind of cancer.

(C) Radium is probably not effective in treating cancer, but it is worth researching.

(D) Radium can effectively treat many types of cancer, but not all.

The Bayeux Tapestry is an embroidered cloth nearly 230 feet long that depicts the events leading up to the Norman conquest of England in 1066. Although it is called "The Bayeux Tapestry," it was neither made in Bayeux, nor is it actually a tapestry. In 1729, scholars rediscovered the Bayeux Tapestry when it was being displayed annually in Bayeux Cathedral, but it is likely that it was commissioned by Bishop Odo, the half-brother of King William, and made in England in the 1070s. The Bayeaux Tapestry is a linen cloth, with images embroidered onto the cloth in colored yarns. In a technical sense, a "tapestry" means a cloth with images woven into the fabric itself, not embroidered; however, many similar embroidered hangings from the period are still referred to as tapestries.

The embroidered images on the Bayeux Tapestry depict a series of scenes with Latin captions, focusing on the relationship and struggle for power between William, Duke of Normandy, and Harold, Earl of Wessex. The events depicted on the Bayeux Tapestry begin during the lifetime of King Edward, when King Edward sent Harold on a mission to Normandy. In Normandy, Harold met William who provided him with soldiers and supplies. Before returning to England, Harold swore an oath to William. This event may be included in the tapestry in order to provide a justification for William's later deeds.

After Harold's return to England, the tapestry depicts the death of King Edward, and the coronation of Harold as the new King of England. Following Harold's coronation, the tapestry depicts the appearance of Halley's Comet, along with images of ghostly ships. Comets were regarded as an evil omen in medieval times, and the scene with the comet foreshadows William's future invasion of England.

The following scenes show William rallying troops and building ships, then sailing to England. The events depicted in the Bayeux Tapestry culminate with the Battle of Hastings, when Williams's Norman army faces the English army of King Harold. The scenes at the end of the tapestry depict this bloody battle, in which William's forces defeated the forces of King Edward. Among the final scenes on the tapestry is the death of King Harold himself at the Battle of Hastings.

With Edward dead and his forces routed, William would go on to be crowned William the Conqueror, and to rule as the first Norman King of England. The Bayeux Tapestry is now exhibited at Musée de la Tapisserie de Bayeux in Bayeux, France, in the region of Normandy.

7. What is this passage primarily about?

   (A) the depiction of Halley's Comet in European art
   (B) the design of an important European artifact
   (C) the details of the Battle of Hastings
   (D) the importance of depicting history through art

8. What can we infer is a likely reason that Halley's Comet was depicted in the Bayeaux Tapestry?

   (A) Halley's Comet is probably included in order to mark the dates of the events depicted in the tapestry.
   (B) The comet was most likely the cause of the events depicted in the tapestry.
   (C) Halley's Comet was probably seen as an evil omen of the Battle of Hastings.
   (D) The comet is probably depicted in order to explain William the Conqueror's decision to invade England.

9. Based on information in the passage, which sentence best explains why the tapestry is named after Bayeux?

   (A) It was originally created in Bayeux, by Bishop Odo, half-brother to William the Conqueror.
   (B) The tapestry was rediscovered by scholars when it was on display in Bayeux Cathedral.
   (C) The main events depicted in the tapestry took place in the Bayeux region of France.
   (D) The tapestry is currently on display in a museum in Bayeux.

10. In line 51, "rallying" most nearly means

    (A) dispersing.
    (B) welcoming.
    (C) racing.
    (D) recruiting.

11. What can we infer from the passage about the relationship between Harold and William?

    (A) Harold and William were ancient enemies, destined to solve their differences in battle.
    (B) Harold and William were not enemies before the death of King Edward.
    (C) Harold and William were allies against King Edward, but their alliance crumbled after his death.
    (D) William tricked Harold, and used him as a pawn to gain control of England.

12. What is the most likely function of the second, third, and fourth paragraphs (lines 22-62)?

(A) to describe in chronological order the events depicted on the Bayeux Tapestry

(B) to relate the order of events that led to the Bayeux Tapestry's creation

(C) to analyze how the Bayeux Tapestry has influenced important historical decisions

(D) to illustrate the artistic skill with which the Bayeux Tapestry's images were depicted

Composed of mostly rock and ice, Pluto is the second-most-massive known dwarf planet in the Solar System. The dwarf planet has five moons: Charon, Nix, Hydra, Kerberos, and Styx, and its mass is 1.31×10^{22} kg, less than 0.24 percent of Earth's mass. The origin of Pluto has been shrouded in uncertainty. Pluto was once believed to be an escaped moon of Neptune, but this hypothesis has been debunked. From its discovery in 1930 until 2006, Pluto was classified as the ninth planet from the Sun. In the late 1970s, following the discovery of minor planet 2060 Chiron in the outer Solar System and the recognition of Pluto's relatively low mass, Pluto's status as a major planet began to be questioned. In the early 21st century, many objects similar to Pluto were discovered in the outer Solar System, notably the scattered disc object Eris in 2005, which is 27% more massive than Pluto. In 2006, the International Astronomical Union (IAU) defined what it means to be a "planet" within the Solar System. This definition excluded Pluto as a planet and added it as a member of the new category "dwarf planet" along with Eris. Numerous scientists hold that Pluto should continue to be classified as a planet.

Researchers on both sides of the debate gathered in 2008 for a conference called "The Great Planet Debate." The conference published a post-conference press release indicating that scientists could not come to a consensus about the definition of a planet. Some members of the public have also rejected the new IAU classification, citing the disagreement within the scientific community on the issue or their own sentimental reasons: they maintain that they have always known Pluto as a planet and will continue to do so regardless of the IAU decision.

13. With which of the following statements would the author most likely agree?

    (A) Pluto should keep its new categorization as a dwarf planet.

    (B) Pluto should revert to its original categorization as a regular planet.

    (C) It is foolish to be sentimentally attached to Pluto's categorization as a planet.

    (D) The debate around Pluto's categorization remains unresolved.

14. Based on information in the passage, we can conclude that the most massive known dwarf planet in the Solar System is

    (A) Pluto.

    (B) 2060 Chiron.

    (C) Eris.

    (D) Earth.

15. What is the central idea of this passage?

    (A) Many planets are difficult to categorize with the IAU's new criteria.

    (B) It is crucial that we reach a consensus about Pluto's categorization.

    (C) Many mysteries remain in the field of astronomy.

    (D) Pluto is officially a dwarf planet, but not everyone agrees.

16. According to the passage, which event originally cast doubt on Pluto's status as a planet?

    (A) the discovery of another minor planet

    (B) the realization that Eris was 27% more massive than Pluto

    (C) the IAU's 2006 redefinition of a planet

    (D) the discovery that Pluto is an escaped moon of Neptune

17. How many moons does Pluto have?

    (A) one

    (B) three

    (C) five

    (D) zero

18. The final sentence suggests which of the following differences between the International Astronomical Union and the general public?

    (A) The International Astronomical Union is unlikely to accept a new definition even if a public consensus is reached.

    (B) The International Astronomical Union has less sentimental reasons than much of the public for deciding whether Pluto should be classified as a planet.

    (C) Unlike the general public's opinions, decisions made by the International Astronomical Union have never been controversial.

    (D) The general public has known that Pluto was a planet for a longer period of time than the the International Astronomical Union.

1   Isadora Duncan was a dancer
2 considered by many to be the
3 progenitor of modern dance. To
4 Duncan, classical ballet, with its strict
5 rules of posture and formation, was
6 "ugly and against nature." She rejected
7 traditional ballet steps, preferring to
8 emphasize improvisation, emotion, and
9 the human form. She said, "I spent long
10 days and nights in the studio seeking
11 that dance which might be the divine
12 expression of the human spirit through
13 the medium of the body's movement."
14 By thus establishing connections
15 between human emotion and the
16 movements of dance, Duncan hoped to
17 restore dance to a form of high art
18 rather than mere entertainment.
19 Breaking with convention, she traced
20 the art of dance back to its roots as a
21 sacred art. She developed free and
22 natural movements inspired by the
23 classical Greek arts, folk dances, social
24 dances, nature, and natural forces. She
25 incorporated the new American
26 athleticism, which included skipping,
27 running, jumping, leaping, and tossing.
28 The athleticism and classical roots of
29 her style are reflected in her innovative
30 costume choice of a Grecian tunic and
31 bare feet, which allowed for a physical
32 freedom that could not be achieved in

33 the traditional corseted ballet costumes
34 and pointe shoes that restrained
35 dancers. With time, she gained a very
36 wide following and set up several
37 schools in Europe and the United States.
38   Duncan's celebrity, however, did
39 not suffice to bring her prosperity. As
40 her performing career waned in the
41 later years of her life, her financial
42 situation degraded, and eventually she
43 had to be maintained in apartments
44 rented by friends and supporters. After
45 one financially unsuccessful tour in the
46 United States, Duncan's creditors nearly
47 prevented her from leaving the country
48 to return to Europe. Duncan also
49 received criticism for her highly
50 controversial political opinions.
51   But while financial problems and
52 public controversy embroiled Duncan
53 in her later years, she is remembered
54 today for her artistic achievements: the
55 creation of modern dance, and the
56 restoration of dance to a high place
57 among the arts. While Duncan's own
58 schools no longer exist, her style of
59 dance continues to be practiced. Her
60 life inspired novels, ballets, and films,
61 and her likeness was included in the
62 bas-relief carved by sculptor Antoine
63 Bourdelle over the entrance of the
64 Théâtre des Champs-Élysées.

19. According to the passage, Isadora Duncan's modern dance was inspired by all of the following EXCEPT

   (A) the heroines of romantic ballet.

   (B) the natural human form.

   (C) American athleticism.

   (D) classical Greek art.

20. As it is used in line 3, "progenitor" most closely means

   (A) practitioner.

   (B) creator.

   (C) instructor.

   (D) competitor.

21. A "bas-relief" (line 62) is most likely

   (A) an ornamental basin.

   (B) a type of sculpture or engraving.

   (C) a type of large basket.

   (D) clothing made of silk or taffeta.

22. It can be inferred from the passage that Isadora Duncan is primarily famous because

   (A) she was a skilled historian.

   (B) she was an excellent dance teacher and opened several schools.

   (C) she inspired thousands of artists to make beautiful jewelry and sculptures.

   (D) she invented a new form of dance.

23. What was innovative about Duncan's costume choice?

   (A) It allowed dancers to move naturally and without restraint, unlike traditional costumes.

   (B) It was white, which diverged from traditionally darker costumes.

   (C) It included newly designed pointe shoes, which were customized to fit each individual dancer.

   (D) It was extremely plain and understated.

24. The main purpose of the second paragraph is to

   (A) explore the connection between art and prosperity in the United States and Europe.

   (B) contrast Isadora Duncan's personal and financial life with her artistic achievements.

   (C) characterize Isadora Duncan as an unstable person who shouldn't be honored today.

   (D) provide evidence for the claim that Duncan was inspired by her personal challenges.

1 From 1949 to 1990, modern-day
2 Germany was split into two states: the
3 Federal Republic of Germany, or West
4 Germany, and the German Democratic
5 Republic (GDR), or East Germany.
6 Although Berlin was located within East
7 Germany, part of it was designated as
8 belonging to West Germany.
9 The Berlin Wall was a barrier
10 constructed by the government of East
11 Germany in 1961 that completely cut
12 off West Berlin from East Berlin. The
13 barrier included guard towers placed
14 along two large concrete walls, with a
15 wide area between them. The leaders of
16 East Germany claimed that the Wall was
17 erected to protect its population from
18 enemies conspiring to prevent the will
19 of the people in building a socialist state
20 in East Germany. In practice, the Wall
21 served to prevent people from leaving
22 East Germany.
23 In 1989, a radical series of
24 political changes occurred in East
25 Germany. After several weeks of unrest
26 on the streets, the East German
27 government announced on November
28 9, 1989 that all GDR citizens could visit
29 West Germany and West Berlin. Crowds
30 of East Germans crossed and climbed
31 onto the wall, joined by West Germans
32 on the other side in a celebratory
33 atmosphere. Over the next few weeks, a
34 euphoric public and souvenir hunters
35 chipped away parts of the wall; the
36 governments later used industrial
37 equipment to remove most of the rest.
38 The fall of the Berlin Wall paved the
39 way for German reunification, which
40 was formally concluded on October 3,
41 1990.

25. According to the passage, the German Democratic Republic was

   (A) located in East Germany.
   (B) located in West Germany.
   (C) located within Berlin.
   (D) conquered by the Federal Republic of Germany in 1949.

26. According to the passage, the East German Government claimed that

   (A) West Germans were planning to launch a military attack on their East German neighbors.
   (B) a socialist state in East Germany is what the East Germans wanted.
   (C) the area between the concrete walls should not be controlled by either government.
   (D) East Germans were free to visit West Germany during the day.

27. It can be inferred from the passage that

   (A) the GDR put limitations on its citizens' freedom.
   (B) the leaders of West Germany did everything they could to have the wall removed.
   (C) most citizens of East Berlin tried to climb over the wall.
   (D) no one was able to travel between East and West Germany from 1949 to 1990.

28. As it is used in line 34, "euphoric" most nearly means

   (A) joyful.
   (B) timid.
   (C) despairing.
   (D) ambivalent.

29. According to the passage, the fall of the Berlin Wall eventually led to

   (A) the Second World War.
   (B) the Cold War.
   (C) the reunification of East and West Germany.
   (D) the rise of a socialist state in East Germany.

30. All of the following questions are answered in the passage EXCEPT

   (A) What was the German Democratic Republic?
   (B) What material was the Berlin wall made from?
   (C) Why did Berliners long for German reunification?
   (D) How did the governments of East and West Germany take the wall down?

UPPER LEVEL CHALLENGE PASSAGES

Use these questions to practice the most challenging questions that you might see on the Upper Level exam only. These types of questions would very rarely appear on the Middle or Lower Levels.

1 A myth is any imaginative
2 interpretation of humanity or of the
3 objects and events in nature outside
4 of humanity, including their
5 appearance, their effects, and the still
6 greater mystery of their causes.
7 Myths may exist in many forms, from
8 a simple myth of explanation to a
9 complicated system of religious
10 myths in which the objects of nature
11 are regarded as gods in human form.
12 As sacred stories, myths are often
13 endorsed by rulers and priests and
14 closely linked to religion or
15 spirituality. In fact, many societies
16 have two categories of traditional
17 narrative: "true stories" or myths,
18 and "false stories" or fables. Myths
19 generally take place in a primordial
20 age, when the world had not yet
21 achieved its current form, and
22 explain how the world gained its
23 current form and how customs,
24 institutions, and taboos were

25 established.
26   Closely related to myth are
27 legend and folktale. Myths, legends,
28 and folktales are different types of
29 traditional story. Unlike myths,
30 folktales can be set in any time and
31 any place, and they are not
32 considered true or sacred by the
33 societies that tell them. Like myths,
34 legends are stories that are
35 traditionally considered true, but
36 they are set in a more recent time,
37 when the world was much as it is
38 today. Legends generally feature
39 humans as their main characters,
40 whereas myths generally focus on
41 superhuman characters. The
42 distinction between myth, legend,
43 and folktale is intended as a useful
44 tool for grouping traditional stories,
45 but in many cultures, it is hard to
46 draw a sharp line between myths and
47 legends.

1. According to the passage, which of the following best describes a myth's relationship to the truth?

   (A) Myths are considered to be true by the societies that tell them.
   (B) Unlike folktales and legends, myths are completely truthful.
   (C) Myths contain no elements of truth, but they are always considered true by those who create them.
   (D) In myths, it is impossible to distinguish fact from fiction.

2. The characters in myths are usually

   (A) gods or other supernatural beings.
   (B) humans much like us.
   (C) humans with animal features.
   (D) recent historical figures.

3. The main purpose of this passage is to

   (A) explain why myths are more important than folktales and legends.
   (B) keep myths from being forgotten by younger generations.
   (C) argue why it is still useful to read and understand mythology.
   (D) define a myth and compare it to other forms of storytelling.

4. As it is used in line 19, "primordial" most nearly means

   (A) primitive.
   (B) exotic.
   (C) urbanized.
   (D) futuristic.

5. It can be inferred from this passage that

   (A) myths are typically not set in modern times.
   (B) myths are less popular than legends.
   (C) myths use more antiquated vocabulary than do folktales and legends.
   (D) myths are a central component of all civilized cultures.

6. A "traditional story" (line 29) is most likely

   (A) a story that deals with serious subject matter and that has been around for hundreds of years.
   (B) a story told in formal language on important occasions.
   (C) a story connected to the culture or customs of a particular society.
   (D) a story that is impossible to forget.

Using mitochondrial DNA, researchers in one study said that they were able to reconstruct the first detailed genetic history of modern-day Europeans. They studied maternally-inherited mitochondrial DNA samples from bones and teeth of the skeletons of 364 people who lived in Central Europe about 5,000 years ago, and they used this information to map the history of human migration in the region.

This research is the result of an 8-year collaborative effort between the Australian Centre for Ancient DNA (ACAD), at the University of Adelaide, the Johannes Gutenberg University of Mainz, the State Heritage Museum in Halle (Germany), and the National Geographic Society's Genographic Project.

"This is the largest and most detailed genetic time series of Europe yet created, allowing us to establish a complete genetic chronology," said the study's joint lead author Dr. Wolfgang Haak. "Focusing on this small but highly important geographic region meant we could generate a gapless record, and directly observe genetic changes in 'real-time' from 7,500 to 3,500 years ago, from the earliest farmers to the early Bronze Age."

The scientists said that their research revealed a pattern of genetic replacement in people who lived in central Europe over a period of several thousand years. This indicates that some rather intricate changes went into producing today's Europeans.

They also pointed out that noticeable changes in the genetic composition of those living in a region we now know as Germany were the result of at least four stages of migration and settlement. The ancestors of the modern German population not only came from a path through the Near East that was previously well-known to historians, but also from Western and Eastern Europe. These different stages of population change over time would not be evident to researchers examining only modern evidence.

"None of the dynamic changes we observed could have been inferred from modern-day genetic data alone, highlighting the potential power of combining ancient DNA studies with archaeology to reconstruct human evolutionary history," said Haak.

7. The main purpose of the passage is to

(A) describe the genetic history of modern Europeans.

(B) discuss a study that explored the genetic history of modern Europeans.

(C) explain the complete range of methods that scientists use to trace ancient human lineages.

(D) argue that research into the genetic history of humans is the future of archeology.

8. How did researchers acquire the DNA for this study?

(A) Researchers took DNA from volunteers in modern Europe.

(B) Researchers were able to inherit mitochondrial DNA from their mothers.

(C) DNA was acquired from the Near East, as well as from Europe.

(D) Researchers extracted the DNA from ancient skeletons.

9. The purpose of the final paragraph is to

(A) describe the method by which ancient genealogies are usually studied.

(B) discuss the dangers of sloppy data interpretation.

(C) provide a contrast to an opinion expressed earlier in the passage.

(D) emphasize the possible benefits of new research techniques.

10. What does Dr. Haak most nearly mean when he says that the researches could observe genetic changes in "real time" (line 30)?

(A) By creating a record of genetic changes without any gaps, they could track changes very precisely through time.

(B) By focusing on a very small region, researchers were able to work quickly enough to track changes in the modern population as they were occurring.

(C) Researchers were able to construct a model that predicted changes before they could actually happen.

(D) Although the changes happened in a past time, the researchers were able to learn about some of them in the 'real time' of the present.

11. As it is used in line 55, "dynamic" most nearly means

(A) somewhat irrelevant.

(B) almost magical.

(C) constantly changing.

(D) generally stable.

12. What role did the University of
    Adelaide play in the events
    described in the passage?

    (A) Researchers at the University of
        Adelaide were part of a larger
        team collaborating on the
        project.

    (B) Dr. Haak, a lead researcher in
        the project, teaches at the
        University of Adelaide.

    (C) Mitochondrial DNA samples
        were extracted from skeletons
        at the University of Adelaide.

    (D) The University of Adelaide
        contributed modern-day genetic
        data from Europeans.

1 I do not claim that I can tell a
2 story as it ought to be told. I only claim
3 to know how a story ought to be told,
4 for I have been almost daily in the
5 company of the most expert story-
6 tellers for many years.
7 There are several kinds of stories,
8 but only one difficult kind—the
9 humorous. I will talk mainly about that
10 one. The humorous story is American,
11 the comic story is English, the witty
12 story is French. The humorous story
13 depends for its effect upon the
14 MANNER of the telling; the comic story
15 and the witty story upon the MATTER.
16 The humorous story may be spun
17 out to great length, and may wander
18 around as much as it pleases, and arrive
19 nowhere in particular; but the comic
20 and witty stories must be brief and end
21 with a point. The humorous story
22 bubbles gently along, the others burst.
23 The humorous story is strictly a
24 work of art—high and delicate art—and
25 only an artist can tell it; but no art is
26 necessary in telling the comic and the
27 witty story; anybody can do it. The art
28 of telling a humorous story—
29 understand, I mean by word of mouth,
30 not print – was created in America, and
31 has remained at home.
32 The humorous story is told
33 gravely; the teller does his best to
34 conceal the fact that he even dimly
35 suspects that there is anything funny
36 about it; but the teller of the comic story
37 tells you beforehand that it is one of the
38 funniest things he has ever heard, then
39 tells it with eager delight, and is the first
40 person to laugh when he gets through.
41 And sometimes, if he has had good
42 success, he is so glad and happy that he
43 will repeat the "nub" of it and glance
44 around from face to face, collecting
45 applause, and then repeat it again. It is a
46 pathetic thing to see.

13. What best describes the main purpose of this passage?

    (A) to explain the difficulties of story-telling
    (B) to list the qualities of a successful story-teller
    (C) to compare and contrast a few specific types of stories
    (D) to explain what makes a story funny

14. According to the author, those who tell humorous stories are

    (A) artists.
    (B) average people.
    (C) French.
    (D) eager to please.

15. According to the passage, humorous stories differ from witty and comic stories in

    (A) the way in which they are told, their length, and their level of difficulty.
    (B) the reaction of the audience and the context in which it is told.
    (C) the way in which they are told and the age of the characters in the story.
    (D) the intonation of the speaker and the number of people listening.

16. According to the passage, what makes comic and witty stories successful?

    (A) They are told in both English and French.
    (B) Their subject matter is funny.
    (C) The story-tellers laugh as they tell their stories.
    (D) They ramble without direction.

17. What does the author mean when he says, "the humorous story bubbles gently along, the others burst" (lines 21-22)?

    (A) Humorous stories are more light-hearted than other types of stories.
    (B) Comic and witty stories are more likely to fail than humorous stories.
    (C) Humorous stories are less direct and more subtle than other types of stories.
    (D) Humorous stories are funnier than other types of stories.

18. The meaning of the word "gravely" as it is used in line 33 is closest to

    (A) seriously.
    (B) menacingly.
    (C) deeply.
    (D) abrasively.

Many units of measurement in use by scientists are defined by natural properties, which are uniform and unchanging. A meter, for example, is defined as the length of the path traveled by light in a vacuum over a very specific, and very short, period of time. Since the speed of light is constant and universal, this distance will always be the same wherever and whenever it is measured. When measuring mass, however, scientists face a problem.

The kilogram, a basic unit of mass that is a reference point for many other measures, is defined not by a universal natural property, but by the mass of a single physical object: a cylindrical piece of platinum and iridium, called the International Prototype Kilogram or IPK. The IPK is, by definition, one kilogram. The IPK is kept in France, but other countries have copies of the IPK which, when first created, had almost exactly the same mass as the IPK. There were small variations in mass between copies, but the discrepancies were recorded. Over time, however, the variations in mass between the IPK and its copies have changed. This means that the standard that defines a kilogram is actually changing over time, and at any given time one country's copy of the IPK may be slightly different from another's. Even worse, because the masses of all of the copies are changing, it's not even clear exactly how much the IPK itself is changing.

Fortunately, the change is very small— too small to be a problem for most everyday purposes. But to scientists who require extremely precise measurements, small differences matter a great deal. Motivated by the need to have a stable unit of measurement, a group of Australian scientists have proposed a solution: to define a kilogram not by the mass of any single artifact, but by defining it as the mass of a certain number of atoms of silicon. This would be a much more specific and stable measure than the IPK.

In order to achieve this objective, the Australian scientists have created nearly perfect spheres of pure silicon. The spheres themselves would not define the mass of a kilogram, however. Instead, they would only be a tool to help create a definition. By measuring the volume and mass of the spheres, scientists will be able to calculate the number of atoms the spheres contain. The kilogram could then be defined by the mass of a precise number of silicon atoms, rather than by the changing mass of any single physical object.

19. As it is used in line 27, "discrepancies" most nearly means

(A) differences.
(B) violations.
(C) rumors.
(D) artifacts.

20. Why is it problematic that the exact mass of the IPK changes over time?

(A) There are copies of the IPK in other countries, and every time the IPK changes, those copies need to be changed as well.
(B) The IPK defines the mass of a kilogram, so if it changes, the definition of a kilogram changes as well.
(C) The changes in the mass of the IPK are too small to detect with everyday scales, so they can go unnoticed.
(D) The IPK is made of expensive platinum and iridium, which are too costly to replace.

21. Based on information in the passage, what is the current mass of the IPK?

(A) one kilogram
(B) slightly more or less than one kilogram
(C) the same as the mass of a silicon sphere
(D) one gram

22. What can we infer about the proposal to change the definition of a kilogram?

(A) The proposal has been rejected by the scientific community, even though some enthusiasts still support it.
(B) Without the technology to create perfect spheres, it could take decades to complete the proposed project.
(C) At the time the passage was written, the proposal had been accepted by the scientific community and the definition of a kilogram had been changed.
(D) At the time the passage was written, the proposal had not yet been accepted by the entire scientific community.

23. Which of the following statements is supported by information in the passage?

(A) The IPK is probably losing mass because of the way that it is stored.
(B) The definition of a kilogram is too political, and scientists should be allowed to define it for themselves.
(C) However hard we try, no unit of measurement can ever be made truly accurate.
(D) Some scientists require much more precise measurements than most of us need in everyday life.

24. Which sentence best summarizes the main point of this passage?

(A) While the mass of a platinum and iridium weight changes over time, silicon is stable and won't change.

(B) What was once thought to be a problem with the definition of the kilogram has actually turned out to be a problem with all units of mass.

(C) There's a problem with the current definition of the kilogram, but scientists are working on a possible solution.

(D) Without a reliable definition for the kilogram, many other units of measurement are also slightly unstable.

THE ESSAY

CHAPTER 5

INTRODUCTION

The last section of the ISEE is a 30-minute essay in response to a prompt. The essay prompts tend to be broad and varied. They will usually ask you to reflect on your own life, thoughts, and values, or to discuss a current issue. You may be asked to state an opinion, to share an experience, to offer a definition, or to present a description. You will have one page of scratch paper to prepare your notes or outline your argument, and two pages of lined paper to write your essay.

Your essay will not be scored, but will be sent to the admissions officers of the schools to which you are applying. Although the essay will not affect your ISEE score, admissions officers consider it an important component of your application. They will look for a strong writing style free from spelling, punctuation, and grammar mistakes. They will also try to get a sense of who you are as a person. With this in mind, choose subjects you would be comfortable talking about during an interview with a principal or admissions officer. Avoid overly dark, violent, or inappropriate subject matter.

HOW TO APPROACH THE ESSAY

Review the following brief strategies to help you prepare for the ISEE essay. Then, turn to the following sections for strategies to help you improve your writing style, master standard essay structure, and approach different types of essay prompts.

TIME MANAGEMENT

You only have 30 minutes to plan and write a thorough response to the essay prompt. Be smart about how you budget your time. Plan to spend no more than a few minutes brainstorming your essay outline. Save a few minutes at the end to edit. Don't spend too long on any one paragraph.

MANAGING YOUR TIME	
Time	Goal
2 – 3 minutes	Brainstorm and plan your essay
5 – 6 minutes	Write your introduction
5 – 6 minutes	Write your second paragraph
5 – 6 minutes	Write your third paragraph
5 – 6 minutes	Write your conclusion
2 – 3 minutes	Re-read or edit your essay
Total: 30 minutes	

WRITE LEGIBLY IN PEN

Make sure the admissions officer can read your handwriting! Take the time to write legibly in cursive or print, whichever is neater. The ISEE requires that you use a blue or black ballpoint pen. Neatly cross out any errors you make. You may also choose to bring an erasable pen. Indent to make sure it is clear where a new paragraph begins.

BE SPECIFIC

Keep your writing clear and to the point. Avoid rambling or repeating yourself. Use specific, precise vocabulary instead of vague words and phrases. Use sophisticated vocabulary, but make sure you use words properly. Use vivid language that incorporates the five senses: sight, smell, taste, touch, and sound.

EDIT YOUR WRITING

Save time at the end of your essay to edit for spelling, punctuation, and grammar. Continue reading the "Writing Basics" section for a review of some common mistakes to look out for.

WRITING BASICS

Like playing an instrument or playing a new sport, writing is a skill acquired through practice. A strong piece of writing is the product of critical thinking. In order to improve your writing and critical thinking skills, make a commitment to read and write daily.

In this section, you'll find some techniques and exercises for building your writing skills. These techniques are suitable for all students, but the specific approach you will use will vary depending on your age and grade level. Work on improving the fundamental content, structure, and mechanics of your writing before tackling more advanced strategies.

WRITING DESCRIPTIVELY

Regardless of your age or grade level, you can improve your writing by learning how to **write descriptively**. You can make your writing more descriptive by:

- using the sensory descriptions of smell, touch and even taste in addition to sight and sound
- identifying key characteristics of your subject
- being able to describe and explain causes and effects

In addition to the writing exercises offered in this section, here are some daily writing ideas:

- Keep a daily journal where you record your thoughts and observations.
- Write "fan fiction" involving characters or events from novels you are reading.
- Write opinion pieces in response to news articles you read.
- Work on writing your very own novel!
- If you get stuck, the Internet offers a plethora of writing ideas.

USING YOUR FIVE SENSES

How do writers bring stories and ideas to life? They write sentences that employ the **five senses**.

Here's an example of descriptive writing from a work of fiction:

> "Toto was not gray; he was a little black dog, with long silky hair and small black eyes that twinkled merrily on either side of his funny, wee nose."
>
> - L. Frank Baum, *The Wizard of Oz*

Look at all the sensory imagery! We can see the dog because we are told he is "little" and "black." He has eyes that "twinkle." We can also get a sense of what it would be like to touch him. He has "silky hair."

Here's another example from an essay:

> "The whistle of the locomotive penetrates my woods summer and winter, sounding like the scream of a hawk sailing over some farmer's yard, informing me that many restless city merchants are arriving within the circle of the town, or adventurous country traders from the other side."
>
> -Henry David Thoreau, *Walden*

This is a description we can hear! First we hear the "whistle" of the train, only to learn that it sounds like a "scream." And, it's not just any scream, but the "scream of a hawk"! Thoreau provides us with many fine visual descriptions: the hawk the author hears is "sailing." The author also makes the suggestion that the town has a shape. Merchants arrive "within the circle of the town."

To get started writing with your five senses, try using some of the following words:

DESCRIPTIVE WORDS	
Sensory Perception	**Description**
Sight words	Color, shape, light, dark, bright, dim…
Smell words	Sweet, acrid, fetid, fragrant, musty, musky, perfumed, pungent, rancid, stinky…

Touch words	Cold, damp, dry, furry, hot, lumpy, rough, sharp, slimy, smooth, sticky, wet…
Hearing words	Bang, chime, chirp, clash, crunch, fizz, jingle, ping, rattle, roar, sizzle, slam, tap, thud…
Taste words	Bitter, sweet, sour, salty, juicy, fruity, rich, sharp, sugary, succulent, tangy, tart, zesty…

Exercise #1: To practice bringing the reader into your essay with vivid sensory descriptions, re-write the following sentences to make them more interesting by using one of the five senses. Have a trusted reader check your work.

1. Alisha and Sam were at the seashore. *(taste)*

    Alisha and Sam could taste the salt in the fresh sea air.

2. I saw a car go by. *(sound)*

3. It was sunset. *(sight)*

4. Robin went into the woods. *(smell)*

5. I walked down the street. *(touch)*

6. They sat down to lunch. *(taste)*

IDENTIFY KEY CHARACTERISTICS

Identifying and defining **key characteristics** is another way to make your writing stronger. Let's go back to the Thoreau example:

"The whistle of the locomotive penetrates my woods summer and winter, sounding like the scream of a hawk sailing over some farmer's yard, informing me that many restless city merchants are arriving within the circle of the town, or adventurous country traders from the other side."

-Henry David Thoreau, *Walden*

Thoreau uses sensory imagery and also identifies the key characteristics of the locomotive. The locomotive seems to serve two functions: (1) it is a noisy distraction, and (2) it informs the author that merchants will soon arrive.

Being able to vividly describe characteristics of people, places, and things is a good skill to keep in mind when writing essays.

Let's try a few together:

What are some characteristics of a good teacher? Can you think of a third?

- *Expertise*
- *Organization*
- _____

Exercise #2: Identify and describe some characteristics on your own. Have a trusted reader check your work.

1. List three characteristics of a good friend:

   (1)

   (2)

   (3)

2. List three characteristics of a helpful person:

   (1)

   (2)

   (3)

3. What is your favorite book? List three qualities that make it interesting:

   (1)

   (2)

   (3)

4. What three things make for a good student?

   (1)

   (2)

   (3)

5. What is your favorite hobby? List three qualities that make it enjoyable:

   (1)

   (2)

   (3)

6. What are three words you'd use to describe yourself?

   (1)

   (2)

   (3)

WRITING ABOUT CAUSES AND EFFECTS

Let's say you are trying to write an essay about how you can help slow down climate change. Before you can start writing, you will need to think about **causes and effects**. In other words, if you don't know the causes of climate change, how can you possibly write about stemming, or eliminating, the effects? Since you already know the effect, namely, climate change, you just need to identify some of the causes:

- Car pollution
- Manufacturing
- Burning of coal for electricity

Now that you have listed some of the causes, you can better write about ways you can prevent climate change. For instance, carpooling reduces car pollution, and turning off lights when you leave the room means electric companies need to use fewer coal resources to keep power plants going. By evaluating causes and effects, you are better able to plan a more thorough, clear, and detailed essay.

Exercise #3: List some causes and effects for the scenarios below. Have a trusted reader check your work.

1. Your school wants to create a dress code.

   Causes:

   - *Parents are concerned that students aren't dressing professionally.*
   - *Some students say that they feel uncomfortable with the pressure to dress in a certain way.*
   - *Teachers are concerned that students aren't paying attention in class because of how their classmates are dressing.*

Effects:

- *The school administration and parent association meet to come to a consensus about appropriate standards of dress in school.*
- *They hope that this will help students focus in class, reduce peer pressure, and learn what type of dress is appropriate for a professional environment.*

2. Your friend needs help.

   Causes:

   Effects:

3. Your community needs to clean up its parks.

   Causes:

   Effects:

4. You need to try something a second time.

   Causes:

   Effects:

5. Your school proposes that bullying become a criminal offense.

   Causes:

   Effects:

Ivy Global

CLEANING UP YOUR GRAMMAR

Use this section to review basic grammar rules and style conventions for essay writing. These concepts will help make your ISEE essay as clean and understandable as possible.

INDENT YOUR WRITING

Indent your paragraphs. Make sure the first line of each new paragraph starts a few spaces over to the right. This helps your reader see where each new paragraph begins.

For example, here are two paragraphs of a sample essay. The first line of each paragraph is indented as marked:

Indent → Learning a second language gives students exposure to different cultures and broadens our understanding of the world we live in. While studying Spanish, I have gained insight into the traditions and customs of different Spanish-speaking countries. This has helped me connect with the many Spanish-speaking immigrants in my apartment building. They appreciate that I can speak with them in their native language, and I have made many new friends that I wouldn't have met if I only spoke English.

Indent → A second language is also important for students entering the global workforce. More and more frequently, companies and organizations need workers who can connect with international clients by speaking their language. In the future, I hope to use my skills in Spanish to work for an organization that serves Spanish-speaking communities in the United States and abroad. I believe that the skills I have developed by studying this language will help me connect with these communities and better understand their needs.

USE PROPER CAPITALIZATION

Follow these rules for **capitalization**:

- Capitalize the first word of a sentence.
- Capitalize **proper nouns**, which are words that name specific people, places, organizations, or events.
- Capitalize the pronoun "I."
- Capitalize the names of languages and nationalities.

- Capitalize the first, last, and main words of titles for books, stories, newspaper articles, movies, songs, plays, or shows.

For example:

- Suzanne turned in her homework to Mrs. Williams.
- I had a lot of fun on my trip to Honolulu, Hawaii.
- The violinist gave his first recital at Carnegie Hall.
- The World Health Organization released a new report about European health care.
- The Revolutionary War was a turning point in American history.

Exercise #4: Correct the following sentences. Check your answers in the answer key at the end of the book.

1. My sister, catherine, lives with her husband in dallas, texas.

2. our history teacher helped us understand the british civil war.

3. i study french with madame bellamy and spanish with señora cabrera.

4. during our trip to san francisco, we drove across the golden gate bridge and attended a concert by the san francisco philharmonic.

PUNCTUATE YOUR SENTENCES

Review these rules for proper **punctuation** in your essays.

A **period** is used at the end of a complete sentence. Periods are also used after initials and abbreviations. For example:

- Mr. Smith called to schedule an appointment with Dr. Orbuch.
- The C.E.O. of General Motors conducted a press interview at 1:00 p.m.

Commas are most frequently used to join together two **clauses** (parts) of a sentence, often before **conjunctions** (connecting words) like "and," "but," "or," "so," "for," "nor," and "yet." Commas are also used after phrases at the beginning of a sentence, before and after descriptive phrases in a sentence, and between three or more items in a list. For example:

- It was a beautiful day outside, so I didn't want to stay in and do homework.
- After Sarah, Emily, and Xiwen finished their paper, they celebrated with ice cream.
- Dr. Romanik, a cardiac specialist, is currently accepting new patients.

Be careful: don't use commas to connect complete sentences without some sort of connecting word! Sentences squished together with a comma are called run-on sentences. Keep reading this section for more information about how to avoid them.

Question marks are used after questions. For example:

- How old are you?
- Where is my notebook?

Exclamation points are used after interjections, or after sentences to show strong emphasis. For example:

- Wow! I never knew there were so many different kinds of spiders!
- Watch out! A car is coming!

Colons are used to introduce examples or items in a list. For example:

- Elaine has three daughters: Amy, Michaela, and Christine.
- Here are the classroom rules: keep your desk clean, don't talk while others are talking, don't eat or chew gum, and don't wear hats indoors.

Semicolons are used to join together complete sentences without a comma or conjunction. For example:

- Victoria was frequently tardy; therefore, she received a low grade.
- The teacher is very angry; I think he is going to call my friend's parents.

Parentheses are used to provide extra information in a sentence. For example:

- Your homework is to read Chapter 5 (pages 60-72).
- In case of an emergency, exit through the north doors (next to the principal's office).

Hyphens are used in compound words and numbers. For example:

- The store's inventory includes twenty-two small, forty-five medium, and thirty-one large T-shirts.
- Susan's ex-husband was a well-known author.

Apostrophes are used to form **contractions** by taking the place of a missing letter, as in the words "can't," "isn't," and "I'm." Apostrophes are also used to signify **possession** when something belongs to someone or something else. To make a singular noun possessive, add an apostrophe and the letter "s." For example:

- Joe's fish
- My uncle's car

For a plural noun ending in the letter "s," add an apostrophe to the end of the word, but do not add another "s." For example:

- Boys' cars
- Heroes' victories

For all plural nouns not ending in the letter "s," add an apostrophe and "s." For example:

- Children's ideas
- People's Republic

Exercise #5: Correct the following sentences. Check your answers in the answer key.

1. Mikes dog is sweet but his sisters dog is unfriendly smelly and loud

2. Listen Im trying to talk to you

3. Students should bring the following items a backpack a pencil an eraser and a ruler

4. After a strong gust of wind all of the partiers hats fell off

5. Is this someones pencil

6. Its my mothers fifty second birthday and I dont have a present for her

7. The mens suits which were designed by Armani were very elegant

8. We wanted to go sailing however the thunder lightning and hail were too dangerous

USE COMMON CONVENTIONS FOR TITLES

Conventions are customs or rules we follow. If you talk about books, stories, poems, or newspaper articles in your ISEE essay, there are some common writing conventions you'll want to make sure you follow.

Underline the titles of novels, newspapers, and magazines. For example:

- <u>The Lion, the Witch, and the Wardrobe</u>
- <u>The New York Times</u>

Put quotation marks around short stories, poems, or article titles. For example:

- "To Build a Fire"
- "Yankees Win the Pennant"

When you first mention a novel, story, poem, or article, provide the author's full name. For example:

- The Lion, the Witch, and the Wardrobe by C.S. Lewis
- "The Raven" by Edgar Allan Poe

When you mention a novel, story, poem, or article for the second, third, fourth, or hundredth time, you only need to use the author's last name. However, *always* use the full name of the novel, story, poem, or article every time!

- In The Lion, the Witch and the Wardrobe, Lewis writes . . .
- Poe shows in "The Raven" . . .

AVOID RUN-ON SENTENCES

A **run-on sentence** joins together too many complete sentences in a row. Break up these long sentences into shorter sentences. You can also avoid run-on sentences by using conjunctions like "and," "or," "but," "so," "if," "because," and "when." These words, and others like them, can properly join together otherwise complete sentences. However, don't use too many of them in a row, or you'll still have a run-on sentence! Here are some examples:

FIXING RUN-ON SENTENCES	
Incorrect	**Correct**
It is cold outside, don't forget your jacket.	It is cold outside. Don't forget your jacket.
It was cold and windy and raining outside, so my mother told me to wear a jacket but I forgot so I was cold.	Because it was cold, windy, and raining outside, my mother told me to wear a jacket. Unfortunately, I didn't heed her warning. As a result, I was cold.
I sang, the crowd applauded.	When I sang, the crowd applauded.
I'll finish my homework then I'll read then I'll walk the dog then I'll have dinner.	After I finish my homework, I will read. Then, I will walk the dog and have dinner.

Exercise #6: Correct the following run-on sentences. Then, check your answers in the answer key.

1. I like to ski, it makes me happy.

2. James went home then did his homework then went to bed.

3. Don't forget to bring your folder it is important.

4. The strangest thing happened on my way to school, our school bus broke down and they made us all get out through the back door and we had to wait beside the road for another bus to pick us up, but it took a long time to come so we were late.

WATCH OUT FOR HOMOPHONES

Homophones are words that sound the same, but are spelled differently and have different meanings. Students often make errors with homophones by substituting one homophone for another. Study the following chart for common homophones and their uses. When using these words in your essay, make sure you are spelling the word correctly for a given context.

COMMON HOMOPHONES		
Homophone	Meaning	Examples
Too	Excessive	Too much, too fast
Two	Number	Two apples, two cars
To	Direction	Went to the store
There	Location	Stay right there, go there
Their	Belonging to them	Their cat, their essays
They're	Contraction for "they are"	They're ready!
By	Author or place	By the lake, by C.S. Lewis
Buy	Purchase	Buy some food

Bye	Farewell	Bye, I'll see you tomorrow!
Here	Location	Right here, come here
Hear	Listen	Hear a song, hear a noise
Whether	Doubt or choice	Whether to go, whether to stay
Weather	Climate	The weather is nice today.
Principal	Leader of a school	The principal's office
Principle	Truth or belief	I stick to my principles.
Its	Belonging to something	Turn the book on its side.
It's	Contraction for "it is"	It's raining outside.
Your	Belonging to you	Your car, your homework
You're	Contraction for "you are"	You're coming tonight.
Than	Comparison	An elephant is bigger than a dog.
Then	Time	Then, I went home.

Exercise #7: The following sentences may contain one, many, or no homophone errors. Rewrite the sentences to make them error free. Answers are provided at the end of the book.

1. "To Build a Fire" was written bye Jack London.

2. Jack borrowed too pens. Than he went home.

3. There coming to our house tomorrow.

4. Your waiting to long to answer.

5. My mother told me to wait they're.

6. Their right hear. Can't you see them?

7. My school has a great principle.

8. Your not serious!

9. The whether is nice outside.

10. I need to bye three binders too take to school. Its important.

AVOID THE PASSIVE VOICE

The **passive voice** re-orders your sentence so it sounds clunky and impersonal. Using the **active voice** instead of the passive voice will strengthen your writing. For every sentence, make sure the "doer" of the verb (or the person performing the action) comes first. See the following chart:

PASSIVE VOICE VS. ACTIVE VOICE	
Passive Voice	**Active Voice**
The soup was heated.	I heated the soup.
The essay was written by Joe.	Joe wrote the essay.
The computer was being used by Alice.	Alice was using the computer.

Exercise #8: Re-write the following sentences in the active voice. Then, check your answers in the answer key.

1. The cookie was eaten by Amanda.

2. The dishes were washed by my brother.

3. My homework was eaten by my dog.

4. The mistake was made by me.

STRUCTURING YOUR ESSAY

An essay is a specialized type of writing that presents an argument using an ordered structure. Like a story, an essay has a beginning, middle, and end. Unlike a story, an essay is organized so that each paragraph serves a specific function in order to support a bigger idea.

Your ISEE essay should contain three main components: an **introduction**, a **body**, and a **conclusion**. Your introduction will generally be a single paragraph outlining your position. Your body will be two or three paragraphs describing different reasons or examples to explain your position. Your conclusion will be your final paragraph, summarizing your argument for the reader.

ESSAY STRUCTURE	
Introduction (first paragraph)	Explain the topic, explain your position, and outline your argument.
Body (2-3 paragraphs)	In each body paragraph, describe a different reason or example that explains your position.
Conclusion (last paragraph)	Summarize your position and your argument.

In this section, we'll discuss steps for writing each component of your ISEE essay.

BRAINSTORMING

Before you start writing, take a moment to brainstorm your essay on the scratch paper provided. Taking time to jot down ideas and outline your structure will help you stay focused when you start writing. Here are some exercises for effective brainstorming.

FREEWRITING

Sometimes, starting an essay can be intimidating: you stare at a blank page in front of you, rack your brain for ideas, and can't decide how you should begin. **Freewriting** is a useful brainstorming technique to help you break out of "writer's block." On your scratch paper, spend a minute writing about whatever comes to mind when you think about the essay topic. Don't stop, think, or edit yourself. Don't worry about spelling, grammar, or whether your ideas are any good—this isn't your actual essay, just a brainstorming exercise to get your creative juices flowing!

After a minute is up, read over what you have written. Circle any ideas that address the prompt clearly and that you could use in your essay. Then, think about how you might organize those ideas into one unifying statement with two or three supporting reasons or examples.

MAKE A LIST

Another brainstorming technique is to make a list of ideas or concepts before deciding what you would like to discuss in your essay. Most prompts will ask you to discuss one main topic. Look at your essay prompt and circle or underline this topic. Then, make a list of any ideas or concepts that come to mind when you think about this topic.

For example, consider the following prompt:

In your opinion, what is the most important school rule?

This prompt is asking you to pick a specific rule and describe why you think it is the most important rule for a school community to follow. You might brainstorm by jotting down a list of rules that you consider important. For example, you could write:

Important rules:

- Attend class every day and be on time.
- Treat others as you would like to be treated.
- Resolve problems in a positive, non-violent way.
- Respect school property and the property of others.
- Follow the school dress code.

Then, think about why each of these rules is important, and decide which would be the most compelling for you to write about.

OUTLINE REASONS OR EXAMPLES

After you have decided on the main focus of your essay, the next step is to list the reasons or examples that you will use to explain your position in your body paragraphs. For the prompt above, maybe you decided that you would like to talk about resolving problems in a positive, non-violent way. Next, take a moment to jot down two or three reasons for this choice. For example, you might write:

My position: The most important school rule is to resolve problems in a positive, non-violent way.

My reasons:

- Using violence to solve problems creates an unsafe environment for the whole school community.
- Learning to talk out our problems helps us build our communication skills and makes us more productive community members.
- Using positive language to resolve a problem helps both sides feel like they are being heard and helps us reach a better understanding.

When you are thinking of reasons or examples to explain your position, try to be as specific as possible, and try not to repeat yourself. If you are having difficulty coming up with reasons for one position, try thinking of reasons for another position. For example, if you were having trouble thinking about reasons why one school rule is important, you could try brainstorming reasons for another school rule on your list.

After you have outlined your position and some reasons and examples that explain this position, you have all of the main components you need to organize your essay! In the rest of this section, we will discuss how to convert this brainstormed outline into your final complete essay.

Exercise #1: For each sample prompt below, use one of the brainstorming methods in this section to identify your position and outline some reasons or examples to explain your position.

1. Describe one thing you do well.

   My position (name one thing I do well):

My reasons:

- *One way in which I excel in this area:*

- *Another way in which I excel in this area:*

- *Optional – a third way in which I excel in this area:*

2. Whom do you admire most? Describe three qualities that you admire in this person.

   My position (name the person I admire):

   My reasons:

   - *One quality this person possesses:*

   - *Another quality this person possesses:*

   - *A third quality this person possesses:*

3. Does technology make people's lives better? Why or why not?

   My position (whether I think that technology does or does not make people's lives better):

   My reasons:

   - *One example that shows how technology does or does not make people's lives better:*

   - *Another example that shows how technology does or does not make people's lives better:*

   - *Optional – a third example that shows how technology does or does not make people's lives better:*

4. If you could visit any place in the world, where would you visit and why?

    My position (name the place I would visit):

    My reasons:

    - *One reason why I would want to visit this place:*

    - *Another reason why I would want to visit this place:*

    - *Optional – a third reason why I would want to visit this place:*

5. Tell us about a time you did something you are proud of.

    My position (name the thing that makes me proud):

    My reasons:

    - *One reason why this makes me proud:*

    - *Another reason why this makes me proud:*

    - *Optional – a third reason why this makes me proud:*

THE INTRODUCTION

After you have outlined the position and reasons you will discuss in your essay, it's time to start writing! The first paragraph of your essay is your **introduction**. In this paragraph, you will explain the topic, your position, and the reasons you will discuss in your essay. In other words, you are *introducing* your readers to everything you will talk about by giving them a short preview of what's ahead.

Your introduction should include the following components:

COMPONENTS OF AN INTRODUCTION	
1-2 sentences	In your own words, explain the essay topic and why this topic is important.
1 sentence	In one sentence, state the position you will discuss in your essay. This sentence is called your **thesis statement**.
1-2 sentences	Introduce the reasons or examples you will discuss in your essay.

Continue reading to learn more about each of these components.

EXPLAIN THE TOPIC

Start your introduction with 1-2 sentences explaining the main topic or issue in the essay prompt. Demonstrate to the reader that you understand the prompt by explaining why this topic or issue is important. Be sure to explain the topic in **your own words** rather than copying the wording of the prompt. Don't begin with "Yes, I agree" or "No, I don't agree"— make sure that you use full sentences.

For example, how would you explain the topic in the sample prompt about school rules? Here it is again:

In your opinion, what is the most important school rule?

In order to show that you understand this topic, start by explaining in your own words why rules are necessary for school communities. You might write:

Schools bring together students, teachers, and staff from different backgrounds, and they might not always see eye-to-eye on every issue. In order to help resolve disagreements and maintain a safe learning environment, school communities need to agree on certain rules to follow.

These sentences introduce the topic of the essay prompt (school rules) and explain why this topic is important. Notice that we used different wording from the prompt in order to demonstrate that we understand the topic and have thought critically about it.

STATE YOUR POSITION

After you have explained the topic in the prompt, answer the question in the prompt by stating your position. The sentence where you explain your own position on the topic is called your **thesis statement**. Your thesis statement should state one main idea that directly answers the question in the prompt. This main idea will be the focus of your whole essay.

For example, what would you write as your thesis statement for the "school rule" prompt? If you are following the structure we brainstormed in the previous section, write a full sentence stating the position we chose. Add this sentence to your introduction:

Schools bring together students, teachers, and staff from different backgrounds, and they might not always see eye-to-eye on every issue. In order to help resolve disagreements and maintain a safe learning environment, school communities need to agree on certain rules to follow. **I believe the most important school rule is to resolve problems in a positive, non-violent way.**

Notice how this thesis statement clearly answers the question in the prompt and presents only one main idea that will be the focus of the essay. Try not to present more than one main idea in your thesis. If you were to write, "I think there are actually two school rules that are important," it would be harder for you to focus your essay. Furthermore, you wouldn't be answering the question convincingly—the prompt asks you to pick one rule that you feel is the *most* important!

INTRODUCE YOUR REASONS OR EXAMPLES

After your thesis statement, use the last one or two sentences of your introduction to briefly introduce the reasons or examples that you will be using to explain your position. Look at the list of reasons that you brainstormed, and pick the two or three that you think are the most important. Then, link them together in one or two complete sentences.

It can be easier to budget your time for the ISEE essay if you only pick two reasons or examples to discuss. Pick the two reasons that you feel are the most important to help you make your point. However, some prompts might specifically ask for three reasons or examples. For example, the second prompt in Exercise #1 on page 238 asks you to discuss "three characteristics" of a person you admire. In order to answer this prompt completely, you would need to pick three characteristics to discuss.

Let's look back at the reasons we brainstormed for the "school rule" prompt. Which do you consider the most important? Perhaps you'd like to discuss the first two reasons. You would link these reasons together as complete sentences to finish your introduction:

> Schools bring together students, teachers, and staff from different backgrounds, and they might not always see eye-to-eye on every issue. In order to help resolve disagreements and maintain a safe learning environment, school communities need to agree on certain rules to follow. I believe the most important school rule is to resolve problems in a positive, non-violent way. **Using violence to solve problems creates an unsafe environment for the whole school community. By contrast, learning to talk out our problems helps us build our communication skills and makes us more productive community members.**

This paragraph effectively introduces the reader to the argument that will be discussed in this essay. It provides background information about the topic, demonstrating that the writer understands the issue. It then states a position on this topic, clearly answering the question and presenting one main idea. Finally, it briefly introduces two reasons explaining this position. These are the reasons that will be discussed further in the essay's body paragraphs.

Exercise #2: Look back at the outlines you brainstormed for the prompts in Exercise #1. Then, on a separate sheet of paper, **write an introduction** for each prompt. First, explain the topic in your own words, then state your position, and finally introduce the reasons or examples you will discuss.

1. Describe one thing you do well.

2. Whom do you admire most? Describe three qualities that you admire in this person.

3. Does technology make people's lives better? Why or why not?

4. If you could visit any place in the world, where would you visit and why?

5. Tell us about a time you did something you are proud of.

THE BODY

After your introduction, the next two to three paragraphs are your **body paragraphs**. These are the most important paragraphs of your essay: in these paragraphs, you will explain your reasons or examples in order to convince the reader of your position.

In each body paragraph, you will explain one of the reasons or examples that you summarized in your introduction. You should include the following components:

COMPONENTS OF A BODY PARAGRAPH	
1-2 sentences	Introduce your first reason or example supporting your position.
2-3 sentences	Explain your reason or example with specific, relevant details.
1-2 sentences	Analyze your reason or example to show how it connects back to the main position in your essay.
Then, transition to your next body paragraph, and repeat!	

Continue reading to learn more about each of these components.

EXPLAIN YOUR REASON OR EXAMPLE

At the beginning of each body paragraph, briefly summarize the reason or example that you will be discussing. Then, explain this reason or example with specific and relevant **details**. Think of a specific person or event that could help you illustrate your point, and describe this in detail to the reader. Try to answer the **5 w's**: the "who," "what," "where," "when," and "why." The more specifically and vividly you are able to describe your reason or example, the stronger your argument will be.

For example, let's look back at the "school rule" prompt. Re-read the introduction we wrote for this prompt in the previous section. After the thesis statement, we listed two reasons to explain our position:

I believe the most important school rule is to resolve problems in a positive, non-violent way. Using violence to solve problems creates an unsafe environment for the whole school community. By contrast, learning to talk out our problems helps us build our communication skills and makes us more productive community members.

In our first body paragraph, we'll need to think of specific and relevant details to explain the first of these reasons—that violence creates an unsafe learning environment. It might be helpful to illustrate our point with a specific event, "showing" rather than "telling" why violence is a problem. We could write:

> Schools become unsafe places for students to learn if we use violence to solve problems. A small push or shove can escalate into a much larger conflict, putting other students and staff members in danger. In my school, two students recently got hurt when they started fighting on the playground at recess. They were arguing over whose turn it was to use the monkey bars, and they began throwing rocks and sticks at each other. Both students ended up with cuts and scrapes, and everyone else on the playground felt unsafe.

In this paragraph, we picked a specific event to demonstrate why violent problem-solving can lead to an unsafe school environment. We explained the "who," "what," "where," "when," and "why" of this event in order to describe this example in detail and to give the reader specific evidence for the point we are making.

ANALYZE YOUR REASON OR EXAMPLE

After explaining your reason or example in great detail, the next step is to **analyze** your reason or example to show how it supports your position. Clearly connect your reason or example back to the main point of your essay. This is the "aha!" part of your paragraph— your reader should say, "Aha! That is why this example is important!"

How would we finish the body paragraph we started above by connecting it directly back to the main point of our essay? First, we should remind ourselves what this main point is: we're trying to argue that solving problems in a positive, non-violent way is the most important school rule. We need to explain why all of these details show that this is true. We might write:

> Schools become unsafe places for students to learn if we use violence to solve problems. A small push or shove can escalate into a much larger conflict, putting other students and staff members in danger. In my school, two students recently got hurt when they started fighting on the playground at recess. They were arguing over whose turn it was to use the monkey bars, and they began throwing rocks and sticks at each other. Both students ended up with cuts and scrapes, and everyone else on the playground felt unsafe. **By resorting to violence to solve their problems, these students put themselves and the rest of my school community in danger. In order to maintain a safe learning environment, schools must enforce non-violent approaches to solving problems.**

The last two sentences of this body paragraph analyze why the details in this paragraph are important. They connect the example in this paragraph directly back to the main point of the essay, making sure the reader understands how this information fits together. It's your job to "connect the dots" for your readers and lead them through the structure of your essay in a clear, logical manner.

TRANSITION TO YOUR NEXT BODY PARAGRAPH

After finishing your first body paragraph, you'll explain your next reason or example in a new paragraph. It is helpful to **transition** into your second body paragraph with a short phrase that links it to your previous point. Then, follow the same steps above to **explain** your second reason or example with specific, relevant details and to **analyze** how your reason or example connects back to your position in the essay.

How would we write a second body paragraph for our "school rule" essay above? We might start with a short transition before stating the next reason we are going to discuss:

> Instead of using violence to solve problems, it is more effective for students to talk out their problems together. A school community functions best when all of its members develop their communication skills and learn to discuss issues in a positive manner.

With the phrase "instead of using violence to solve problems," we effectively transitioned from the previous paragraph, where we talked about violence, to this new paragraph, where we will talk about a better problem-solving approach.

How would you continue this body paragraph? First, explain this topic with specific, relevant details. Try to think of a specific event or person you could describe. Then, analyze how these details connect back to the main position in the essay. Give this a try on a separate sheet of paper, and have a trusted reader check your work!

After you have finished explaining all of your reasons or examples, the body of your essay is complete. By this point, the reader should have a very clear idea of how you have arrived at the point you are making, and what type of detailed evidence supports this point.

Exercise #3: Look back at the outlines you brainstormed for the prompts in Exercise #1, and the introductions you wrote for these prompts in Exercise #2. Then, on a separate sheet of paper, **write the body paragraphs** for each prompt. In each paragraph, discuss one reason or example you outlined in your introduction. Explain this reason or example with specific, relevant details, and then analyze how this reason or example connects back to your main position.

1. Describe one thing you do well.

2. Whom do you admire most? Describe three qualities that you admire in this person.

3. Does technology make people's lives better? Why or why not?

4. If you could visit any place in the world, where would you visit and why?

5. Tell us about a time you did something you are proud of.

Ivy Global

THE CONCLUSION

The last paragraph of your essay is your **conclusion**. In this paragraph, you'll summarize your position and examples, in slightly different words. The point of this paragraph is to ensure that your reader understands how you put together your argument. Make sure you stay on topic: don't talk about any new reasons or examples, and don't be overly general. All you need to do is end with a strong statement about why your argument is important.

Here are the components you should include:

COMPONENTS OF A CONCLUSION	
1 sentence	Summarize your main point, in slightly different words.
1-2 sentences	Summarize your reasons or examples, in slightly different words.
1 sentence	End with a strong concluding statement about why your argument is important.

For example, let's look at the "school rule" prompt one more time. Re-read the introduction and body we wrote for this prompt in the previous sections. How would we write a conclusion to summarize our argument and tie our reasons together, in slightly different words? We might write:

Because talking through our problems is essential for a safe, productive learning environment, I believe that non-violent problem-solving is the most important rule that a school can enforce. Resorting to violence to solve problems puts other students and staff in danger and severely damages the safe environment that schools aim to create. However, by talking through our problems, we can learn to communicate in a positive way that respects the different viewpoints of our peers. Developing our communication skills will help us build a school community that embraces its diversity of students and staff, preparing us to excel not only as students, but also as global citizens.

This concluding paragraph re-states the main point of our essay: non-violent problem-solving is the most important school rule. It also summarizes our two main reasons: violence creates an unsafe school environment, and talking through problems builds our community. It ends with a strong statement about the importance of communication skills in school and beyond, emphasizing the significance of the main point in this essay. Notice how the conclusion stays focused on the position and reasons we have already discussed in the essay, but it doesn't repeat the same wording—it uses new language to summarize the argument and make sure the point is clear for the reader.

Exercise #4: Look back at the introductions you wrote for the prompts in Exercise #2 and the body paragraphs you wrote in Exercise #3. Then, on a separate sheet of paper, **write the conclusion** for each prompt. Summarize your main position and reasons or examples, and end with a strong statement that shows why your argument is important.

1. Describe one thing you do well.

2. Whom do you admire most? Describe three qualities that you admire in this person.

3. Does technology make people's lives better? Why or why not?

4. If you could visit any place in the world, where would you visit and why?

5. Tell us about a time you did something you are proud of.

ESSAY CHECKLIST

When you finish writing your essay, make sure to save time at the end for editing. Re-read your essay not only to correct grammar or spelling mistakes, but also to make sure that you have all of the structural components you need. Here is a checklist to help you out:

INTRODUCTION

- ☐ Do I explain the topic in my own words?
- ☐ Do I have a thesis statement stating my position? Does my thesis statement clearly answer the question?
- ☐ Do I introduce 2-3 reasons or examples that explain my position?

BODY PARAGRAPHS (2 OR 3)

- ☐ Do I introduce a reason or example that I listed in my introduction?
- ☐ Do I explain my reason or example in as much specific detail as possible, giving the "who," "what", "where," "when," and "why"?
- ☐ Do I analyze my reason or example, clearly demonstrating how it connects to my main position?
- ☐ Do I briefly transition from one body paragraph to the next?

CONCLUSION

- ☐ Do I summarize my position, in slightly different words?
- ☐ Do I summarize my reasons or examples?
- ☐ Do I end with a strong concluding sentence about why my argument is important?

Exercise #5: Use this checklist to edit the introductions, body paragraphs, and conclusions you wrote for the prompts in Exercises #2, #3, and #4. When you are done, have a trusted reader check your work.

In the previous section, we reviewed some general strategies for structuring an ISEE essay in response to any prompt. In this section, we will explore in greater detail the different types of prompts you might see on the ISEE, and specific strategies for approaching these prompts. Make sure that you have a solid understanding of basic essay structure before you approach these more advanced strategies.

The ISEE essay prompts might ask different types of questions. You might be asked to **describe** a person or event, or define characteristics or qualities. You might be asked to take a side on an issue and **persuade** the reader of your opinion. Finally, you might be asked to **consider the causes and effects** of a particular issue. Continue reading for more information about these types of questions.

DESCRIPTIVE ESSAY STRATEGIES

Some ISEE prompts will ask you to describe a person or event, or define characteristics and qualities. For example, the prompt might ask:

- What do you want to be when you grow up?
- What three qualities make for a good teacher?
- What is your favorite subject in school? What characteristics make this subject appealing?

To answer these types of prompts, you will want to use the following **descriptive writing** strategies. First, stick to topics you know. The topics are defined broadly, so the specific subject matter is largely up to you to decide. For example, if you are asked to write about your favorite subject in school, it makes sense to choose a subject you know well.

Before you start writing, choose two or three qualities you can use to describe your subject, and think of the reasons why you chose these. Some prompts will specify how many characteristics or qualities you are required to describe: in some cases, you'll be asked to identify two qualities, and in some cases, you'll be asked to identify three qualities. In your body paragraphs you'll want to explain the importance of the qualities you select and explain how these qualities relate to your topic.

The following chart offers one way you can structure a descriptive essay in response to the following prompt:

Which three qualities make a good teacher?

DESCRIPTIVE ESSAY APPROACH	
Introduction Paragraph	Establish the three qualities you'd like to discuss: *I admire teachers who set ambitious goals. Teachers who show expertise and organization place their students in a position to succeed.*
Body Paragraph 1	Establish why one of these qualities is important: *A teacher must have expertise. Joshua Bell developed mastery of the violin by learning from the expert violin master, Josef Gingold …*
Body Paragraph 2	Establish why the second of these qualities is important: *In order to learn, we must be organized. Watson and Crick's discovery of DNA was the result of the scientists' attempt to organize and understand the work of other scientists …*
Body Paragraph 3	Establish why the third of these qualities is important: *Teachers should set ambitious goals. Had John F. Kennedy not set the ambitious goal of sending people to the moon, the Apollo missions would never have taken place …*
Conclusion Paragraph	Summarize your description: *While there are other important qualities that make a good teacher, the most important qualities, in my view, are ambition, organization, and expertise.*

Exercise #1: For each prompt below, identify your position, some qualities you'd like to discuss, and why each quality is important. Have a trusted reader evaluate your work.

1. What do you want to be when you grow up?

   Identify your position (name what you want to be when you grow up):

   One reason why I aspire to this goal:

Explain why this is important:

Second reason why I aspire to this goal:

Explain why this is important:

2. What is your favorite subject in school? What characteristics make this subject appealing?

   Identify the subject:

   Name one characteristic:

   Explain why this is important:

   Name a second characteristic:

   Explain why this is important:

3. What three qualities define a good student?

   Name one quality of a good student:

   Explain why this is important:

   Name another quality of a good student:

   Explain why this is important:

   Name a third quality of a good student:

   Explain why this is important:

4. What is the most meaningful book you have read recently, and why was it meaningful to you?

   Identify your position (name the book you want to discuss):

Name one meaningful thing about the book:

Explain why this was meaningful to you:

Name a second meaningful thing about the book:

Explain why this was meaningful to you:

SAMPLE DESCRIPTIVE ESSAY

In the following **sample descriptive essay**, the author gives a specific answer to the prompt using two main reasons. As you read, look for the main structure of the essay (introduction, body paragraphs, and conclusion), and identify how the author uses specific details to illustrate the qualities and characteristics she considers important.

Whom do you admire, and why?

I admire my grandmother for her creativity and for her independent-mindedness. She showed her creativity in the countless paintings and other artwork she made throughout her life, and she showed her independent mind by going back to work while she was still raising her children.

My grandmother's creativity is apparent in the many beautiful paintings that adorn the walls in the homes of her four children. My aunt's dining room boasts a large oil painting of herself and her siblings playing in a stream; in my bedroom, I have a small watercolor of an African violet, my grandmother's favorite flower. She was able to evoke the fuzz of the violet's leaves by painting a fine sheen of gray over the green. My grandmother also made the beautiful quilt on my bed. As an aspiring artist, I am inspired by my grandmother's creative work.

In addition to being creative, my grandmother was also very independent. When she was raising my mother and her siblings in the 1960s, it was unusual in her community for a mother to work outside the home. My grandmother was not happy working only as a wife and mother, however, so she took a job as a teacher at the local elementary school. Her friends and even her husband were surprised by this choice. They didn't understand why she would want to devote so much time to a job when my grandfather made enough money to support their family comfortably. The work made her happy, however, so she did it in spite of others' objections. I admire her choice to pursue her own happiness even when that led her down an unusual path.

My grandmother enjoyed using her creativity to make beautiful things, and she was able to reap the rewards of a teaching career due to her independent-mindedness. I admire her for these qualities, and hope that I share them.

Exercise #2: Analyze the sample essay above. What are the author's position, characteristics, and reasons for discussing these characteristics?

1. Identify the subject:

2. Identify the first characteristic the author describes:

3. Explain why this is important:

4. Identify the second characteristic the author describes:

5. Explain why this is important:

PERSUASIVE ESSAY STRATEGIES

Some ISEE prompts will ask you to argue for or against an idea, urge the reader to act a certain way, or convince the reader to agree with a certain position on an issue. For example, the prompt might ask:

- Do we learn more from our mistakes or from our successes?
- Do you think money is important to a happy life?
- Should schools require their students to wear uniforms?

To answer these types of prompts, you will want to use the following **persuasive writing** strategies:

- In your thesis statement, clearly state your position on the prompt or issue presented. The thesis statement should let your reader clearly know what opinion you hold. Your entire essay should support your thesis statement.
- Explain why you hold the position you hold. Take a side. Don't sit on the fence.
- Use concrete examples to support your position: history, science, literature, or current event examples work best. Well-described personal examples can also be effective.

A four-paragraph essay works well for most persuasive prompts. The essay should contain an introduction in which you state your position and introduce your supporting examples, two body paragraphs explaining and supporting your opinion, and a conclusion paragraph where you summarize your argument. For some prompts, it may be useful to provide three reasons for your opinion, in which case you should write three shorter body paragraphs.

PERSUASIVE ESSAY APPROACH	
Paragraph Type	**Content**
Introduction Paragraph	In your thesis statement, take a side on the issue presented. Introduce two reasons why you believe what you believe.
Body Paragraph: Evidence/Support	Introduce your first supporting reason and provide specific details about this reason. Make sure to clearly relate this example back to your thesis.
Body Paragraph: Evidence/Support	Transition from your first reason to your second reason. Provide specific details about this reason. Explain how this reason supports your thesis.

Conclusion Paragraph	Summarize your reasons and your thesis.

A successful persuasive essay needs strong specific examples or reasons to demonstrate your position or opinion. The best examples are "big picture" examples from history, literature, or current events. Examples from your personal life can be effective, but these examples can be more difficult to clearly narrate in the limited time provided.

Think about important people or events that you have studied in history class, in books you have read recently, or events you have read about in newspapers. Consider your knowledge of government and politics. Be as specific as possible—for instance, instead of discussing "wars" in general, discuss a specific war or battle. Make sure you select topics about which you know a great deal. Provide names, places, dates, and other detailed background information for every example you choose.

Before you start writing, take a few minutes to brainstorm examples for both sides of the argument. Then, pick the side that has the stronger examples—it doesn't necessarily have to be the side you agree with.

Let's say you choose the following topic:

Do we learn more from our mistakes or from our successes?

Let's brainstorm!

BRAINSTORMING EXAMPLES	
We learn more from our mistakes because…	We learn more from our successes because…
Only 705 of the Titanic's 2,224 passengers and crew survived when the ship hit an iceberg in 1912. The ship didn't have enough lifeboats for every passenger. The disaster led to better regulation later, with governments in both Britain and America requiring all ships to have enough lifeboats to accommodate all passengers.	Gregor Mendel set out to study variation in plants. He cultivated pea plants in his monastery and, as a result of his observations, he was able to develop his important Laws of Inheritance. For every trait, an individual possesses two alleles. Only one allele is passed on to offspring from each parent. This discovery helps account for genetic variation in individuals.

Alexander Fleming was a brilliant researcher, but he wasn't tidy. Before going on vacation, he stacked his Petri dishes on a bench in his laboratory. When he returned, he noticed that one of the dishes had been mistakenly left without a lid and had grown a mold. The mold killed the bacteria in the Petri dish. Fleming had discovered Penicillin, a lifesaving antibiotic.	Early success often has a positive impact on later success. Wolfgang Amadeus Mozart was a child prodigy. By age five, he was proficient on the piano and had already begun to compose music. His early experience allowed him to develop into a lifelong learner. In his maturity, he became a musician capable of composing the *Requiem*.
Last year, I wrote an article for the school newspaper that won a district award. Yet, before I wrote the winning story, I wrote several drafts with which I wasn't pleased. I revised my work and showed it to teachers. Finally, after several attempts, I wrote a story with which I was pleased. This story went on to win the district award.	In grade five I made it my summer goal to read a complete play by Shakespeare in the original Early Modern English. I worked very hard, and by the end of the summer, I completed *Romeo and Juliet*. I gained the confidence after the summer to try to read challenging books during the school year. I am now working on reading H.G. Wells' *The Time Machine*.

Exercise #3: Practice brainstorming examples for the following prompts. Think of two "big picture" examples for each side of the issue. Then, decide which side has the stronger examples. Have a trusted reader review your work.

1. Do you think money is important to a happy life? Why or why not?

   I think money is important to a happy life because . . .

   Example One:

   Example Two:

   I think money is not important to a happy life because . . .
   Example One:

   Example Two:

2. Which do you think is more important, kindness or intelligence?

   Kindness is more important than intelligence because . . .

   Example One:

Example Two:

Intelligence is more important than kindness because . . .

Example One:

Example Two:

3. Do you prefer group work or individual work?

    I prefer group work because . . .

    Example One:

    Example Two:

    I prefer individual work because . . .

    Example One:

    Example Two:

4. If you had the power to read your best friend's mind, would you use it? Why or why not?

    I would choose to read my best friend's mind because . . .

    Example One:

    Example Two:

    I would not choose to read my best friend's mind because . . .

    Example One:

    Example Two:

UPPER LEVEL STRATEGY: WRITING A COUNTERARGUMENT

Students often wonder how to conclude essays. One way to effectively conclude your essay is to include a counterargument. In a **counterargument**, you identify an objection to your thesis or position and then refute or disprove that objection.

When developing a counterargument, imagine an intelligent skeptic reading your essay. If a friend held an opposing view to yours, how would he or she respond to your argument? Express your counterargument fairly. A strong, fairly presented, well-refuted counterargument lends credibility to your writing and can make the difference between an acceptable essay and an excellent one.

Let's say you've just finished writing a stellar essay about the benefits of wearing school uniforms. You've argued your position using strong examples and now it's time to conclude your essay. But, before you set your pen to page, imagine what would happen if you showed your essay to a friend who doesn't believe students should have to wear school uniforms. What would your friend say? You friend might say, "Uniforms make students less creative; less able to express themselves."

Or, let's say you show your essay to a school principal who doesn't believe students should be asked to wear uniforms. Your principal might say, "Uniforms promote elitism."

Or, let's say you show your essay to a mother who doesn't believe her child should wear uniforms. The parent might say, "Uniforms are too expensive."

The responses above are objections to your position. A strong counterargument presents an objection and responds to it. There are several ways you can respond to an objection. The following chart provides a few counterarguments you might use to defend your position on uniforms:

COUNTERARGUMENT EXAMPLES		
Objection	**How to respond**	**Counterargument**
Uniforms make students less creative; less able to express themselves.	Show ways in which the objection is valid, but not important.	*While adolescents require opportunities to express themselves, clothing is neither the best nor the only medium.*
Uniforms promote elitism.	Show ways in which the objection is flawed.	*Some have gone as far as to claim that uniforms promote elitism, but elitism is a mental state. Mental states can be occasioned by many factors, clothing being only one factor among many.*
Uniforms are too expensive.	Minimize the objection or compare and contrast it to your position.	*While uniforms can indeed be costly, everyday clothes can sometimes be even more expensive.*

Exercise #4: Practice writing counterarguments for the following prompts. Have a trusted reader evaluate your work.

1. Do you think money is important to a happy life?

    My opinion:

    One objection to my opinion:

    My response to this objection:

2. Which do you think is more important, kindness or intelligence?

    My opinion:

    One objection to my opinion:

    My response to this objection:

3. Do you prefer group work or individual work?

    My opinion:

    One objection to my opinion:

    My response to this objection:

4. If you had the power to read your best friend's mind, would you use it? Why or why not?

    My opinion:

    One objection to my opinion:

    My response to this objection:

SAMPLE PERSUASIVE ESSAY

In the following sample persuasive essay, the author gives a specific answer to the prompt using two main reasons. As you read, observe how the writer follows the structure discussed above.

Do we learn more from our mistakes or from our successes?

While success is the result of mastery and learning, learning itself is often the result of a willingness to learn from errors or mistakes. People grow when they are given the opportunity to properly evaluate and correct for their failures. This is evident in the sciences, but it is also true in my life. Alexander Fleming invented Penicillin because he was able to properly evaluate the repercussions from an error he made. In my own life, my ability to evaluate my own shortcomings has helped me to develop as a writer.

Alexander Fleming was a brilliant researcher, but he wasn't very tidy. Before going on vacation, he stacked his Petri dishes on a bench in his laboratory. However, he made a crucial mistake: he failed to cover one of the dishes with a lid. The dishes contained strains of Staphylococci. Staphylococci are sometimes harmless bacteria, but pathogenic strains can cause food poisoning and respiratory disease. When Fleming returned home from his vacation, he noticed that one of the lidless dishes had grown a mold. Where the mold grew, the Staphylococci had been eradicated. Fleming had made the error of not properly storing his Petri dishes. Yet, Fleming's willingness to explore the implications of the mold on his Petri dishes led to the discovery of Penicillin, a life-saving antibiotic. In this case, a careless mistake led to a discovery that changed medicine forever.

In the sciences, errors can sometimes lead to discovery; the same is true for those who work in language arts. I often write for my school newspaper. Last year, I wrote several drafts for an important story about school uniforms, but I wasn't pleased with any of my drafts. The structure wasn't quite right and I didn't like how the story ended. My advisor told me to revise my work. I knew I needed to work harder. Finally, after several false starts and a couple of outright failures, I wrote a draft with which I was pleased. This story went on to win a district journalism award. In this case, my ability to learn from failure allowed me to write a better story.

Some might claim that early success has a lasting effect on later success, and for this reason failure at all cost should be avoided. This claim might seem valid at first. For example, Wolfgang Amadeus Mozart was a child prodigy whose early successes allowed him to become a successful composer at a young age. Yet Mozart was no stranger to failure. As an adult, he failed to accept many good appointments and fell into debt. However, this time of failure was essential to Mozart's growth as an artist.

During this time he wrote important pieces, most notably Symphony Number 31. Mistakes, failures, errors, and difficulties create opportunities for learning. In the sciences, Fleming discovered Penicillin, a life-saving drug. Failure also tempers those who work in the arts. One doesn't have to be Mozart to learn this lesson; I learned its value as a writer for my school paper.

Exercise #5: Evaluate the sample essay. Have a trusted reader evaluate your summary.

1. What is the author's thesis?

2. What is the author's first reason and evidence?

3. What is the author's second reason and evidence?

4. What is one objection the author presents?

5. What is the author's response to the objection?

CAUSE-AND-EFFECT ESSAY STRATEGIES

Some ISEE prompts will ask you to describe an issue or situation and analyze its possible causes and effects. For example, the prompt might ask:

- What would you do if you saw a student bullying another student?

- What is one problem facing the world today and what is one thing you can do to help solve this problem?

- What is the most important lesson you have learned? How have you changed as a result?

Writing a strong **cause and effect essay** will require you to employ all the skills you have learned thus far. You'll need to identify causes, explain effects, and offer solutions. In other words, this essay will require you to describe, explain, and narrate.

Before you start writing, you'll want to make sure you narrow the topic sufficiently to ensure that you can respond adequately in 30 minutes. For instance, if you have been asked to identify ways you can help your community, it probably doesn't make sense to choose a big unfeasible topic like eliminating homelessness. Instead, you might choose to write about how you would like to volunteer at a soup kitchen.

Include an introduction that provides clear background information and adequately identifies both the causes and effects of an issue. Before you explain how your solution (your desire to volunteer at a soup kitchen) relates to the issue, you'll also want to describe and explain some of the causes and effects of homelessness.

Sometimes the prompt will only present the effects of an issue and it is your job to establish the causes. In some cases, the prompt will present you with a problem and ask you to develop a solution. Even if you have only been asked to develop a solution, a strong essay will explain the causes and effects that led you to decide on a particular course of action.

After you have adequately framed the causes and effects relating to a given issue, you'll want to offer solutions or explain how things can be done differently to improve the situation. Here, you'll want to employ not only your critical thinking skills, but also your ability to narrate possibilities and show potential outcomes.

Cause and effect essays require advanced writing abilities. How you structure your writing will depend on the requirements of the topic. Your goal should be to write an essay that is both logical and clear.

Let's plan a cause and effect essay together in response to the following prompt:

What are some things you could start doing today to prevent continued climate change?

CAUSE AND EFFECT ESSAY APPROACH	
Establish causes	Climate change is the result of greenhouse gas emissions. These emissions are caused by energy use. I use quite a bit of energy. For instance, sometimes I forget to turn off the light when I leave a room.
Establish effects	Leaving the lights on has negative consequences for the environment. Climate change results in more severe storms, like Hurricane Sandy. It also destroys polar ice, which affects many species.
Offer solutions	By remembering to turn off the lights when I leave the room, I can make a small but important positive impact on the environment. By biking to soccer practice instead of having my parents drive me, I can help prevent climate change.

Exercise #6: For the following topics, establish causes, effects, and offer solutions. Have a trusted reader look over your responses.

1. What would you do if you saw a student bullying another student?

   Establish causes:

   Establish effects:

   Offer solutions:

2. What is one problem facing the world today and what is one thing you can do to help solve this problem?

   Name the problem:

   Establish causes:

   Establish effects:

   Offer solutions:

3. What is the most important lesson you have learned? How have you changed as a result?

Name the lesson:

Establish causes:

Establish effects:

Offer solutions:

SAMPLE CAUSE AND EFFECT ESSAY

In the following **sample cause and effect essay**, the author identifies causes, effects, and offers a solution to a problem. As you read, look at how the author identifies causes, effects, and a solution to a problem.

What are some things you could start doing today to prevent continued climate change?

Human industrial activity has led to the 20th century being the warmest in recorded history. Scientific consensus links the recent trend of increased global temperature to the release of carbon dioxide into the atmosphere. The burning of fossil fuels in industry and for personal uses further exacerbates a problem many scientists currently deem irreversible. Societies will have to limit their output of carbon dioxide if we hope to see the global temperature stop increasing over the next century. Individuals can help mitigate the problem by being conscientious of their energy use.

Climate change is a problem worth addressing because it holds negative consequences for both people and the environment. Increased global temperatures are linked to more severe storms, like hurricanes Katrina and Sandy. The economic costs of these storms are in the billions of dollars, and there is no measuring the toll of human suffering when one considers the thousands who have lost homes, businesses, and loved ones due to these weather events. Climate change also increases the rate at which species go extinct. Besides the obvious loss of arctic habitat for penguins and polar bears, animals in other regions of the world suffer from changed habitats. Ignoring climate change means sanctioning the loss of an ecological heritage humanity cannot stand to lose.

There are several things I can do to help play a role in preventing further climate change. Leaving on lights when I am not using them has negative consequences for the environment. Power plants burn fossil fuels so that we may use electricity. Using more electricity means that power plants must burn more fossil fuels, meaning more carbon dioxide is released into the atmosphere. Therefore, turning off lights when I am not in the room or using them is a small but important way I can play a role in preventing further climate change. Another way I can help is by biking to soccer practice instead of having my parents drive me. I can also take public transit on the weekends rather than choosing to drive. Fewer cars on the road means fewer sources of carbon dioxide.

Resolving climate change permanently will clearly require global cooperation between governments and industry. While the problem might initially seem unmanageably large, there are definitely measures I can take in my daily life to play a role in resolving this incredibly important global issue.

Exercise #7: Analyze the sample essay above. What are the author's causes, effects, and solutions?

1. What causes does the author establish?

2. What effects does the author name?

3. What solutions does the author provide?

SAMPLE ESSAY PROMPTS
SECTION 5

In this section, you will find 20 sample essay prompts to prepare you for the types of prompts you might find on the ISEE. For each of the following prompts, on a separate sheet of paper, write a practice 30-minute essay using the structure and brainstorming exercises we discussed in this chapter. Have a trusted reader evaluate your work.

1. What is one problem that you have faced, and how did you solve it?

2. Describe how you would spend a perfect afternoon.

3. If you could do something over again, what would it be, and why?

4. Where would be your favorite place to live? Explain your choice.

5. What are three things that your school could do to improve the quality of education for its students?

6. Do you think it is more important to develop one skill, or to try many things?

7. Tell us about an influential person in your life. Why have you chosen this person?

8. If you could do one thing to improve your neighborhood, what would it be? Describe in detail how this would benefit your community.

9. Do you think it is ever acceptable to tell a lie? Explain why or why not.

10. Who is your favorite teacher? Describe three qualities that you admire in this person.

11. Do you think that all students should be required to participate in a school club or sport?

12. What is one book that has changed the way you think about something?

13. Tell us about something you learned from a friend. Why was it a valuable lesson?

14. What do you think is the best way to handle a disagreement?

15. If you could meet one famous person, past or present, who would it be and why?

Prompts 16-20 are Upper Level Only.

16. Do you think it is important for students to be involved in their local communities? Why or why not?

17. Your school is considering cutting its art and music programs in order to balance its budget. Do you agree with this decision? Why or why not?

18. What do you consider the biggest issue facing our country today, and how do you think this issue should be addressed?

19. Tell us about an experience that has helped shape who you are today.

20. How do you think that governments could improve access to education in disadvantaged communities?

VOCABULARY BUILDING

CHAPTER 6

INTRODUCTION

Vocabulary building is the best long-term way to improve your Verbal Reasoning and Reading Comprehension scores. In this chapter, learn some effective and fun strategies for learning ISEE-level words. Although this process might seem intimidating at first, learning words can be fun when you make some of these activities a regular part of your study schedule. And remember that vocabulary building is not just helpful for the ISEE—learning words will help you improve your reading, writing, and speaking skills in school and beyond!

VOCABULARY BUILDING STRATEGIES

The words you will encounter on the ISEE are commonly found in middle- and high-school level academic texts, but some words may be more advanced or less familiar depending on your age. The best way to expose yourself to more advanced vocabulary is to read as much as possible. Read a wide variety of genres—fiction, nonfiction, poetry, newspaper articles— and look up words you don't know. Pay attention to any words that are unfamiliar in the ISEE practice exercises you are working on, and look them up as well.

At the end of this section, you will also find a list of 500 words that will help you start preparing for the level of vocabulary that commonly appears on the ISEE. Use these words as a starting point, and supplement this list with your own personal words from your reading and practice exercises. In order to make this process more fun and effective, use the following strategies when you are learning and reviewing new words.

LEARN THE DEFINITION WITH A PERSONAL TRIGGER

When you learn a new word, the first step is to learn its definition. Some words have more than one meaning, and sometimes the ISEE will ask you to identify a less common meaning for a word. Therefore, make sure you learn **all possible meanings** for any new word you look up.

When you learn a word's definition, it is just as important to learn how a word is **used in a sentence**. Pay attention to any sample sentences that demonstrate how the word is used, and look up more examples in a dictionary or online.

Finally, come up with a **personal trigger** to help you build a personal connection with the word. This can be as simple as writing your own personal sentence for the word. The more personal, the better—if the sentence relates to your own personal life, you'll have an easier time remembering it! For example, if your word is "irritable," you might write a personal sentence like "My aunt Martha is sometimes irritable and grouchy." This way, when you think of the word "irritable," you'll think of your grouchy aunt!

If you can't think of a personal story to connect with your word, see if you can come up with **a wacky way to remember the word** based on what it sounds like. For example, "confluence" means convergence or coming together. A wacky way to remember confluence might be to think of the flu. If one person in a group has the flu and then all of the people come together, chances are they will all get the flu!

KEEP A VOCABULARY JOURNAL

Keep your own personal vocabulary journal as you work your way through this book's word list and as you do your own outside reading. A vocabulary journal is the best way to personalize your vocabulary learning because it allows you to keep track of any words that are new to you. Any time you come across a new word in this book's word list, in an ISEE practice test, or in your own reading, write it down in your journal. Include the definition and an example. It is also sometimes helpful to note the context in which you first encountered the word. For particularly difficult words include a personal trigger or wacky association. Make sure you also understand whether the word is a noun, verb, adjective, or adverb (see pages 44-45 for a review of these types of words). If you find it helpful, you can write "N" for noun, "V" for verb, "Adj" for adjective, and "Adv" for adverb.

Use the following sample entries as a model to start your own journal.

My Vocabulary Journal
Date: _____

Abduct

Definition: to kidnap

Sentence: Susan was abducted by aliens and taken to a faraway planet.

Personal trigger: Think of the word "duck," as to crouch down. If you see an alien ship coming to abduct you, you'd better duck!

Abscond

Definition: to depart in a sudden and secret manner, particularly to avoid capture or legal prosecution

Sentence: The cashier absconded with the money.

Personal trigger: Abscond has "scon" in it, which is close to "scone." Think of a baker absconding from the bakery and bringing lots of scones with him.

Akimbo

Definition: with hands on hips and elbows extending outwards

Sentence: Jeremy stood with arms akimbo, looking very cross.

Personal trigger: Akimbo rhymes with limbo. It certainly wouldn't be easy to do the limbo with arms akimbo!

MAKE FLASHCARDS

Make **flashcards** to help you practice the words in this book's word list and in your own vocabulary journal. Write the word on the front and the definition, type of word, and personal example sentence or trigger on the back. Here is an example:

Front	Back
Unique	*Definition: (Adj) the only one of its kind* *Sentence: Marjorie has a unique sense of style – she comes up with clothing combinations that I've never seen anyone else wear.*

If a word has multiple meanings, make sure you include all of these on your flashcard. For example:

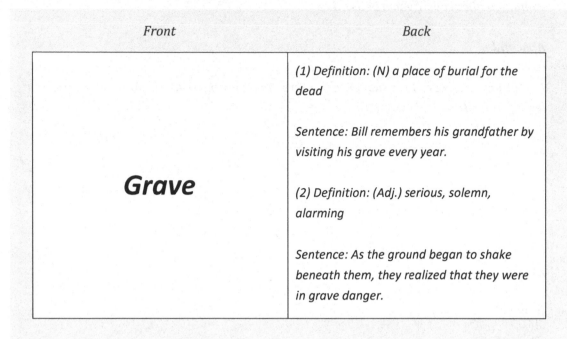

Front	Back
Grave	*(1) Definition: (N) a place of burial for the dead* *Sentence: Bill remembers his grandfather by visiting his grave every year.* *(2) Definition: (Adj.) serious, solemn, alarming* *Sentence: As the ground began to shake beneath them, they realized that they were in grave danger.*

Take your flashcards with you throughout the day, and flip through them during your spare time as you're waiting in line or riding in the car, bus, or train. After you have mastered a word and can remember it easily, put it in a different pile and test yourself just on the words you have more difficulty remembering. As you learn new words, go back to your previous flashcard piles every so often and make sure you still remember your old words.

PRACTICE USING NEW WORDS

As you learn new words, practice using them as frequently as you can in your daily life. Use them when you talk with friends and parents and look out for them in your reading. Some students find it helpful (and fun!) to write a short story using as many vocabulary words as they can think of. You can keep the story going on for as long as you like, and keep adding new words each day.

Take a look at the following sample short story, which uses many of the words from this book's vocabulary list:

Yesterday morning, my parents told me that our family would be taking a surprise vacation to Hawaii. We had all been working too hard, and they could see that we were **fatigued**. I have very **compassionate** parents! I was very excited about the trip, but my older brother, Jim, was **apathetic**. "I've been to Hawaii already," he told me, "so I don't really care if I go again." When I told my best friend about the trip, I thought she would be happy for me, but instead she was irate. "Without me?!" she yelled. "You're taking a trip and leaving me here alone!?" My best friend is very **fickle**. Just that morning she had been in such a good mood. Usually when she gets angry like this, I become **meek** and **submissive**, and do whatever she says. But this time, I decided to stand up for what I wanted. I've always wanted to visit Hawaii, and am **resolute** about going on this trip.

As you work through the vocabulary list and add to your own journal, try finishing this story, or come up with your own!

CREATE A STUDY SCHEDULE

When you learn new words, remember that practice makes perfect! The more you repeat and review your words, the better you will remember them. Aim to work consistently, learning a small number of words on a daily basis, so you don't become overwhelmed. Creating a structured study schedule will help you set goals and track your progress. If you have a structured schedule to follow, you'll be more likely to stick with it. Set a goal for the number of words you would like to learn before your test, and divide this number by the days you have available. It may be helpful to set aside certain days of the week, like Saturdays or Sundays, to review the new and old words you have been learning.

Here is a sample study schedule for three weeks:

Week	Monday	Tuesday	Wednesday	Thursday	Friday	Saturday	Sunday
1	5 words	5 words	5 words	5 words	5 words	Review Week 1 words	Break
2	5 words	5 words	5 words	5 words	5 words	Review Week 2 words	Review Week 1 and 2 words
3	5 words	5 words	5 words	5 words	5 words	Review Week 3 words	Review Week 1, 2, & 3 words

If you keep up this schedule, you'll learn 75 words in 3 weeks, 150 words in 6 weeks, and 300 words in 12 weeks! Adjust the number of words you learn per night to fit the amount of time you have before your test, but make sure you are working at a pace that is feasible for you. If you are an older student, you may be able to remember 10 or more words per night. Don't forget to review both your new and your old words on a regular basis.

WORD ROOTS, PREFIXES AND SUFFIXES

In English grammar, many words can be broken into basic parts. Learning these basic parts will help you decipher unfamiliar vocabulary and speed up your vocabulary building process. Learning only 30 key word parts can help you decode over 10,000 words!

In this section, learn about the basic parts that make up English words and practice breaking down words into these parts. Learn some of the most common word parts by working your way through the list at the end of this section.

WORD ROOTS

The **root** of a word is the main building block that carries a specific meaning. If different words have the same root, they are related in meaning. Therefore, looking for a word's root or thinking of other words that have the same root can help you guess at a word's meaning. Knowledge of French, Spanish, German, or Latin can be helpful here, because many English word roots are similar to words in these languages.

For example, you might guess that the word root "act" means "to do." The words ACTION, ACTOR, and ACTIVE all involve doing things because they all have this same word root.

For a more advanced example, look at the word AMIABLE. If you know that "ami" in French and "amigo" in Spanish mean "friend," you can guess that this word might have something to do with friends. In fact, AMIABLE means "friendly."

This is because AMIABLE contains the word root "am," which has to do with love or liking. Can you think of some other words with the roots "am," "ami," or "amor," which relate to love or liking? Here is a list to get started:

- AMICABLE: friendly
- AMITY: friendly or peaceful relations
- ENAMOR: to fill with love

As another example, consider the word BENEFICENT, which contains the word root "ben." This root is related to the words "bien" in French and "bene" in Italian, which mean "good." We can guess that BENEFICENT means something good. In fact, it means "performing acts of kindness or charity."

Here are some other English words with the root "ben":

- BENEFICIAL: favorable, resulting in good
- BENEVOLENT: kind, well-meaning
- BENIGN: gentle, kind, not harmful

Exercise #1: Look at the list of word roots at the end of this section to find the meaning of the underlined roots below. Then, look up the definition of each word in a good dictionary. Notice how the root influences the meaning of the word! The first word has been filled out for you.

WORD	ROOT MEANING	DEFINITION OF WORD
bibliography	*biblio: related to books*	*a list of books referred to in a scholarly work*
carnivore		
chronology		
civilian		
fidelity		
mortuary		
potential		
sacred		
vacuous		
eloquent		

Ivy Global

PREFIXES

Sometimes a word has a **prefix**, which is a small component that comes before the root. Not all words have prefixes—in fact, as you saw in Exercise #1, many words start with roots. However, when a word has a prefix, the prefix can significantly change the word's meaning.

For example, the word UNHAPPY has two parts: the prefix "un" and the root "happy." The prefix "un" means "not," so UNHAPPY means "not happy."

As a more advanced example, consider the word INCORRIGIBLE. "In" is another prefix that often means "not"—for instance, "inadequate" means "not adequate." So, INCORRIGIBLE means "not corrigible." What does "corrigible" mean? We can think of another word with the root "corr": "correct." "Corrigible" means "able to be corrected" or "correctable." Therefore, INCORRIGIBLE means "not able to be corrected." It is often used to describe a person who is so bad or so stubborn that his or her behavior cannot be improved!

Exercise #2: Look at the list of prefixes at the end of this section to find the meaning of the underlined prefixes below. Then, look up the definition of each word in a good dictionary. Notice how the prefix influences the meaning of the word! The first word has been filled out for you.

WORD	PREFIX MEANING	DEFINITION OF WORD
<u>amphi</u>bian	*amphi: both*	*an animal that can live both in water and on land*
<u>circum</u>ference		
<u>contra</u>dict		
<u>dys</u>functional		
<u>inter</u>mediate		
<u>poly</u>gon		
<u>peri</u>meter		
<u>trans</u>parent		

SUFFIXES

A word might also have a **suffix**, which is a small component that comes at the end of a word. Not all words have suffixes. However, when they do, the suffix frequently changes the word's meaning or function. A suffix might change a word to a noun, verb, adjective, or adverb.

Take a moment to review the definitions of nouns, verbs, adjectives, and adverbs:

TYPES OF WORDS			
Word Type	**Definition**	**Examples**	**Sample Sentence**
Noun	a person, place, or thing: "things" can also include qualities or categories that you might not be able to touch or see	teacher, lawyer, city, Italy, animal, car, water, tool, hunger, comfort, curiosity, trust, emotion, science, art, biology	The young <u>puppy</u> ran quickly.
Verb	an action word: what the subject of the sentence (the main noun) is "doing"	run, hit, dig, carve, learn, hear, enjoy, understand, become, be	The young puppy <u>ran</u> quickly.
Adjective	a word that describes, identifies, or defines a noun	soft, sharp, green, full, loud, wet, happy, thoughtful, diligent, humorous, good	The <u>young</u> puppy ran quickly.
Adverb	a word that describes a verb, adjective, or another adverb: often ends in "-ly"	quickly, desperately, sadly, suddenly, freely, quietly, strangely, well	The young puppy ran <u>quickly</u>.

Notice how many of the adverb examples in the chart above end with the suffix "-ly." This is because the suffix "-ly" is a very common way to change an adjective into an adverb. For example, if you start with the adjective QUICK and add "-ly," you'll have the adverb QUICKLY.

As another example, let's start with the adjective MUSIC. If we add the suffix "-al," we'll get the adjective MUSICAL, which means "related to music." The suffix "-al" can change a noun to an adjective. Here are some other English words that use this suffix:

- ACCIDENTAL: by accident

- FUNCTIONAL: working, relating to a specific function
- GLOBAL: relating to the whole world (the globe)

Suffixes can be added to other suffixes to create longer and longer words! For example, if we start with the adjective GLOBAL and add the suffix "-ize," we'll have the verb GLOBALIZE. If we then add the suffix "-ation," we'll have the noun GLOBALIZATION.

Exercise #3: Look at the list of suffixes at the end of this section to find the meaning of the underlined suffixes below. Then, look up the definition of each word in a good dictionary. Notice how the suffix influences the meaning of the word! The first word has been filled out for you.

WORD	SUFFIX MEANING	DEFINITION OF WORD
manage<u>able</u>	*able: capable of*	*able to be managed or controlled*
critic<u>ize</u>		
apti<u>tude</u>		
aer<u>ate</u>		
defens<u>ible</u>		
futil<u>ity</u>		
ten<u>sion</u>		
triumph<u>ant</u>		
eco<u>logy</u>		

CHALLENGE TACTIC: PUTTING IT ALL TOGETHER

Now that you know the meaning of some common roots, prefixes, and suffixes, let's look at how you would break down a complicated word with several of these parts in combination. For example, consider the word COLLABORATE. You probably know that this word means "to work together," but did you know that you could break it into a prefix, root, and suffix?

- "col" is a prefix that means "with"
- "labor" is a root that means "work"
- "ate" is a suffix that turns a word into a verb

Therefore, we can break down COLLABORATE as follows:

COL + LABOR + ATE

↑   ↑   ↑

with   *work*   *verb*

From these parts, we see that COLLABORATE is a verb that literally means to work with someone else.

Exercise #4: Look at the list of roots, prefixes, and suffixes at the end of this section. Use this information or your own knowledge to break the following words into parts and guess at their combined meaning. Then, check your answer with the answer key at the end of the book. The first word has been filled in for you.

#	WORD	WORD PARTS	MEANING
1.	prenatal	*pre + nat + al*	*before birth (adjective)*
2.	inaudible		
3.	amorphous		
4.	synchronize		
5.	rejuvenate		
6.	incredulous		
7.	ambivalent		

8.	philanthropy		
9.	vivisection		
10.	retrospective		

COMMON WORD ROOTS, PREFIXES, AND SUFFIXES

Here is a list of some of the most common roots, prefixes, and suffixes that make up words in the English language. Remember that roots carry a word's basic meaning, prefixes come before a root and change its meaning, and suffixes come at the end of words and tell you whether they are nouns, verbs, adjectives, or adverbs. Start learning some of these basic word parts to cement your vocabulary knowledge and help decipher new, unfamiliar vocabulary.

COMMON ROOTS		
ag, act	do	action, activity, agent
ambul	walk, move	ambulance, ambulatory, amble
ami, amo	love	amiable, amorous
anim	mind, soul, spirit	animal, animate, unanimous
anthro	human	anthropology, philanthropy
aud, audit	hear	audible, auditorium, audience
auto	self	automobile, autobiography, autograph
belli	war	belligerent, rebellious, bellicose
ben	good	benefactor, beneficial, benevolence
biblio	book	bibliography, Bible
bio	life	biography, biology
carn	flesh, meat	carnivore, carnal, incarnate
chron	time	chronic, chronology, synchronize
cid, cis	cut, kill	incision, homicide, insecticide
civi	citizen	civilization, civilian, civil

corp	body	corporation, corporeal, corpse
dem	people	democracy, demographic
dic, dict	speak	dictate, contradict, prediction, verdict
domin	master	dominant, domain, domineering
err	wander	error, erratic, errand
eu	good, beautiful	eulogize, euphoria, euphemism
fall, fals	deceive	fallacious, infallible, falsify
fid	faith	fidelity, confide, confidence
graph, gram	writing	grammar, telegram, graphite
loqu, locut	talk	soliloquy, loquacious, elocution
luc	light	elucidate, lucid, translucent
magn	great	magnify, magnate, magnanimous
mal	bad	malevolent, malediction, malicious
mori, mort	die	mortuary, immortal, moribund
morph	shape, form	amorphous, metamorphosis
nat	born	innate, natal, nativity
nom	name	misnomer, nominal
nov	new	novice, innovate, renovate, novelty
omni	all	omniscient, omnipotent, omnivorous
pac, pas, pax	peace	pacify, pacific, pacifist, passive
path, pass	disease, feeling	pathology, sympathetic, apathy, antipathy

phil	love	philanthropist, philosophy, philanderer
port	carry	portable, porter, transport, export
poten	able, powerful	potential, omnipotent, potentate, impotent
psych	mind	psyche, psychology, psychosis, psychopath
reg, rect	rule	regicide, regime, regent, insurrection
sacr, secr	holy	sacred, sacrilegious, sacrament, consecrate
scribe, script	write	scribe, describe, script
somn	sleep	insomnia, somnolent, somnambulist
spec, spic	see, look	spectators, spectacles, retrospect, conspicuous
tang, tact, ting	touch	tactile, tangent, contact, contingent
terr	land	terrain, terrestrial, subterranean
urb	city	urban, urbane, suburban
vac	empty	vacation, vacuous, evacuate, vacant
ver	truth	veracity, verify, veracious
verb	word	verbose, verbatim, proverb
viv, vit	alive	revival, vivacious, vitality

COMMON PREFIXES		
ambi, amphi	both	ambidextrous, ambiguous, ambivalent
an, a	without	anarchy, anemia, amoral
anti	against	antibody, antipathy, antisocial

Ivy Global

circum	around	circumnavigate, circumspect, circumscribe
co, col, com, con	with, together	coauthor, collaborate, composition, commerce
contra, contro	against	contradict, contravene, controversy
di, dif, dis	not, apart	digress, discord, differ, disparity
dia	through, across	diagonal, diameter, dialogue
dys	abnormal, bad	dysfunction, dyslexia, dystopia
e, ex, extra, extro	out, beyond	expel, excavate, eject, extrovert
in, il, im, ir (1)	not	inefficient, inarticulate, illegible, irrepressible
in, il, im, ir (2)	in, upon	invite, incite, impression, illuminate
inter	between, among	intervene, international, interjection, intercept
intra	within	intramural, introvert, intravenous
mis	bad, hatred	misdemeanor, mischance, misanthrope
mono	one	monarchy, monologue, monotheism
non	not, without	noncommittal, nonentity, nondescript
pan	all, every	panacea, panorama, pandemic
peri	around, near	perimeter, periphery, periscope
poly	many	polygon, polygamist, polyglot
post	after	postpone, posterity, postscript, posthumous
pre	before	preamble, prefix, premonition, prediction

pro	forward, for, before	propulsive, proponent, prologue, prophet
re, retro	again, back	reiterate, reimburse, react, retrogress
sub, suc, sup, sus	under, less	subway, subjugate, suppress
super, sur	over, above	superior, supernatural, supervise, surtax
syn, sym, syl , sys	with, together	symmetry, synchronize, synthesize, sympathize
trans	across	transfer, transport, transpose
un	not	unabridged, unkempt, unwitting

COMMON SUFFIXES		
able, ible	ADJ: capable of	edible, presentable, legible
ac, ic, ical	ADJ: like, related	cardiac, mythic, dramatic, musical
acious, icious	ADJ: full of	malicious, audacious
ant, ent	ADJ/N: full of	eloquent, verdant
ate	V: make, become	consecrate, enervate, eradicate
en	V: make, become	awaken, strengthen, soften
er (1)	ADJ: more	bigger, wiser, happier
er (2)	N: a person who does	teacher, baker, announcer
cy, ty, ity	N: state of being	democracy, accuracy, veracity
ful	ADJ: full of	respectful, cheerful, wonderful
fy	V: to make	magnify, petrify, beautify
ism	N: doctrine, belief	monotheism, fanaticism, egotism

Ivy Global

ist	N: dealer, doer	fascist, realist, artist
ize, ise	V: make	victimize, rationalize, harmonize
logy	N: study of	biology, geology, neurology
oid	ADJ: resembling	ovoid, anthropoid, spheroid
ose/ous	ADJ: full of	verbose, lachrymose, nauseous, gaseous
osis	N: condition	psychosis, neurosis, hypnosis
tion, sion	N: state of being	exasperation, irritation, transition, concession
tude	N: state of	fortitude, beatitude, certitude

ISEE CORE VOCABULARY

SECTION 3

The following words will help you prepare for the vocabulary you will encounter on the Lower, Middle, and Upper levels of the ISEE. These words are sorted by subject category to help you learn groups of words with similar or related definitions. When you learn a word, pay attention to its part of speech (is it a noun, verb, adjective, or adverb?) and to other possible definitions of the word. Although any of these words might appear on any level of the ISEE, younger students may want to focus on the less difficult vocabulary first before tackling more challenging words.

Use this section as a study aid and write your own personal sentence for each word to help you remember it. To help cement your learning, try making separate flashcards for each word, writing the word on the front, and writing all of its definitions and your own personal sentence on the back. In order to master as many words as possible before your ISEE exam, create a daily schedule and make sure to review old words while you are learning new ones.

#	WORD	LEVEL	DEFINITION	SAMPLE SENTENCE	GROUP
1	colleague	6	N: a co-worker or fellow classmate	The young doctor impressed his colleagues with the difficult diagnosis.	Relationships & Emotions
2	compatible	7	ADJ: capable of getting along well with other people or things	George and Larry seem to have compatible personalities, as they get along quite well.	Relationships & Emotions

3	accommodate	8	V: (1) to be agreeable, acceptable, suitable, (2) to adapt. ADJ: accommodating	(1) This table is meant to accommodate six diners. (2) Jose worked to accommodate himself to the difficult economic times.	Relationships & Emotions
4	amiable	10	ADJ: friendly, kind, likeable	Kelly was an amiable hostess, friendly and welcoming to all of her guests.	Relationships & Emotions
5	congenial	10	ADJ: friendly, sociable, suited to one's needs	The college aimed to create a congenial atmosphere for both professors and students.	Relationships & Emotions
6	aloof	10	ADJ: emotionally distant	The grandfather was generally aloof and uninterested in playing with his grandchildren.	Relationships & Emotions
7	nonchalant	9	ADJ: casual, calm, unconcerned	The mayor's nonchalant attitude toward the disaster lost him many supporters.	Relationships & Emotions
8	apathetic	8	ADJ: showing no interest or concern. N: apathy	Politicians are wondering why voters are so apathetic this election year.	Relationships & Emotions
9	indifferent	8	ADJ: showing no interest or concern. N: indifference	I really don't care where we go for dinner tonight—I am entirely indifferent.	Relationships & Emotions
10	sentimental	6	ADJ: very emotional	Although he had long outgrown it, Neil felt a sentimental attachment to his baby blanket.	Relationships & Emotions

11	hysterical	8	ADJ: having excessive and uncontrollable emotion. N: hysteria	When she heard the news, Susan reacted with hysterical sobbing.	Relationships & Emotions
12	benevolent	10	ADJ: kind, generous. N: benevolence	Queen Elizabeth was a benevolent ruler, generous and responsive to the needs of her people.	Relationships & Emotions
13	compassionate	5	ADJ: kind, sympathetic. N: compassion	Mrs. White was a firm instructor but also compassionate towards her students.	Relationships & Emotions
14	empathy	6	N: an understanding of the feelings of others. ADJ: empathetic	Caring and considerate, Liam always expressed deep empathy towards others.	Relationships & Emotions
15	charismatic	8	ADJ: charming. N: charisma	With his naturally magnetic and charming personality, he was a charismatic leader.	Relationships & Emotions
16	engaging	6	ADJ: interesting, charming, attractive	The students found the hands-on activity more engaging than simply reading a textbook.	Relationships & Emotions
17	gracious	7	ADJ: charming, generous, polite	Always a good sport, the losing player was still gracious in defeat.	Relationships & Emotions
18	courteous	6	ADJ: polite. N: courtesy	The staff was courteous and helpful when asked for advice.	Relationships & Emotions

19	cordial	9	ADJ: polite, friendly	The president extended a cordial invitation to the Chinese and Korean ambassadors.	Relationships & Emotions
20	tact	7	N: consideration and sensitivity in dealing with others. ADJ: tactful	Diplomats must display tact when dealing with sensitive issues between nations.	Relationships & Emotions
21	emulate	8	V: to copy or imitate, to look up to	An excellent team player, Christine is a role model whom everyone should emulate.	Relationships & Emotions
22	flatter	6	V: to praise excessively or dishonestly. N: flattery	At first flattered by his employee's compliments, the boss realized that she was only angling for a pay raise.	Relationships & Emotions
23	fidelity	8	N: faithfulness, loyalty	The knight served his king with utmost fidelity.	Relationships & Emotions
24	steadfast	8	ADJ: determined, loyal, steady	Maria's steadfast commitment to the cause won her great recognition.	Relationships & Emotions
25	fickle	7	ADJ: not reliable or dependable, changing opinions frequently	The fans were fickle, abandoning the team whenever it began to lose.	Relationships & Emotions
26	headstrong	6	ADJ: stubborn, disobedient	Elizabeth showed a headstrong determination to do things her own way.	Relationships & Emotions

27	obstinate	8	ADJ: stubborn, disobedient. N: obstinacy	Despite evidence to the contrary, Alex obstinately refused to admit he had made a mistake.	Relationships & Emotions
28	exasperate	6	V: to annoy, irritate. ADJ: exasperating	The mother was exasperated by her daughter's whining.	Relationships & Emotions
29	infuriate	7	V: to anger or enrage. ADJ: infuriating	The judge's decision against him infuriated the defendant.	Relationships & Emotions
30	indignant	10	ADJ: outraged, angry at something unjust.	The new ruling inspired an onslaught of indignant letters of protest.	Relationships & Emotions
31	mock	6	V: to ridicule or make fun of. N: mockery	When her neighbors painted their house bright pink, Quinn unfairly mocked their color choice.	Relationships & Emotions
32	malicious	7	ADJ: intending to harm or cause suffering. N: malice	Jenny was deeply hurt by the malicious rumors spread about her.	Relationships & Emotions
33	exploit	6	(1) V: to take advantage of, (2) N: a bold action or deed	(1) The drug company exploited the system by abusing the patients' trust. (2) The daring exploits of Robin Hood are legendary.	Relationships & Emotions
34	belittle	7	V: to put someone down, to express a negative opinion	Mary refused to be belittled by the school bully, and she stood up to his unkind actions.	Relationships & Emotions

35	jeer	7	V: to laugh at with scorn, N: a scornful laugh	Ryan and Alim got in trouble for jeering at a classmate who made a mistake.	Relationships & Emotions
36	snub	8	V: to behave coldly towards, to ignore	Mary could not understand why her friends now snubbed her and ignored her in the hall.	Relationships & Emotions
37	condescend	6	V: to look down on, to display arrogance. ADJ: condescending	The arrogant judge finally condescended to speak with the poor woman.	Relationships & Emotions
38	disdain	6	N: arrogance, scorn, V: to display scorn. ADJ: disdainful	The criminal showed disdain for the law.	Relationships & Emotions
39	hypocrite	7	N: someone who says one thing and does another. ADJ: hypocritical	Sam's father forced all of his children to eat their vegetables, but he hypocritically never ate his own.	Relationships & Emotions
40	admonish	8	V: to scold or warn strongly	The players were admonished for not paying close enough attention during the game.	Relationships & Emotions
41	reprimand	8	(1) V: to scold or warn strongly, (2) N: a strong warning	(1) The policeman reprimanded the careless driver but did not issue a ticket. (2) The student received a strong reprimand from the teacher for forgetting his homework.	Relationships & Emotions

42	vivacious	9	ADJ: lively, spirited	Catherine's vivacious and enthusiastic personality made her a great team member.	Relationships & Emotions
43	animated	7	ADJ: lively, spirited. N: animation	She approached the challenge with an energetic, animated attitude.	Relationships & Emotions
44	extrovert	8	N: a sociable, outgoing person. ADJ: extroverted	Outgoing and sociable, Elaine is a true extrovert.	Relationships & Emotions
45	introvert	8	N: a person who has a quiet, reserved personality. ADJ: introverted	James is friendly but introverted, keeping his thoughts and feelings to himself.	Relationships & Emotions
46	reserved	8	ADJ: quiet, shy, not showing one's feelings. N: reservation	Mark is a reserved person, not likely to share his feelings openly.	Relationships & Emotions
47	timid	6	ADJ: shy, lacking confidence	The timid animals ran away as we approached.	Relationships & Emotions
48	meek	7	ADJ: humble, tame	Despite his meek attitude, he was actually a courageous opponent.	Relationships & Emotions
49	docile	9	ADJ: obedient, tame	Sarah was a docile and obedient student who never questioned what the teacher said.	Relationships & Emotions
50	subdued	8	ADJ: quiet, low-key, hushed. V: subdue	The painting should be displayed in a room with soft, subdued lighting.	Relationships & Emotions

Ivy Global

51	submissive	7	ADJ: giving in to orders, obedient. V: submit	Nova was an overly submissive dog, easily dominated by more assertive animals.	Relationships & Emotions
52	passive	8	ADJ: lacking in energy or will, submissive	Gordon is a passive group member, preferring to let others take charge and make decisions.	Relationships & Emotions
53	cynical	8	ADJ: believing the worst about people or events	Many young voters are cynical about politicians and their campaign promises.	Overcoming Obstacles
54	dejected	9	ADJ: depressed, sad. N: dejection	Eric was dejected after hearing the bad news.	Overcoming Obstacles
55	initiate	6	V: to begin	Customers can use the online forum to initiate discussion about the product.	Overcoming Obstacles
56	fatigue	7	N: exhaustion, tiredness. ADJ: fatigued	After his third night with little sleep, Michael suffered from severe fatigue.	Overcoming Obstacles
57	feeble	6	ADJ: weak, faint, lacking strength	Aaron gave a rather feeble excuse for why he forgot his homework.	Overcoming Obstacles
58	diligent	7	ADJ: steadily persevering to complete a task. N: diligence	Mary is a diligent student, studying every day to improve her grades.	Overcoming Obstacles

59	industrial	7	ADJ: of or relating to production and manufacturing. N: industry	Factories and new inventions boomed during the Industrial Revolution.	Overcoming Obstacles
60	valiant	8	ADJ: showing courage or determination. N: valor	Although it was defeated, the team made a valiant effort during the soccer match.	Overcoming Obstacles
61	resolute	7	ADJ: determined, firm, unyielding. N/V: resolve	Martia's hard work and resolute determination earned her great success in her career.	Overcoming Obstacles
62	emphatic	7	ADJ: forceful, spoken with emphasis	When asked whether he would change his mind, Peter made an emphatic refusal.	Overcoming Obstacles
63	endeavor	7	V: to make an attempt, N: an attempt	Scientists are currently endeavoring to find a cure for cancer.	Overcoming Obstacles
64	endure	5	V: to suffer, to put up with something unpleasant. N: endurance	Residents of Siberia have to endure extremely cold, dark winters.	Overcoming Obstacles
65	withstand	7	V: to resist, to stand up to something	Strong as they were, the walls of the fortress could not withstand the attack.	Overcoming Obstacles
66	resilient	8	ADJ: springing back, recovering quickly. N: resilience	Policemen have to be resilient in order to cope with and bounce back from the stress of their work.	Overcoming Obstacles

Ivy Global

67	robust	9	ADJ: strong, sturdy	There are few plants robust enough to survive the Arctic climate.	Overcoming Obstacles
68	pragmatic	9	ADJ: practical, useful. N: pragmatist	The software's pragmatic design was intended to make it easier to use.	Overcoming Obstacles
69	fret	8	V: to worry unnecessarily	Relax, enjoy, and don't fret the small stuff!	Overcoming Obstacles
70	adversity	8	N: hardship, difficulty, misfortune. ADJ: adverse	Martin Luther King, Jr. had to overcome great adversity in his struggle for racial equality.	Overcoming Obstacles
71	plight	7	N: a difficult or extremely unpleasant situation	After the earthquake, the world was concerned about the plight of the citizens of Haiti.	Overcoming Obstacles
72	predicament	6	N: a difficult or extremely unpleasant situation	The doctor was faced with a difficult predicament: how could he treat the patient's infection if the patient was allergic to antibiotics?	Overcoming Obstacles
73	rigor	8	N: something very hard to endure. ADJ: rigorous	The rigorous curriculum was designed to challenge the students and teach them how to manage a heavy workload.	Overcoming Obstacles
74	strenuous	7	ADJ: requiring hard effort or energy	Mountain climbing is a strenuous activity, requiring strength as well as endurance.	Overcoming Obstacles

75	toil	6	V: to labor, to work hard, N: hard work	At noon, the farmhands came back for lunch and a chance to rest from their toil under the hot sun.	Overcoming Obstacles
76	tedious	8	ADJ: boring, tiring, long	The chapters in the textbook were long and stuffed with so much information that they were tedious to read.	Overcoming Obstacles
77	trek	6	N: a very long journey on foot, V: to go on a long journey on foot	The guide took us on a long trek through the jungle in order to reach the village.	Overcoming Obstacles
78	grimace	7	N: a facial expression indicating pain, V: to contort one's face in pain	We grimaced as the frigid gust of December air whipped across our faces.	Overcoming Obstacles
79	wince	6	V: to flinch in fear or pain	Jose winced as the doctor touched his swollen, bruised ankle.	Overcoming Obstacles
80	daunting	8	ADJ: discouraging, inspiring fear	Balancing the budget appeared a daunting task, but it was the new president's goal.	Overcoming Obstacles
81	bleak	6	ADJ: hopeless, depressing, bare	After the stock market crash, the future of the economy looked bleak.	Overcoming Obstacles
82	dread	5	N: great fear, terror, V: to feel great fear or terror	The students dreaded the approaching exam week.	Overcoming Obstacles

83	grim	7	ADJ: (1) gloomy, dark, bleak, (2) relentless, unyielding	(1) The earthquake destroyed the village so thoroughly that its hopes of recovery look grim. (2) With grim determination, he plodded forward through the blowing snow.	Overcoming Obstacles
84	ail	8	V: to be ill or unwell. N: ailment	The government proposed a bailout to rescue the ailing car manufacturers.	Overcoming Obstacles
85	deteriorate	6	V: to become worse, to disintegrate	The abandoned house had deteriorated after years of exposure to harsh weather.	Overcoming Obstacles
86	falter	8	V: to be unsteady or weak, to stumble	After keeping up his pace for ten kilometers, the runner began to falter.	Overcoming Obstacles
87	relinquish	6	V: to give up, abandon, release	After several days of bombardments, the rebels relinquished control of the military base.	Overcoming Obstacles
88	concede	9	V: (1) to yield or surrender, to give in, (2) to admit to be true. N: concession	(1) The losing candidate graciously conceded defeat and congratulated his opponent. (2) The journalist conceded that his report may have been influenced by his own personal opinions.	Overcoming Obstacles

89	pessimist	6	N: a person who expects a bad outcome. ADJ: pessimistic	Always a pessimist, Andrew expected to fail the test.	Overcoming Obstacles
90	optimist	6	N: a person who expects a good outcome. ADJ: optimistic	Despite the rough start to the season, the coach was optimistic about the team's improvement.	Overcoming Obstacles
91	versatile	7	ADJ: having a wide variety of skills, flexible. N: versatility	Susan was a versatile actress, able to adapt easily from theatre to film acting.	Overcoming Obstacles
92	apt	8	ADJ: able, skillful, fitting. N: aptitude	The poems are accompanied by humorous and apt illustrations.	Overcoming Obstacles
93	capacity	7	N: (1) the capability to perform, produce, or hold, (2) the maximum amount that can be produced or held	(1) With continued training, Mark will have the capacity to win the 100 meter dash. (2) The theatre has a capacity of 450 audience members.	Overcoming Obstacles
94	merit	6	N: (1) excellence in achievement or performance, (2) deserving of aid or recognition. V: to deserve aid or recognition	(1) Scholarships will be given based on financial need and academic merit. (2) The environmental program merits further consideration by the government.	Overcoming Obstacles

95	surpass	7	V: to exceed	With their popular new blockbuster, the filmmakers aim to surpass their previous record of success.	Overcoming Obstacles
96	feat	7	N: a great achievement	The heroes were rewarded for their feats of bravery.	Overcoming Obstacles
97	exuberance	8	N: joyful enthusiasm. ADJ: exuberant	HIs youthful exuberance always keeps his parents on their toes.	Overcoming Obstacles
98	bliss	8	N: extreme happiness. ADJ: blissful	As the child stuffed the cake into his mouth, his face showed pure bliss.	Overcoming Obstacles
99	ecstasy	8	N: extreme happiness. ADJ: ecstatic	For some, sky-diving is ecstasy; for me, it is terrifying.	Overcoming Obstacles
100	elation	8	N: extreme happiness. ADJ: elated	The elation you feel when you cross the finish lIne makes running a marathon worth all the difficulty.	Overcoming Obstacles
101	jubilation	8	N: extreme happiness. ADJ: jubilant	When the team scored the winning goal, the crowd exploded with jubilation.	Overcoming Obstacles
102	awe	6	N: wonder, respect, admiration	We felt a sense of awe as we gazed at the Grand Canyon.	Overcoming Obstacles

103	acclaim	9	N: praise, approval. V: to praise or approve	The author's first novel received widespread public acclaim, and we eagerly await her second book.	Overcoming Obstacles
104	exalt	9	V: to praise, glorify, honor, to heighten. N: exaltation	Salvador Dali's paintings are works of art that exalt the imagination.	Overcoming Obstacles
105	astute	10	ADJ: intelligent, smart, sharp	Michael was an astute businessman with an excellent sense of timing.	Language & Intellect
106	keen	6	ADJ: (1) sharp, intelligent, (2) cutting, painful, (3) eager	(1) Jordan's keen eyesight was able to spot the eagle from many yards away. (2) Having not eaten for many days, the prisoner felt a keen pang of hunger. (3) We are keen to hear the report from the new committee.	Language & Intellect
107	methodical	7	ADJ: in a careful, organized manner	The experiment was conducted in a very organized, methodical fashion.	Language & Intellect
108	meticulous	9	ADJ: paying strict attention to detail	Amy was meticulous about hygiene and took every precaution to keep her house sanitized.	Language & Intellect
109	impeccable	9	ADJ: perfect, without fault	The intensive music course helped Gregory develop an impeccable sense of rhythm.	Language & Intellect

110	immaculate	9	ADJ: without fault or error, completely clean or perfect	The new car looked immaculate sitting in the driveway; it was shining and spotless.	Language & Intellect
111	omniscient	9	ADJ: all-knowing, infinitely wise. N: omniscience	Many religions believe in an omniscient, all-knowing god.	Language & Intellect
112	profound	8	ADJ: deep, significant, important	The Battle of Gettysburg had a profound effect on the rest of the Civil War.	Language & Intellect
113	superficial	8	ADJ: not deep, not significant	The wound was only superficial and did not require stitches.	Language & Intellect
114	prolific	10	ADJ: producing a lot of offspring or materials quickly	Karen was a prolific writer and published a new book almost every year.	Language & Intellect
115	ornament	6	N: a decoration, V: to decorate.	The shield was ornamented with gold and gemstones.	Language & Intellect
116	embellish	7	V: (1) to decorate or add detail to, (2) to make something look or sound better than it actually is	(1) The scarf was embellished with embroidery and beads. (2) Tony said he hadn't actually lied, but had only embellished the truth.	Language & Intellect
117	ornate	8	ADJ: flowery, highly decorated or ornamented	The castle's ornate decorations were overwhelming.	Language & Intellect
118	vivid	5	ADJ: bright, striking, intense, graphic	Vincent Van Gogh used vivid yellows, oranges and reds in his paintings.	Language & Intellect

119	thesis	7	N: the central argument that an author proves through evidence	The thesis of the essay argued that technology makes our lives easier but not necessarily better.	Language & Intellect
120	ambivalent	10	ADJ: having mixed feelings about a topic or a person. N: ambivalence	Leo felt ambivalent towards his newborn baby sister, unsure whether he liked the new addition to the family.	Language & Intellect
121	articulate	8	(1) V: to put into words, (2) ADJ: well-spoken, using elegant language	(1) Overwhelmed by emotion, Samantha struggled to articulate what she was feeling. (2) Abraham Lincoln was a highly articulate and persuasive speaker.	Language & Intellect
122	eloquent	8	ADJ: well-spoken, using elegant language. N: eloquence	The author's eloquent language makes the novel a pleasure to read.	Language & Intellect
123	monotonous	7	ADJ: flat, all the same, lacking in variety. N: monotony	Nobody likes to listen to flat, monotonous voices.	Language & Intellect
124	concise	7	ADJ: brief and to the point. N: concision	Good writers avoid wordiness and use concise language to make their point.	Language & Intellect
125	succinct	8	ADJ: brief and to the point	Your summary should be succinct and should not exceed 200 words.	Language & Intellect

126	elaborate	6	V: to add detail to, to make complex, ADJ: complex, detailed	As his story began to unravel, Joseph's elaborate lie was revealed.	Language & Intellect
127	redundant	7	ADJ: more than is needed, overly repetitive. N: redundancy	The phrase "past history" is redundant and should be avoided.	Language & Intellect
128	extraneous	8	ADJ: extra, unnecessary	Monica cleared all of the extraneous clothes out of her closet.	Language & Intellect
129	cliché	6	N: an overused phrase or remark	The phrase "to think outside the box" is a cliché and is highly overused.	Language & Intellect
130	vulgar	8	ADJ: coarse, common, rude N: vulgarity	Edward was sent to the principal's office for his vulgar behavior.	Language & Intellect
131	profane	7	ADJ: rude, vulgar, unholy. N: profanity	The book was banned from school libraries for its profane language.	Language & Intellect
132	coherent	7	ADJ: logical and orderly. N: coherence	The play had a highly coherent plot, making it easy for the audience to follow.	Language & Intellect
133	legible	6	ADJ: able to be read	Work to keep your handwriting clear and legible.	Language & Intellect
134	cite	8	V: to mention, make reference to. N: citation	In a research paper, it is important to cite the sources you use.	Language & Intellect

135	document	7	(1) V: to record in detail, (2) N: writing that provides information	(1) The film documents the devastation and recovery efforts of the Philippines after the recent typhoon. (2) A contract is a document that outlines a legal agreement between two parties.	Language & Intellect
136	inquire	7	V: to ask about. N: inquiry	The doctor inquired about the medical history of the patient.	Language & Intellect
137	orate	8	V: to give a speech. N: oration, orator	Stephen was a fine orator who could make even the longest speech interesting.	Language & Intellect
138	monologue	7	N: a dramatic speech by one character	Drama students applying to the program must memorize and recite a monologue.	Language & Intellect
139	soliloquy	9	N: a speech where a character talks out loud to himself	Hamlet's speech to himself is one of Shakespeare's most recognizable soliloquies.	Language & Intellect
140	prologue	7	N: an introduction to a play or book	The novel's prologue sets the scene and provides interesting background information.	Language & Intellect
141	epilogue	7	N: a short piece of writing at the end of a play or book	In the story's epilogue, we see a glimpse of the characters' lives thirty years in the future.	Language & Intellect

142	excerpt	7	N: a selection from a larger literary work. V: to take a selection from a larger work	The Critical Reading portion of the test contains many excerpts from short stories and poems.	Language & Intellect
143	synopsis	7	N: a summary or outline	Can you give a short synopsis of the movie's plot without spoiling the ending for me?	Language & Intellect
144	genre	8	N: a style of literature or art	Students must identify the genre of the passage and answer questions about style.	Language & Intellect
145	memoir	7	N: an autobiography	At the age of 80, Grandma decided it was time to write her memoir.	Language & Intellect
146	narrative	6	N: a story V: narrate	Dickens's Christmas Carol is a narrative of greed, sorrow, and making amends.	Language & Intellect
147	epic	6	(1) N: a very long poem about a hero's adventures, (2) ADJ: long and impressive	(1) Homer's Odyssey is an epic about the adventures of Odysseus. (2) Frodo Baggins undertook an epic journey to Mount Doom.	Language & Intellect
148	saga	7	N: a story telling the adventures of a hero	The Vikings enjoyed playing music and telling sagas of their gods and heroes.	Language & Intellect

149	parody	9	N: a spoof, a humorous imitation	"Weird Al" Yankovic creates parodies of popular songs.	Language & Intellect
150	protagonist	7	N: the main character in a story	Leonardo DiCaprio played the protagonist in the movie *Inception*.	Language & Intellect
151	metaphor	7	N: a poetic or symbolic comparison between two objects or ideas. ADJ: metaphorical	The poem used the metaphor of the changing seasons to represent human life and death.	Language & Intellect
152	parallel	6	ADJ: (1) similar, related, (2) not intersecting	(1) The newspaper noticed that the two wars were strikingly parallel. (2) The pinstripe tie had a pattern of parallel lines.	Language & Intellect
153	abstract	7	(1) ADJ: existing only in ideas or theory, not concrete, (2) a short summary of a scientific article	(1) The only way to test an abstract theory is to put it into practice in the real world. (2) The scientists submitted an abstract of their experiment to the journal.	Language & Intellect
154	anonymous	7	ADJ: having no name or known identity	The police received an anonymous phone call with information about the crime.	Language & Intellect
155	counsel	9	(1) V: to give advice. (2) N: advice	(1) The Cabinet counsels the President on issues of domestic and international policy. (2) The elders provided wise counsel to the young leaders.	Law & Politics

156	advocate	8	(1) V: to argue in favor of a person or idea, (2) N: someone who supports a person or idea	(1) Health experts advocate moderation when consuming alcohol. (2) He has a strong reputation as an advocate for women's and children's rights.	Law & Politics
157	champion	6	(1) N: a hero, someone who holds first place. (2) V: to fight for a cause	(1) The Junior Girls Volleyball Team was the district champion this year. (2) Susan B. Anthony championed early on the cause of women's rights.	Law & Politics
158	contemplation	7	N: long and thoughtful observation. V: contemplate	The poet spent a week in the wilderness in the contemplation of nature's beauty.	Law & Politics
159	objective	6	(1) ADJ: based on evidence, not influenced by personal experience or emotion, (2) N: a goal	(1) The scientists were asked to provide objective evidence for their claims. (2) The team's objective was to score more goals in the second half.	Law & Politics
160	subjective	6	ADJ: based on personal experience or emotion	The critic gave her subjective opinion of the painting, explaining her personal feelings about its style and subject matter.	Law & Politics
161	bias	5	N: prejudice, unequal favor to one side, V: to make prejudiced. ADJ: biased	The judge was accused of being biased in his decision.	Law & Politics

162	legislate	7	V: to pass a law. N: legislation	The committee legislated the new health care reform bill.	Law & Politics
163	ratify	8	V: to formally approve, sign off on. N: ratification	192 nations have formally ratified the Kyoto Protocol on climate change.	Law & Politics
164	decree	7	V: to order, N: an order	The king decreed that no commoner would be allowed to wear purple, the color of royalty.	Law & Politics
165	coerce	8	V: to force someone to do something through threats and intimidation. N: coercion	The king coerced his citizens into paying higher taxes.	Law & Politics
166	comply	8	V: to act according to someone's laws or commands	Robin Hood refused to comply with King John's harsh tax policy.	Law & Politics
167	censor	7	V: to forbid the distribution of material considered harmful or inappropriate	Wartime letters are censored to remove sensitive military information.	Law & Politics
168	prohibit	6	V: to ban or forbid. N: prohibition	School rules prohibit the use of cell phones during class.	Law & Politics
169	felon	6	N: someone who has been convicted of a serious crime	The notorious felon was sentenced to life in prison.	Law & Politics
170	lethal	5	ADJ: deadly	Chocolate can be lethal to dogs.	Law & Politics

171	plead	7	V: to humbly request help. N: plea	Knowing he was defeated, the enemy knight pleaded for mercy.	Law & Politics
172	pardon	6	V: to forgive, N: formal forgiveness	The convict was ordered to kneel before the king and beg pardon for his crime.	Law & Politics
173	condone	8	V: to forgive or excuse	The teacher could not condone such rude behavior in her classroom.	Law & Politics
174	thwart	9	V: to prevent someone from doing something	George's parents thwarted his winter vacation plans by insisting that he study for three hours every day.	Law & Politics
175	mediate	10	V: to resolve differences between conflicting sides. N: mediator	The U.N. sent peacekeepers to mediate between the warring groups.	Law & Politics
176	righteous	8	ADJ: following just and moral principles. N: righteousness	Defending the homeless man was a righteous act.	Law & Politics
177	virtuous	6	ADJ: morally excellent	A truly virtuous person performs acts of kindness for their own sake, not for recognition.	Law & Politics
178	notorious	8	ADJ: having a bad reputation, well-known for bad reasons	The government was notorious for its human rights abuses.	Law & Politics

179	repress	8	V: to put down by force or intimidation N: repression, ADJ: repressive	The government was quick to repress the rebellion.	Law & Politics
180	oppress	7	V: to keep down by force or authority. N: oppression, ADJ: oppressive	Many countries around the world still oppress their citizens and deny them their rights.	Law & Politics
181	authoritarian	9	ADJ: requiring absolute obedience, enforcing strong or oppressive policies	The authoritarian government restricted public debate and opposition.	Law & Politics
182	tyrant	8	N: a cruel and oppressive ruler. ADJ: tyrannical	Hitler is known as one of the most ruthless tyrants of the 20th century.	Law & Politics
183	lax	8	ADJ: loose, not strict. N: lassitude	A lax attitude towards airport security could put all passengers in danger.	Law & Politics
184	resign	8	V: (1) to accept a hopeless situation, (2) to step down from a position of power. N: resignation, ADJ: resigned	(1) As the game came to a close, the team resigned itself to defeat. (2) Richard Nixon was the first US President to resign from office.	Law & Politics
185	endorse	9	V: to give support or approval N: endorsement	The board endorsed the decisions recommended by the paper.	Law & Politics
186	novice	7	N: a beginner	Although a novice to the sport, Sarah showed a great potential for soccer.	Law & Politics

Ivy Global

187	naïve	8	ADJ: inexperienced, lacking knowledge of the world. N: naïveté	The citizens were naïve to believe that the new mayor would be better than the old one.	Law & Politics
188	diplomacy	8	N: negotiations between nations or groups. ADJ: diplomatic	Peacemakers hoped that successful diplomacy would keep the two countries from going to war.	Law & Politics
189	allegiance	6	N: loyalty, commitment	In order to gain citizenship, immigrants must pledge allegiance to their new country.	Law & Politics
190	intervene	6	V: to come between or get involved, often to prevent an action N: intervention	When the industry was on the brink of failure, the government intervened to save the economy.	Law & Politics
191	autonomous	9	ADJ: independent, self-ruling. N: autonomy	India became an autonomous nation in 1947 after many years of British rule.	Law & Politics
192	sovereign	8	(1) N: a ruler or head of government. (2) ADJ: independent, self-ruling. N: sovereignty	(1) The Queen is the sovereign of Britian, but today she has a mostly ceremonial role. (2) The United States Constitution united the sovereign states into one federal government.	Law & Politics
193	convene	7	V: to gather, to hold a meeting N: convention	The committee will convene every month.	Law & Politics

194	converge	9	V: to come together	The city was founded where the two rivers converged.	Law & Politics
195	consensus	7	N: general agreement	The jury arrived at the consensus that the defendant was guilty.	Law & Politics
196	dissent	8	(1) V: to protest or disagree. (2) N: disagreement or protest	(1) The jury was almost unanimous in their decision; only one juror dissented. (2) A strong democratic government should be able to tolerate non-violent dissent.	Law & Politics
197	transgress	8	V: to violate a law, boundary, or duty. N: transgression	The leader was accused of transgressing the appropriate limits of his power.	Law & Politics
198	explicit	7	ADJ: very specifically and clearly stated	Parents must give their explicit consent for students to attend the field trip.	Law & Politics
199	overt	8	ADJ: open and observable, not secret or concealed	There was overt hostility between the two leaders; it was clear that they hated each other.	Law & Politics
200	negligent	9	ADJ: neglectful, careless, irresponsible. N: negligence	Alan demonstrated negligent behavior by talking on his cell phone while driving.	Law & Politics
201	inadvertent	9	ADJ: accidental, unintentional	Susan was embarrassed when she inadvertently mispronounced the teacher's name.	Law & Politics

202	universal	8	ADJ: characteristic of all people, nationalities, or ethnicities. N: universality	Many wonder whether we can ever agree on a universal standard for right and wrong.	Law & Politics
203	venerate	10	V: to respect or admire greatly, to worship. ADJ: venerable	The saint was venerated by Catholics across the world.	Status & Conduct
204	revere	7	V: to idolize or worship. N: reverence	Mahatma Gandhi was revered by many as the leader of the Indian Independence Movement.	Status & Conduct
205	pompous	8	ADJ: arrogant and self-important	His arrogant speech made the politician seem pompous and stuck-up.	Status & Conduct
206	pretentious	7	ADJ: arrogant and self-important	Allan tried to avoid sounding pretentious while describing his accomplishments.	Status & Conduct
207	haughty	6	ADJ: arrogant, scornful, feeling superior to others. N: haughtiness	The duchess showed a haughty attitude towards members of the lower class.	Status & Conduct
208	unruly	8	ADJ: wild, uncontrollable, disobedient	The substitute teacher found the class unruly and disrespectful of her authority.	Status & Conduct
209	insolent	10	ADJ: rude or disrespectful to authority. N: insolence	The student was sent to the principal's office for his insolence towards the teacher.	Status & Conduct

210	conceited	6	ADJ: self-centered	They were concerned that her success was causing Karen to become conceited.	Status & Conduct
211	vain	5	ADJ: (1) self-centered, (2) useless, without effect. N: vanity	(1) Elaine was so vain that she admired her reflection every time she passed by a shiny surface. (2) The police tried in vain to catch the criminal, but he was just too fast for them.	Status & Conduct
212	smug	7	ADJ: pleased with oneself, self-satisfied	Knowing he was right, Paul gave a smug grin.	Status & Conduct
213	refined	7	ADJ: polished, highly developed, purified. N: refinement	Marie developed a refined taste for French wine after her year abroad.	Status & Conduct
214	prominent	7	ADJ: important, well-known. N: prominence	Martin Luther King, Jr. was a prominent leader of the Civil Rights Movement.	Status & Conduct
215	renown	8	N: fame. ADJ: renowned	Michael Jackson achieved great renown for his unique musical and performance style.	Status & Conduct
216	affluent	8	ADJ: wealthy. N: affluence	Many feel that the affluent nations should do more to help those less fortunate.	Status & Conduct
217	thrive	7	V: to boom, flourish, grow	A large number of scavenging animals thrive in the city environment.	Status & Conduct

218	prosperous	5	ADJ: thriving, economically well-off. N: prosperity	The now prosperous businessman earned his success over many years of hard work.	Status & Conduct
219	meager	8	ADJ: lacking in amount or quality	The company struggled to survive on its meager budget.	Status & Conduct
220	benefactor	8	N: a person who helps people or organizations, often by donating money	The gala was held to thank the benefactors who donated to the university.	Status & Conduct
221	charitable	7	ADJ: motivated by generosity, raising funds for the disadvantaged. N: charity	During the holidays, many people consider donating to charitable organizations.	Status & Conduct
222	humanitarian	7	ADJ: devoted to the well-being of other people. N: someone devoted to the well-being of other people	After the earthquake, many countries sent humanitarian aid to Haiti.	Status & Conduct
223	philanthropy	8	N: generous assistance to those in need, devotion to the well-being of other people	Bill Gates has become a well-known philanthropist who has donated much of his personal wealth to charity.	Status & Conduct

224	liberal	6	ADJ: (1) giving freely or loosely, (2) broad or open-minded, progressive	(1) The paper cited many sources and was liberal in its use of quotations. (2) The politician was socially liberal, arguing for more government aid programs for the needy and unemployed.	Status & Conduct
225	miser	10	N: one who hoards money rather than spending it. ADJ: miserly	Ebenezer Scrooge was miserly and unwilling to share even a cent of his money.	Status & Conduct
226	procure	8	V: to get, acquire or obtain	The fundraiser aimed to raise money to procure new equipment for the hospital.	Status & Conduct
227	vend	7	V: to sell something. N: vendor	You can buy chips and cookies from the vending machine downstairs.	Status & Conduct
228	peddle	7	V: to sell something. N: peddler	The salesman peddled his wares from door to door.	Status & Conduct
229	entrepreneur	8	N: someone who starts a business	The city's small business subsidy was meant to encourage entrepreneurs to move there.	Status & Conduct
230	prudent	9	ADJ: careful and sensible	Jane was prudent in her spending and careful to save for an emergency.	Status & Conduct
231	thrifty	6	ADJ: careful in spending money	During the Great Depression, families had to become thrifty in order to make do with what they had.	Status & Conduct

232	frugal	6	ADJ: avoiding wasteful or excessive spending	University students often have to live a frugal lifestyle.	Status & Conduct
233	extravagant	7	ADJ: excessive, unrestrained, often relating to spending money	The society was known for its extravagant parties, with expensive food and entertainment.	Status & Conduct
234	lush	8	ADJ: extravagant, abundant, rich	The king treated his guests to a lush five-course dinner.	Status & Conduct
235	mediocre	9	ADJ: second-rate, average or inferior in quality	Compared to the great masterpieces of Leonardo Da Vinci and Michelangelo, this painting seems mediocre and second-rate.	Status & Conduct
236	stark	8	ADJ: bare, simple, without decoration or disguise	The landscape was stark and barren of any trees.	Status & Conduct
237	squander	7	V: to waste, to spend carelessly	James won a million dollars through the lottery, and then squandered it all on expensive cars and clothes.	Status & Conduct
238	frivolous	7	ADJ: not serious or sensible, often related to spending money	The government's frivolous spending cost the taxpayers a lot of money.	Status & Conduct
239	spontaneous	6	ADJ: impulsive, without planning	Her art appeared spontaneous, as if she had applied paint in an entirely impulsive, unplanned manner.	Status & Conduct

240	whim	7	N: an impulse or sudden desire	On a whim, Amanda decided to buy a motorcycle.	Status & Conduct
241	restrained	7	ADJ: held back, kept under control	The elegance of the composition is subtle and restrained, not over the top.	Status & Conduct
242	destitute	9	ADJ: extremely poor	The shelter provided housing for destitute families.	Status & Conduct
243	impoverished	7	ADJ: extremely poor	The region was impoverished by the prolonged drought.	Status & Conduct
244	aristocrat	7	N: a member of the upper class. ADJ: aristocratic	The aristocrats came under attack during the French Revolution.	Status & Conduct
245	elite	8	ADJ, N: upper-class, superior in intellect or status	Many of Rome's wealthy elite owned large estates where they could escape the city.	Status & Conduct
246	eminent	9	ADJ: important, well-known, respected	Einstein was probably the most eminent physicist of the 20th century.	Status & Conduct
247	hierarchy	7	N: organized ranking of status and authority. ADJ: hierarchical	European society during the Middle Ages had a strict social hierarchy.	Status & Conduct
248	promote	6	V: (1) to advertise or support a person or cause, (2) to raise in rank or importance	(1) The group promoted awareness of illiteracy in the community. (2) The employee was promoted to the status of manager.	Status & Conduct

249	demote	7	V: to reduce to a lower rank or position	The boss decided not to fire the employee, but rather to demote him.	Status & Conduct
250	subordinate	7	(1) N: lower in rank or importance, (2) V: to reduce in rank or importance	(1) The states have some degree of independence, but are subordinate to the federal government. (2) Critics argued that the party system subordinated the interests of the general population to the interests of the individual parties.	Status & Conduct
251	suppress	8	V: to hold back, keep down	She suppressed her feelings of disappointment and tried to smile.	Status & Conduct
252	inconsequential	9	ADJ: unimportant, insignificant	The committee frequently spent too much time on inconsequential details Instead of dealing with bigger issues.	Status & Conduct
253	creed	7	N: a statement of belief	Many Catholics follow the Nicene Creed, a statement of their beliefs that is over 1000 years old.	Time, History, & Tradition
254	conviction	7	N: (1) unshakably strong belief, (2) the final judgment that a person is guilty of a crime	(1) Maria had strong religious convictions. (2) The defendant appealed to the higher court to overturn his conviction.	Time, History, & Tradition

255	pious	9	ADJ: faithful to one's religious beliefs	Mother Theresa was admired by many for her pious and charitable behavior.	Time, History, & Tradition
256	conform	8	V: to obey customs, rules, or styles. N: conformist, conformity	Students who do not conform to the dress code will not be allowed to attend the dance.	Time, History, & Tradition
257	convention	7	N: (1) a meeting or assembly, (2) a custom or standard. ADJ: conventional	(1) Hundreds of fans attended the Star Trek convention dressed in costume. (2) In many cultures, it is convention that a visitor bring a gift to a sick patient in hospital.	Time, History, & Tradition
258	orthodox	8	ADJ: traditional, customary, conventional	The musician's alternative music was far from orthodox.	Time, History, & Tradition
259	uniform	8	(1) ADJ: always the same, consistent, even. (2) N: a distinctive or official outfit worn by a particular group	(1) The finely woven fabric had a smooth, uniform texture. (2) Our school uniforms are green and white.	Time, History, & Tradition
260	anomaly	8	N: an unusual or unexpected event. ADJ: anomalous	The unusually warm winter was an anomaly in a region known for its snow and freezing temperatures.	Time, History, & Tradition
261	atypical	7	ADJ: unusual or unexpected	Barry's bad mood is atypical; he is generally a very cheerful person.	Time, History, & Tradition

Ivy Global

262	radical	8	(1) ADJ: extreme or revolutionary. (2) N: a person who has extreme or revolutionary ideas	(1) The new CEO proposed radical changes in the way the company was structured. (2) Extremists and radicals exist in every major religion.	Time, History, & Tradition
263	chronological	6	ADJ: arranged in order of time. N: chronology	The chart shows a history of events in chronological order.	Time, History, & Tradition
264	contemporary	8	ADJ: belonging to the present or same time	The students were asked to research three contemporary events currently in the news.	Time, History, & Tradition
265	simultaneous	6	ADJ: occurring at the same time	The phone and the doorbell rang simultaneously.	Time, History, & Tradition
266	premonition	8	N: a foreboding, a feeling of evil to come	Jake stocked up on supplies because he had a premonition that a horrible snowstorm was coming.	Time, History, & Tradition
267	ominous	8	ADJ: threatening, menacing, foretelling evil	I had an ominous feeling that something was going to go wrong.	Time, History, & Tradition
268	precursor	8	N: something that comes before and indicates the approach of something or someone	What looks like a harmless skin spot can sometimes be the precursor to a cancerous growth.	Time, History, & Tradition

269	precedent	9	N: a previous act or decision that serves as a guide for later situations	The court considered the case carefully, as it knew that their decision could serve as a precedent for future cases.	Time, History, & Tradition
270	predecessor	8	N: a person who holds an office or position before another	George W. Bush was Barack Obama's predecessor as President of the United States.	Time, History, & Tradition
271	lineage	8	N: an individual's series of ancestors	The family traced its lineage back to the first French traders to settle in North America.	Time, History, & Tradition
272	pedigree	8	N: an individual's or animal's series of ancestors	The puppies share a strong, healthy pedigree.	Time, History, & Tradition
273	residual	9	ADJ: left over, remaining. N: residue	After the building was completed, construction crews cleaned up the residual building material.	Time, History, & Tradition
274	remnant	9	N: a leftover	The land contains only the remnants of the massive forest that once grew there.	Time, History, & Tradition
275	duration	7	N: a time period over which something lasts or continues	Zinc is said to shorten the duration of cold symptoms.	Time, History, & Tradition
276	durable	5	ADJ: lasting for a long time. N: durability	Linda hoped that her boots were durable enough to survive Toronto's winters.	Time, History, & Tradition

Ivy Global

277	sustain	7	V: (1) to prolong or extend, (2) to undergo or endure, (3) to provide with necessary nourishment and support. N: sustenance	(1) Janice sustained her cheerful and optimistic attitude even when disaster struck. (2) The plants could not sustain the blistering heat with little water, and they quickly wilted. (3) The emergency supplies will sustain us in case we are snowed in.	Time, History, & Tradition
278	prophesy	7	V: to predict or reveal something before it has happened. ADJ: prophetic, N: prophet	Some claim that the ancient Mayans prophesied the end of the world in 2012.	Time, History, & Tradition
279	foreshadow	8	V: to suggest or indicate what might happen next	The education reform in Poland foreshadows great changes in its school system.	Time, History, & Tradition
280	foresight	8	N: looking ahead, knowing in advance, preparing for the future	The city planners had the foresight to accommodate the need for mass transit in the city's future.	Time, History, & Tradition
281	foretell	7	V: to predict, to tell what is going to happen	Many realized that the economy was unstable, but no one foretold the sudden stock market crash.	Time, History, & Tradition
282	subsequent	8	ADJ: following in time, later	Although first edition of the book contained many printing errors, subsequent editions corrected these mistakes.	Time, History, & Tradition

283	imminent	10	ADJ: about to happen, occur, take place very soon	The doctors determined that the patient's health was not in imminent danger.	Time, History, & Tradition
284	impending	10	ADJ: about to happen, occur, take place very soon	The hero had only two choices: to embark on the dangerous quest, or to face impending doom.	Time, History, & Tradition
285	inevitable	7	ADJ: unavoidable, unable to be prevented	The team was playing so poorly that everyone knew defeat was inevitable.	Time, History, & Tradition
286	recollect	6	V: to remember. N: recollection	The witness stated that she could not recollect the specific details of the crime.	Time, History, & Tradition
287	reminisce	8	V: to recall the past, particularly pleasant memories	Blaine looked forward to seeing many of his former classmates and reminiscing about the past.	Time, History, & Tradition
288	nostalgia	9	N: longing for the past. ADJ: nostalgic	The film conveys a sense of bittersweet nostalgia for lost youth.	Time, History, & Tradition
289	remorse	8	N: a feeling of deep regret. ADJ: remorseful	Now a changed man, he felt remorse over his past misdeeds.	Time, History, & Tradition
290	commemorate	8	V: to remember through a ceremony or service	Memorial Day commemorates those who lost their lives serving their country.	Time, History, & Tradition

Ivy Global

291	homage	10	N: respect, tribute, honor	Remembrance Day events pay homage to those who served in the military.	Time, History, & Tradition
292	antiquated	9	ADJ: old-fashioned, out-of-date	Eliza was happy when her school finally replaced its antiquated computers with newer laptops.	Time, History, & Tradition
293	archaic	8	ADJ: ancient, old-fashioned	Mosaics lined the walls of the ruin, with an unrecognizable archaic script carved underneath.	Time, History, & Tradition
294	obsolete	7	ADJ: not current, no longer in use, out-of-date	Technology is changing so rapidly that new products may become obsolete within a year or even a few months.	Time, History, & Tradition
295	renovate	6	V: to renew, to restore to a better condition. N: renovation	The apartment was recently renovated with all-new kitchen and bathroom appliances.	Time, History, & Tradition
296	innovation	7	N: a new way of doing something, a creation of something new	The general economy is experiencing a fundamental change fuelled by technological innovation.	Time, History, & Tradition
297	novelty	8	N: (1) the state of being new or interesting, (2) a new product	(1) The novelty of the toy quickly wore off, and the child became bored with his birthday present. (2) The store sells wigs, glasses, hats, props, and other novelties.	Time, History, & Tradition

298	habitual	9	ADJ: usual, regular, according to habit	Matt was not a habitual Mac user and found the different operating system frustrating.	Time, History, & Tradition
299	intermittent	8	ADJ: stopping and starting irregularly	The snow continued lightly into the evening and became intermittent by midnight.	Time, History, & Tradition
300	artifact	7	N: a man-made object	The museum has a display of ancient Egyptian art and artifacts.	Time, History, & Tradition
301	mosaic	7	N: art consisting of glass or stone tiles	The cathedral is decorated by mosaics on the walls, ceiling, and floor.	Time, History, & Tradition
302	intuition	7	N: instinctive, irrational knowledge. ADJ: intuitive	Scientists must rely on both their analytical logic and their well-developed intuition.	Truth & Deception
303	presume	7	V: to assume without proof. ADJ: presumption	Austin was presumed dead in the shipwreck, though his body was never found.	Truth & Deception
304	imply	6	V: to suggest, to state indirectly. N: implication	Although he did not say so directly, the president implied that he did not agree with the military's position.	Truth & Deception
305	insinuate	10	V: to make an indirect, often negative, suggestion. N: insinuation	The reporter insinuated that the company had been lying to the public.	Truth & Deception

306	allege	10	V: to declare, report. N: allegation	The defendant alleged temporary insanity.	Truth & Deception
307	assert	7	V: to make a claim, to state as true N: assertion	Emily was not shy about asserting her opinion.	Truth & Deception
308	testify	6	V: to give evidence for, often in court. N: testimony	The witnessed testified that she had seen the suspect lurking outside of her house.	Truth & Deception
309	certify	8	V: to provide evidence for	The expert certified that the violin was, indeed, an authentic Stradivarius.	Truth & Deception
310	decode	7	V: to figure out, interpret	The language is so ancient and unusual that expert linguists cannot decode it.	Truth & Deception
311	enlighten	8	V: to shed light upon, to make clear	The seminar was meant to enlighten the audience about the application process.	Truth & Deception
312	illuminate	6	V: to shed light upon, to make clear. N: illumination	The paintings on display were illuminated by well-placed lights.	Truth & Deception
313	clarity	7	N: clearness, ability to be understood. V: clarify	A good essay will demonstrate sound logic and clarity.	Truth & Deception
314	fathom	10	(1) V: to come to understand, (2) N: a unit of water depth	(1) We really could not fathom why the singer was so popular. (2) The shipwreck was 130 fathoms underwater.	Truth & Deception

315	feasible	9	ADJ: achievable, possible, able to be done	Sending humans to Mars will likely be possible in the future, but is currently not feasible.	Truth & Deception
316	plausible	9	ADJ: possible, reasonable	The hypothesis sounded plausible but had never been proven.	Truth & Deception
317	credible	8	ADJ: believable. N: credibility	The defense attorney questioned whether the witness was credible.	Truth & Deception
318	legitimate	6	ADJ: legal, authorized, valid. V: to make legal, to authorize. N: legitimacy	Critics wondered whether the election was legitimate, or whether it had been rigged.	Truth & Deception
319	acknowledge	7	V: to notice or accept. N: acknowledgement	The organization's donation to the charity was acknowledged with great thanks.	Truth & Deception
320	frank	9	ADJ: honest, open	The criminal could have shortened his prison sentence by making a full and frank confession.	Truth & Deception
321	integrity	6	N: (1) wholeness, unity, (2) honesty	(1) The engineers ran tests on the bridge to determine its structural integrity. (2) The reporter's deceptive tactics drew questions about his journalistic integrity.	Truth & Deception
322	gullible	8	ADJ: easily deceived or tricked	People should not be so gullible as to believe everything they read in advertisements.	Truth & Deception

Ivy Global

323	devise	8	V: to invent, to create a plan	The research team devised a new method of gathering data.	Truth & Deception
324	devious	9	ADJ: misleading, deceitful	Martha deviously managed to trick her opponent.	Truth & Deception
325	crafty	7	ADJ: sly, skilled in deception	Always crafty, Pete fooled his parents into thinking he had eaten his vegetables.	Truth & Deception
326	wily	6	ADJ: sly, skilled in deception	The police hunted for the escaped criminal, but he proved too wily to be caught.	Truth & Deception
327	blatant	6	ADJ: obvious, offensive	John's action showed a blatant disrespect for authority.	Truth & Deception
328	conspicuous	9	ADJ: obvious, easy to notice	Camouflage uniforms are meant to make the army less conspicuous among the trees.	Truth & Deception
329	confide	7	V: to tell a secret to, to entrust	Brian knew he could always confide in his parents.	Truth & Deception
330	discreet	8	ADJ: respectful of privacy or secrecy. N: discretion	I hope you will be discreet and not mention this secret to anyone else.	Truth & Deception
331	subtle	7	ADJ: fine, delicate, not obvious	Mary dropped subtle hints about what she wanted for her birthday, but her boyfriend did not notice.	Truth & Deception

332	oblivious	8	ADJ: lacking awareness, forgetful	Many people are oblivious to the serious dangers of climate change.	Truth & Deception
333	sarcastic	7	ADJ: ridiculing or making fun of	"Oh, of course, you're always right," Amy's mother said in a sarcastic manner when Amy wouldn't admit that she was wrong.	Truth & Deception
334	cryptic	8	ADJ: difficult to understand or decipher	The anonymous message was cryptic and mysterious.	Truth & Deception
335	enigma	8	N: a mystery, a difficult problem. ADJ: enigmatic	The cause of Type 1 diabetes is still an enigma.	Truth & Deception
336	ambiguous	8	ADJ: unclear, having more than one possible meaning	The report is ambiguous about whether health care will be affected by the government's cutbacks.	Truth & Deception
337	dubious	8	ADJ: (1) doubtful, uncertain; (2) disbelieving, not convinced	After losing the election, the senator's political future looked dubious.	Truth & Deception
338	skeptical	6	ADJ: disbelieving, doubting	It is a good idea to be skeptical about the claims made in advertisements.	Truth & Deception
339	absurdity	6	N: something unreasonable, contradictory, ridiculous	Sartre's plays expose the absurdity of everyday life.	Truth & Deception

340	delusion	9	N: a false belief, not real or logical. V: delude. ADJ: delusional	The man suffered from delusions of grandeur, believing he was destined to save the world.	Truth & Deception
341	mirage	10	N: an illusion	As he walked through the desert he thought he glimpsed a shining oasis on the horizon, but this was just a mirage.	Truth & Deception
342	distort	7	V: (1) to deform or alter an object's original shape, (2) to falsely change the meaning of something	(1) The reflection was distorted as a ripple moved across the water's surface. (2) The media were accused of distorting the facts.	Truth & Deception
343	obscure	6	ADJ: unclear, dark, V: to make dark or unclear	The English class found the poem difficult because of its obscure vocabulary.	Truth & Deception
344	baffling	6	ADJ: puzzling and frustrating. V: baffle	The instructions are absolutely baffling, so confusing that they are impossible to follow.	Truth & Deception
345	perplex	7	V: to confuse, to puzzle. ADJ: perplexed, perplexing	The scientists were perplexed by the odd results of the experiment.	Truth & Deception
346	bewilder	8	V: to confuse, to puzzle ADJ: bewildered	We were bewildered by the government's sudden policy reversal.	Truth & Deception

347	muddle	6	V: to confuse, mix up, N: a confused or disorganized mess. ADJ: muddled	The paper's argument was unclear and muddled.	Truth & Deception
348	convoluted	8	ADJ: complex and intricate	The movie's plot was so convoluted that many viewers could not understand what was happening.	Truth & Deception
349	contend	9	V: (1) to dispute, compete, or struggle against, (2) to claim to be true	(1) The final two teams contended for the championship title. (2) The defendant contended that the judge was biased in his decision.	Truth & Deception
350	contradict	5	V: to oppose or deny	In the second paragraph of your essay, you contradict what you stated in the first paragraph.	Truth & Deception
351	irony	8	N: (1) contradiction between what is expected and what actually occurs, (2) sarcasm	The fireman found it ironic that their own firehouse burned to the ground in the middle of the night.	Truth & Deception
352	erroneous	8	ADJ: wrong, mistaken, in error	After further testing disproved their conclusions, the scientists concluded that their earlier theories were erroneous.	Truth & Deception

353	debunk	9	V: to disprove or expose something as false	The evidence given in this passage debunks the legend that Betsy Ross sewed the first American flag.	Truth & Deception
354	refute	9	V: to disprove or expose something as false	The police force refuted any accusations of wrongdoing.	Truth & Deception
355	mourn	6	V: to feel sadness or sorrow, particularly over a death. ADJ: mournful	Millions mourned the death of Michael Jackson.	War & Conflict
356	woe	7	N: grief, sorrow, suffering	Overspending is a major cause of our financial woes.	War & Conflict
357	melancholy	8	ADJ: depressed, sad, gloomy, N: a depressed or gloomy feeling	The violin's melancholy melody brought the listeners to tears.	War & Conflict
358	morose	9	ADJ: depressed, sad, gloomy	Cheer up-- I hate to see you looking so morose!	War & Conflict
359	somber	8	ADJ: depressing, gloomy, dark	The mood at the funeral was somber.	War & Conflict
360	dismal	7	ADJ: depressing, gloomy	The day outside looked gray, rainy, and dismal.	War & Conflict
361	hail	8	V: (1) to praise, (2) to greet joyfully, (3) to rain small ice particles. N: small ice particles	(1) The new movie was hailed as a stunning achievement. (2) "Hail Caesar!" cried the crowd as the emperor arrived. (3) The weatherman said that it would hail over the weekend.	War & Conflict

362	turmoil	7	N: violent disturbance or protest, disorder	The stock market crash created turmoil in the global economy.	War & Conflict
363	uproar	6	N: a state of noise, excitement, and confusion	The fans were in an uproar over the referee's controversial call.	War & Conflict
364	irate	9	ADJ: extremely angry	The irate passengers had to wait for over an hour for their luggage.	War & Conflict
365	livid	9	ADJ: (1) extremely angry, (2) grayish-blue, bruise-colored	(1) The players' irresponsible behavior made their coach livid with rage. (2) The doctors removed the dressing to reveal the livid wound.	War & Conflict
366	ferocity	7	N: the condition of being wild and fierce. ADJ: ferocious	The army displayed great ferocity on the battlefield.	War & Conflict
367	recede	6	V: to withdraw or move back. N: recession	As the tide went out, the waters receded and exposed meters of wet sand.	War & Conflict
368	impasse	10	N: a deadlock, a point that cannot be passed	The two leaders have reached an impasse in their peace talks, and negotiations between the two countries are unable to continue.	War & Conflict

369	impenetrable	7	ADJ: (1) dense, unable to be penetrated, (2) impossible to understand	(1) Entering the cave, we were faced with a deep, impenetrable darkness. (2) The book was so dense and hard to understand that the students complained it was impenetrable.	War & Conflict
370	deft	9	ADJ: skillful, quick in action	With his quick fingers, Mike is a deft mechanic.	War & Conflict
371	haste	8	N: speedy or quick action. V: hasten	In her haste to leave, Sarah forgot her wallet on the table.	War & Conflict
372	denounce	9	V: to speak out against	The traitor was denounced for his disloyalty to his country.	War & Conflict
373	reproach	8	(1) V: to express disapproval or criticism. (2) N: shame, disgrace	(1) The media were reproached for exaggerating the story. (2) Despite the scandal in his company, the CEO claimed to be above reproach and entirely blameless.	War & Conflict
374	ensnare	7	V: to catch or trap	The tiger was ensnared in the hunter's trap.	War & Conflict
375	assail	9	V: to attack violently	The army waited until nightfall to assail the enemy camp.	War & Conflict
376	vulnerable	6	ADJ: capable of being wounded or hurt	A turtle's shell protects its vulnerable midsection and inner organs.	War & Conflict

377	debilitate	8	V: to make weak. ADJ: debilitated	The city was debilitated by the devastating flu epidemic.	War & Conflict
378	impair	8	V: to weaken, diminish, make worse. N: impairment	Alcohol impairs judgment and slows reaction time.	War & Conflict
379	detrimental	8	ADJ: causing harm. N: detriment	Smoking can have detrimental effects on your health.	War & Conflict
380	mangle	6	V: to mutilate, to destroy or injure severely	The mangled wreckage of the building was all that remained from the fire.	War & Conflict
381	obliterate	8	V: to destroy or remove completely	The computer virus rewrote the hard drive, obliterating all of its data.	War & Conflict
382	terminate	5	V: to bring to an end	The renter had the right to terminate his rental agreement by giving two months' written notice.	War & Conflict
383	slay	6	V: to murder	The hero slayed the fearsome dragon.	War & Conflict
384	adversary	7	N: opponent	I was not looking forward to competing against Brian in the chess match because he was such a strong adversary.	War & Conflict
385	animosity	10	N: deep hatred	The revolutionaries felt great animosity towards the oppressive military leaders.	War & Conflict
386	hostile	6	ADJ: very unfriendly.	The city seemed strange, cold, and hostile to the	War & Conflict

			N: hostility	new immigrants.	
387	affliction	8	N: great suffering, pain, or distress	When we suffer from bodily pain, there is bound to be mental affliction as well.	War & Conflict
388	anguish	6	N: great suffering, pain, or distress	The woman let out a cry of anguish as she watched her city burn.	War & Conflict
389	lament	8	V: to express sorrow or regret, N: an expression of sorrow or regret	The poor man lamented his sorry fate.	War & Conflict
390	atrocity	8	N: an extremely cruel or unjust act. ADJ: atrocious	The war criminal was brought to international trial for the atrocities he had committed.	War & Conflict
391	bane	8	N: something causing misery or death	Injuries are the bane of any athlete.	War & Conflict
392	hazard	7	(1) N: a danger or risk. ADJ: hazardous. (2) V: to speculate	(1) The building was inspected for fire hazards. (2) I am unsure of the answer, but will hazard a guess.	War & Conflict
393	volatile	9	ADJ: explosive, likely to change suddenly or violently	The United Nations sent in peacekeepers to help stabilize the volatile region.	War & Conflict
394	calamity	7	N: a tragedy, an event resulting in great loss	Critics were concerned that the new financial policy would bring about economic calamity for the country.	War & Conflict

395	catastrophe	7	N: a disaster, tragedy. ADJ: catastrophic	Typhoon Haiyan was a huge catastrophe for the Philippines.	War & Conflict
396	sinister	8	ADJ: threatening, menacing, dark	The bombing was revealed to be part of a sinister conspiracy.	War & Conflict
397	evade	7	V: to escape or dodge. N: evasion, ADJ: evasive	The spy evaded capture by the enemy army.	War & Conflict
398	subside	8	V: to die down or wear off	The thunderstorm eventually subsided and the sky began to clear.	War & Conflict
399	fortify	7	V: to strengthen. N: fortification	The city fortified its defenses in preparation for the upcoming attack.	War & Conflict
400	prevail	7	V: to be greater in number, power, or importance	Despite their poor performance during the first three quarters, the team made an amazing comeback and prevailed at the end of the game.	War & Conflict
401	sentry	7	N: a lookout, someone who keeps watch	The checkpoint was guarded by sentries who searched all vehicles that tried to pass through.	War & Conflict
402	vigilant	7	ADJ: carefully observant, on the lookout for possible danger	The army remained vigilant, knowing the enemy could strike at any time.	War & Conflict
403	tactician	8	N: a person who is skilled at planning tactics or strategies	Bruce was an inspiring leader, a brave fighter, and a brilliant tactician.	War & Conflict

404	hypothesis	7	N: an educated guess that has not yet been proven. ADJ: hypothetical	The scientists tried to prove their hypothesis by conducting experiments.	Science & Analysis
405	compile	8	V: to gather together. N: compilation	The new report compiled data from surveys in fifty communities.	Science & Analysis
406	cumulative	8	ADJ: adding together, incorporating everything up to the present	Jason found that the cumulative effects of sleep deprivation were making him unable to concentrate.	Science & Analysis
407	comprehensive	7	ADJ: thorough, covering a wide area, including everything	The book gives a comprehensive history of Chinese culture and politics.	Science & Analysis
408	criterion	7	N: a standard against which other things can be judged. PL: criteria	Amy's application was denied because she did not meet a single criterion or requirement for the job.	Science & Analysis
409	scrutiny	6	N: intense examination or inspection. V: scrutinize	The legislators will carry out an in-depth scrutiny of the bill before it is passed.	Science & Analysis
410	fundamental	7	ADJ: involving basic or essential principles	The fundamental law of gravity states that what goes up must come down.	Science & Analysis
411	innate	10	ADJ: natural, present at birth	The ability to acquire language is innate in most human beings.	Science & Analysis

412	congenital	7	ADJ: present at birth	Edgar had a congenital heart defect that went undetected for years.	Science & Analysis
413	hereditary	7	ADJ: inherited, passed from parents to children	Cholesterol levels are largely hereditary, though exercise and diet contribute as well.	Science & Analysis
414	heterogeneous	9	ADJ: having many different elements or parts	The study surveyed a heterogeneous sample of patients, differing in age, gender, and ethnicity.	Science & Analysis
415	homogeneous	9	ADJ: all of the same kind, having consistent or identical parts. V: homogenize	The ballet company had a fairly homogenous set of dancers, all the same height, weight, and build.	Science & Analysis
416	saturate	8	V: to fill or soak completely. N: saturation	A wetland is a flat area saturated by water, like a marsh or swamp.	Science & Analysis
417	dilute	5	V: to weaken or lessen in strength, to water down	The dye was too dark, so Erin diluted the color by adding water.	Science & Analysis
418	humid	5	ADJ: damp, having a great deal of water vapor in the air. N: humidity	The rainforest climate is warm and humid.	Science & Analysis
419	irrigate	6	V: to supply with water. N: irrigation	The farmer irrigated his crops with a system of sprinklers and hoses.	Science & Analysis
420	deluge	8	N: a flood or downpour	We were caught in the sudden deluge without an umbrella.	Science & Analysis

421	erosion	7	N: the process of wearing away by water or wind. V: erode	As the cliffs are being worn away by erosion, visitors should watch out for falling stones and debris.	Science & Analysis
422	corrode	8	V: to cause to deteriorate, to eat away by water, air, or acid. N: corrosion	Old batteries will eventually corrode and should be replaced.	Science & Analysis
423	tarnish	9	V: to make dirty, often a metal through exposure to air	The silver had tarnished over time, but polishing revealed its shiny surface.	Science & Analysis
424	dehydrate	6	V: to remove water, to dry out. N: dehydration	Halfway through the race, Adam started to feel dehydrated and stopped for a drink of water.	Science & Analysis
425	arid	8	ADJ: dry, lacking rainfall	Deserts are highly arid regions that receive very little rainfall.	Science & Analysis
426	parch	8	V: to dry out through heat	As the summer progressed with no rain, the land looked parched.	Science & Analysis
427	altitude	6	N: height, elevation above sea level	Passengers must remain seated until the plane reaches its cruising altitude.	Science & Analysis
428	excavate	6	V: to dig up. N: excavation	The team of archeologists was excavating the ruins of an ancient Roman city.	Science & Analysis

429	incision	9	N: the result of cutting. ADJ: incisive	The surgeon made an incision in the patient's abdomen so he could begin operating.	Science & Analysis
430	apparatus	7	N: equipment	The firefighters used breathing apparatus so they could tackle the flames.	Science & Analysis
431	remedy	8	N: a cure or solution, V: to cure or set right	Currently there are many treatments but no remedy for diabetes.	Science & Analysis
432	phenomenon	7	N: an observable event or occurrence. PL: phenomena	It is an unusual phenomenon that water weighs less as a solid (ice) than as a liquid.	Science & Analysis
433	acoustics	7	N: the study of the properties of sound	The architect of the concert hall had to consider carefully the acoustics of his design so the music could be heard well.	Science & Analysis
434	auditory	7	ADJ: relating to the process of hearing	Sound is received by the ear and carried along the auditory nerve to the brain.	Science & Analysis
435	cacophony	9	N: a loud, harsh, disagreeable noise	There was a cacophony in the band room as all the players warmed up at the same time.	Science & Analysis
436	din	8	N: a loud, harsh, disagreeable noise	We could hardly have a conversation over the din of the leaf blower next door.	Science & Analysis

Ivy Global

437	muted	8	ADJ: softened, hushed, quiet	The painter preferred muted purples and blues over brighter colors.	Science & Analysis
438	olfactory	9	ADJ: relating to the sense of smell	Dogs have a much keener olfactory sense than do humans.	Science & Analysis
439	pungent	10	ADJ: having a strong or sharp taste or odor	The French cheese smelled pungent but tasted delicious.	Science & Analysis
440	rancid	9	ADJ: having a sour or stale taste or smell due to decomposition	The meat had been sitting out for too long and had gone rancid.	Science & Analysis
441	entice	8	V: to lure or attract, often through appearance or smell. ADJ: enticing	The enticing smell from the oven summoned us into the kitchen.	Science & Analysis
442	glutton	7	N: a person who is greedy, particularly about eating. ADJ: gluttonous	Augustus Gloop was a glutton who gorged himself on chocolate and candy.	Science & Analysis
443	ravenous	8	ADJ: extremely hungry	It had been so long since breakfast that we were ravenous.	Science & Analysis
444	voracious	9	ADJ: greedy or extremely hungry	Nathan has a voracious appetite; he eats and eats and never seems to get full.	Science & Analysis
445	tactile	8	ADJ: relating to the sense of touch	The sculpture was meant to be tactile; in fact, the display invited visitors to touch it.	Science & Analysis

446	tangible	8	ADJ: able to be felt or touched	The prosecutor knew that he could not win his case without tangible proof.	Science & Analysis
447	audible	7	ADJ: able to be heard	The actor spoke quietly but was still audible from the stage.	Science & Analysis
448	taut	8	ADJ: under tension, stretched tightly	The boat's cover should be stretched taut so it does not collect any water.	Science & Analysis
449	contour	7	N: a smooth, curved outline	The road followed the contours of the countryside, rising and falling along with the hills and valleys.	Science & Analysis
450	amorphous	10	ADJ: having no defined shape	The dress was billowy and amorphous, without a fitted shape or structure.	Science & Analysis
451	translucent	6	ADJ: allowing light to pass through	Amethyst can vary in color from translucent lilac to deep purple.	Science & Analysis
452	hue	6	N: a quality or shade of color	The baby ate so many carrots that his skin took on an orange hue.	Science & Analysis
453	solitary	6	ADJ: alone, by oneself	The prisoners were kept in solitary confinement for three nights.	Size, Location & Motion

454	void	7	(1) ADJ: containing nothing, empty. (2) ADJ: invalid, cancelled, having no legal force. (3) N: emptiness, open space	(1) This argument is entirely nonsensical and void of logic. (2) Josh disassembled his computer himself instead of shipping it back to the company, thereby rendering his warranty void. (3) Many ancient religions state that the earth was once a dark, formless void before life was created.	Size, Location & Motion
455	null	10	ADJ: having no value or force	The contract was declared null and void.	Size, Location & Motion
456	equivalent	7	ADJ: of equal value or size	The recipe calls for 150 milliliters of cream, or the equivalent.	Size, Location & Motion
457	ample	7	ADJ: large, more than enough	Aunt Christie piled our plates high with ample servings of turkey.	Size, Location & Motion
458	plentiful	8	ADJ: in full supply, in large amounts	It had been a good growing season, and the harvest was plentiful.	Size, Location & Motion
459	bounty	7	N: (1) a large or generous amount of something, (2) a reward for catching a criminal	(1) After the harvest, they gathered to give thanks for nature's bounty. (2) The bounty hunter captured the fugitive and received his reward.	Size, Location & Motion
460	foster	8	V: to help grow, to nurture or promote	The pep rally was meant to foster team spirit.	Size, Location & Motion

461	pervasive	8	ADJ: spreading throughout, penetrating or affecting everything	The Internet is pervasive in business, education, and entertainment.	Size, Location & Motion
462	prevalent	8	ADJ: frequent, common, widespread	After coming home from Cuba, Carrie missed the street music and dancing so prevalent in that culture.	Size, Location & Motion
463	transcend	9	V: to exceed, to go beyond limitations, to excel	Music is a universal language, able to transcend national and cultural boundaries.	Size, Location & Motion
464	elongate	6	V: to make longer, stretch out	Pluto has an elongated, oval-shaped orbit.	Size, Location & Motion
465	constraint	8	N: a restriction, something that limits or holds back. V: constrain	You are free to be as creative as you wish within the constraints of the assignment.	Size, Location & Motion
466	minute	9	(1) ADJ: small and detailed, (2) N: a unit of time.	The minute details of this painting are very impressive.	Size, Location & Motion
467	dearth	10	N: a lack or insufficiency	Ontario is suffering from a dearth of qualified doctors.	Size, Location & Motion
468	deficient	7	ADJ: inadequate, lacking	Anna's blood tests revealed that she was deficient in iron.	Size, Location & Motion
469	meager	8	ADJ: lacking in amount or quality	The company struggled to survive on its meager budget.	Size, Location & Motion

Ivy Global

470	scant	9	ADJ: lacking, in short supply	The available data is too scant to allow a full understanding of the issue.	Size, Location & Motion
471	scarce	8	ADJ: lacking, inadequate, not enough	Fresh water is quickly becoming scarce in many regions of the world.	Size, Location & Motion
472	deficit	8	N: a lack, where need or expenses are greater than supply or income	Scientists are concerned that we may face an energy deficit in upcoming years.	Size, Location & Motion
473	wane	7	V: to decline, grow smaller	Our enthusiasm waned as we realized that the task would be very difficult.	Size, Location & Motion
474	sparse	6	ADJ: scattered, not dense	The region is largely bare, with sparse vegetation.	Size, Location & Motion
475	sporadic	10	ADJ: scattered, irregular, infrequent	The city's development was sporadic, occurring in starts and stops over the years.	Size, Location & Motion
476	aimless	8	ADJ: without purpose or direction	Unsure what direction to take, they wandered in an aimless manner through the forest.	Size, Location & Motion
477	meander	8	V: to ramble without direction	The river meandered slowly through the countryside, winding its way to the ocean.	Size, Location & Motion
478	fluctuate	9	V: to change irregularly, to have unpredictable ups and downs	Ian was tired all the time because his sleep schedule fluctuated greatly.	Size, Location & Motion

Ivy Global

479	arbitrary	6	ADJ: random	The teams for this competition were created arbitrarily and are meant to be entirely random.	Size, Location & Motion
480	kinetic	8	ADJ: relating to motion	The wind turbine turns the wind's kinetic energy into electricity.	Size, Location & Motion
481	dynamic	6	ADJ: active, moving, changing	New members are necessary to keep the organization growing and dynamic.	Size, Location & Motion
482	fluid	6	ADJ: (1) flowing, changing, N: (2) a substance that flows and changes shape according to its container	The dancer leapt forward in a fluid, graceful motion.	Size, Location & Motion
483	limber	8	ADJ: flexible, moving quickly and lightly	Kate is a skilled and limber soccer player.	Size, Location & Motion
484	agile	8	ADJ: graceful, moving quickly and lightly	Border collies are known as a quick and agile breed.	Size, Location & Motion
485	nimble	6	ADJ: graceful, moving quickly and lightly	Jack nimbly cleared the obstacle.	Size, Location & Motion
486	vigor	8	N: energy, strength. ADJ: vigorous	After half-time, the team charged onto the field with renewed vigor.	Size, Location & Motion

487	invigorate	8	V: to make lively and energetic	They were feeling tired and thought a walk in the fresh air might invigorate them.	Size, Location & Motion
488	dormant	7	ADJ: inactive, asleep	Volcanoes may lie dormant for hundreds of years before suddenly erupting.	Size, Location & Motion
489	sedate	9	ADJ: (1) calm, quiet, V: (2) to calm down	After sprinting for the first mile, Matt continued at a more sedate pace.	Size, Location & Motion
490	serene	7	ADJ: calm, peaceful	Susan gave a serene smile, calmly unaffected by the commotion around her.	Size, Location & Motion
491	tranquil	8	ADJ: calm, peaceful	The lake was perfectly tranquil, with no wind to ruffle the still waters.	Size, Location & Motion
492	remote	7	ADJ: distant, located far away	The shipwrecked sailor was stranded on a remote island.	Size, Location & Motion
493	vacant	7	ADJ: (1) empty, not occupied; ADJ: (2) empty of thought or interest	When the aging president suddenly suffered a heart attack, his position was left vacant.	Size, Location & Motion
494	abyss	9	N: a bottomless gulf or pit	The bridge across the abyss appeared rickety and about to fall apart.	Size, Location & Motion
495	chasm	7	N: a deep gorge or valley	The spectacular waterfalls are located where the river hurls itself into a deep chasm.	Size, Location & Motion

496	evacuate	6	V: to empty completely	Residents were instructed to evacuate the building when the fire alarm sounded.	Size, Location & Motion
497	inhabit	7	V: to live or reside in some place	No people and very few animals inhabit Antarctica.	Size, Location & Motion
498	domestic	7	ADJ: (1) relating to the home, (2) relating to the internal affairs of a nation	The store sells refrigerators, washing machines, and other domestic appliances.	Size, Location & Motion
499	rural	6	ADJ: relating to the countryside	The area is largely rural, comprised of farmland and very few major towns.	Size, Location & Motion
500	rustic	7	ADJ: characteristic of country life, rough or unfinished	The cabins were rustic, with wood fire stoves and no indoor plumbing.	Size, Location & Motion

ANSWER KEYS

SYNONYM STRATEGIES

EXERCISE #3: WORD CONNOTATIONS (PAGES 41-43)

2. –

3. +

4. There are two possible meanings for this word, one positive and one weather-related (neutral).

5. –

6. –

7. +

8. –

9. +

10. –

11. +

12. –

SYNONYM PRACTICE QUESTIONS

WARM-UP QUESTIONS (PAGES 46-47)

1. C
2. B
3. D
4. A
5. B
6. A
7. C
8. B
9. D
10. C

BASIC QUESTIONS (PAGES 48-50)

1. C
2. B
3. D
4. B
5. D
6. D
7. C
8. C
9. C
10. D
11. B
12. A
13. A
14. A
15. D
16. A
17. D
18. B
19. A
20. B
21. B
22. B
23. A
24. C
25. D

26. D	28. A	30. D	32. D
27. B	29. D	31. C	

MEDIUM QUESTIONS (PAGES 51-56)

1. B	13. B	25. B	37. C	49. A
2. A	14. D	26. B	38. C	50. B
3. A	15. C	27. B	39. A	51. D
4. C	16. D	28. B	40. B	52. D
5. A	17. B	29. C	41. B	53. C
6. B	18. C	30. D	42. C	54. D
7. C	19. C	31. A	43. D	55. C
8. B	20. C	32. C	44. B	56. A
9. C	21. A	33. A	45. D	57. C
10. D	22. B	34. D	46. A	58. A
11. A	23. D	35. B	47. B	59. C
12. B	24. A	36. A	48. B	60. C

DIFFICULT QUESTIONS (PAGES 57-61)

1. B	12. B	23. C	34. C	45. B
2. C	13. A	24. D	35. A	46. D
3. D	14. B	25. C	36. D	47. C
4. D	15. C	26. B	37. C	48. D
5. C	16. B	27. C	38. A	49. A
6. A	17. A	28. D	39. D	50. D
7. D	18. D	29. D	40. B	51. B
8. B	19. A	30. A	41. A	52. B
9. C	20. D	31. B	42. D	53. B
10. A	21. A	32. B	43. A	54. C
11. D	22. B	33. A	44. C	55. C

Ivy Global

MIDDLE LEVEL CHALLENGE QUESTIONS (PAGES 62-66)

1. D	11. B	21. A	31. D	41. B
2. B	12. C	22. C	32. C	42. D
3. C	13. D	23. D	33. A	43. A
4. A	14. B	24. C	34. D	44. D
5. D	15. D	25. A	35. D	45. A
6. D	16. D	26. B	36. A	46. C
7. C	17. B	27. D	37. C	47. C
8. D	18. D	28. C	38. D	48. B
9. B	19. A	29. C	39. B	49. D
10. B	20. B	30. A	40. C	50. B

UPPER LEVEL CHALLENGE QUESTIONS (PAGES 67-70)

1. B	9. B	17. B	25. C	33. B
2. A	10. C	18. D	26. C	34. A
3. C	11. D	19. B	27. D	35. B
4. D	12. D	20. B	28. A	36. C
5. C	13. D	21. A	29. C	37. D
6. B	14. C	22. D	30. D	38. B
7. C	15. A	23. C	31. C	
8. A	16. B	24. C	32. B	

SENTENCE COMPLETION STRATEGIES

EXERCISE #3 (PAGE 82)

1. even though
2. but
3. instead
4. as a result
5. despite
6. therefore
7. Although
8. furthermore

SENTENCE COMPLETION PRACTICE QUESTIONS

WARM-UP QUESTIONS (PAGES 87-88)

1. A	3. C	5. A	7. C	9. C
2. B	4. C	6. B	8. B	10. B

BASIC QUESTIONS (PAGES 89-94)

1. A	10. D	19. C	28. A	37. A
2. C	11. B	20. A	29. A	38. C
3. A	12. A	21. D	30. A	39. C
4. A	13. B	22. B	31. B	40. B
5. B	14. A	23. C	32. C	41. D
6. A	15. C	24. D	33. B	42. A
7. A	16. B	25. C	34. B	43. A
8. B	17. B	26. A	35. D	44. B
9. B	18. C	27. D	36. D	45. D

MEDIUM QUESTIONS (PAGES 95-100)

1. B	10. C	19. A	28. A	37. B
2. C	11. B	20. A	29. C	38. A
3. A	12. D	21. C	30. B	39. B
4. C	13. B	22. B	31. C	40. A
5. C	14. D	23. C	32. D	41. D
6. B	15. A	24. D	33. D	42. A
7. C	16. B	25. A	34. B	43. C
8. C	17. D	26. D	35. D	44. B
9. D	18. C	27. B	36. C	45. B

Ivy Global

DIFFICULT QUESTIONS (PAGES 101-106)

1. A	10. C	19. A	28. B	37. B
2. B	11. A	20. C	29. D	38. A
3. A	12. D	21. B	30. D	39. A
4. A	13. A	22. C	31. C	40. B
5. B	14. B	23. A	32. C	41. B
6. C	15. D	24. C	33. A	42. B
7. C	16. A	25. C	34. C	43. D
8. B	17. A	26. C	35. D	44. A
9. D	18. C	27. B	36. D	45. C

MIDDLE LEVEL CHALLENGE QUESTIONS (PAGES 107-108)

1. C	4. D	7. C	10. C	13. D
2. B	5. A	8. A	11. A	14. A
3. A	6. D	9. B	12. B	

UPPER LEVEL CHALLENGE QUESTIONS (PAGES 109-111)

1. C	4. A	7. B	10. A	13. A
2. B	5. C	8. A	11. C	14. A
3. D	6. D	9. D	12. B	15. D

READING COMPREHENSION PRACTICE QUESTIONS

BASIC PASSAGES (PAGES 156-167)

1. B	8. A	15. C	22. B	29. C
2. D	9. C	16. A	23. B	30. D
3. B	10. D	17. A	24. D	31. B
4. D	11. A	18. D	25. A	32. A
5. A	12. A	19. B	26. C	
6. D	13. D	20. A	27. A	
7. B	14. A	21. D	28. A	

MEDIUM PASSAGES (PAGES 168-182)

1. A	9. A	17. A	25. D	33. C
2. C	10. B	18. B	26. B	34. B
3. A	11. A	19. B	27. D	35. A
4. B	12. D	20. D	28. A	36. D
5. C	13. A	21. C	29. C	
6. D	14. D	22. B	30. D	
7. C	15. B	23. A	31. A	
8. C	16. B	24. A	32. A	

DIFFICULT PASSAGES (PAGES 183-195)

1. B	8. D	15. C	22. B	29. D
2. C	9. A	16. D	23. A	30. A
3. A	10. A	17. A	24. A	31. C
4. C	11. C	18. A	25. B	32. D
5. C	12. C	19. A	26. A	33. C
6. B	13. C	20. D	27. C	34. C
7. B	14. B	21. D	28. B	35. B

MIDDLE LEVEL CHALLENGE PASSAGES (PAGES 196-206)

1. A	7. B	13. D	19. A	25. A
2. B	8. C	14. C	20. B	26. B
3. A	9. B	15. D	21. B	27. A
4. D	10. D	16. A	22. D	28. A
5. A	11. B	17. C	23. A	29. C
6. D	12. A	18. B	24. B	30. C

UPPER LEVEL CHALLENGE PASSAGES (PAGES 207-216)

1. A	6. C	11. C	16. B	21. A
2. A	7. B	12. A	17. C	22. D
3. D	8. D	13. C	18. A	23. D
4. A	9. D	14. A	19. A	24. C
5. A	10. A	15. A	20. B	

WRITING BASICS

EXERCISE #4 (PAGE 228)

1. My sister, Catherine, lives with her husband in Dallas, Texas.
2. Our history teacher helped us understand the British Civil War.
3. I study French with Madame Bellamy and Spanish with Señora Cabrera.
4. During our trip to San Francisco, we drove across the Golden Gate Bridge and attended a concert by the San Francisco Philharmonic.

EXERCISE #5 (PAGE 230)

1. Mike's dog is sweet, but his sister's dog is unfriendly, smelly, and loud.
2. Listen! I'm trying to talk to you! *or* Listen, I'm trying to talk to you!
3. Students should bring the following items: a backpack, a pencil, an eraser, and a ruler.
4. After a strong gust of wind, all of the partiers' hats fell off.
5. Is this someone's pencil?
6. It's my mother's fifty-second birthday, and I don't have a present for her.
7. The men's suits, which were designed by Armani, were very elegant.
8. We wanted to go sailing; however, the thunder, lightning, and hail were too dangerous.

EXERCISE #6 - SOME POSSIBLE SOLUTIONS OUT OF MANY (PAGE 232)

1. I like to ski. It makes me happy.

   When I ski, it makes me happy.

2. James went home, did his homework, and went to bed.

   After James got home, he did his homework. Later, he went to bed.

3. Don't forget to bring your folder. It is important.

4. The strangest thing happened on my way to school. Our school bus broke down! They made us all get out through the back door, and we had to wait beside the road for another bus to pick us up. Because it took a long time to come, we were late.

EXERCISE #7 (PAGES 233-234)

1. "To Build a Fire" was written by Jack London.

2. Jack borrowed two pens. Then he went home.

3. They're coming to our house tomorrow.

4. You're waiting too long to answer.

5. My mother told me to wait there.

6. They're right here. Can't you see them?

7. My school has a great principal.

8. You're not serious!

9. The weather is nice outside.

10. I need to buy three binders to take to school. It's important.

EXERCISE #8 (PAGE 234)

1. Amanda ate the cookie.

2. My brother washed the dishes.

3. My dog ate my homework.

4. I made the mistake.

ROOTS, PREFIXES, AND SUFFIXES

EXERCISE #4 (PAGES 282-283)

2. in + aud + ible: not able to be heard (verb)
3. a + morph + ous: without shape (adjective)
4. syn + chron + ize: to occur at the same time (verb)
5. re + juven + ate: to make young again (verb)
6. in + cred + ulous: not believing, full of disbelief (adjective)
7. ambi + val + ent: valuing both sides of an issue, being undecided (adjective)
8. phil + anthrop + y: love of humanity, charity (noun)
9. vivi + sect + ion: cutting into a living animal (noun)
10. retro + spect + ive: backward-looking (adjective)